STANDARD LEVEL
HIGHER LEVEL

PEARSON BACCALAUREATE

Psychology

CHRISTIAN BRYAN • ALAN LAW
SERIES EDITOR: CHRISTIAN BRYAN

Supporting every learner across the IB continuum

Published by Pearson Education Limited, Edinburgh Gate, Harlow, Essex, CM20 2JE.

www.pearsonglobalschools.com

Edited by Paula Clarke
Proofread by Sze Kiu Yeung
Typeset by Phoenix Photosetting, Chatham, Kent

Indexed by Indexing Specialists (UK) Ltd

First published 2013

18 17 16 15 14 13
IMP 10 9 8 7 6 5 4 3 2 1

British Library Cataloguing in Publication Data
A catalogue record for this book is available from the British Library

ISBN 978 1 447 95152 0
ISBN eBook only 978 1 447 95153 7

Printed in Italy by Lego S.p.a.

Acknowledgements
We would like to thank Ellen Vriniotis of ACS Athens, Rizma Rizwan of City and Islington College, Ellen Dittmar of Western Academy of Beijing, Susanna Joachim of Nymphenburger Schulen, Kania Grazyna of 33 Liceum IMM Kopernika, Sami Sorvali of Kannas School , Diane Howlett of Szczecin International School , Brian Hull of AIS Kuwait , Jacques Weber of British International School of Jeddah, Michael Ashleman of Wellington, Baljit Nijjar, Alison Walford, and Peter Giddens for their invaluable help in the development of this series by piloting of the concept material and reviewing this title from a teacher, and EAL perspective.

Every effort has been made to contact copyright holders of material reproduced in this book. Any omissions will be rectified in subsequent printings if notice is given to the publishers.

Dedication
Posvyaschayu etu knigu moemy lyubimomu synu Fyodoru i ego zamechatelnoi mame (moei prekrasnoy zhene) Tatyane Evgenyevne. – *Christian Bryan*

Contents

Introduction

Welcome to your Essential Guide to Psychology. This book has been designed to solve the key problems of many Diploma students:

- relating material you have been taught to the syllabus goals and outcomes
- remembering it from one lesson to the next
- recalling it months later in an exam situation
- demonstrating your understanding of it in an exam situation within a strict time limit.

Who should use Essential Guides?

Essential Guides have been carefully designed with all IB (International Baccalaureate) students in mind as they serve as highly effective summaries and revision guides.

However, they have also been created with the particular interests in mind of IB **students whose first language is not English**, and who would like further support. As a result, the content in all Essential Guides has been edited by an EAL (English as an additional language) expert to make sure that the language used is clear and accessible, key terms are explained, and essential vocabulary is defined and reinforced.

Key features of an Essential Guide

Reduced content: Essentials guides are not intended to be comprehensive textbooks - they contain the essential information you need to understand and respond to each Learning Outcome (LO) published in the IB subject guide. This allows you to understand, review, and revise material quickly and still be confident you are meeting the essential aims of the syllabus. The content is precise and to the point. We have reduced the number of words as much as possible to ensure everything you read has clear meaning, is clearly related to the LO, and will help you in an exam.

Format and approach: The content of the book is organized according to the Learning Outcomes (LOs). Each LO is looked at separately so that you can study each one without having read or understood previous LOs. This allows you to use the book as a first-text, or a revision guide, or as a way to help you understand material you have been given from other sources. The content is explained as clearly as possible, and you can be sure the information relates directly to the LO at the top of each page.

Sub-headings: The pages are organized using logical sub-headings to help you understand the most important points of the LO. This organization also provides you with a guide on what an effective exam answer would look like. The sub-headings can be used to help you during revision, as a planning model before you start writing your answer, or for the actual answer to help you focus the examiner on how you are addressing the question.

Opening sentences: These are suggestions on how to refer to the LO at the very start of your answer in the exam. They are intended either to be memorized or to give you suggestions about how your writing should look when you first begin writing in an exam. For example:

Opening sentence:

In this answer I will discuss the use of PET and MRI scans in investigating the relationship between brain functions and behaviour.

Model sentences: These are intended to summarize key material in a way that you can use in an exam. We have done the phrasing for you so that you can focus on planning what content to include. For example:

Model sentence: **A third example of how neurotransmitters can affect behaviour can be seen in the following study with acetylcholine and memory:**

Vocabulary and synonym boxes: These are included to help identify and support your understanding of subject-specific and difficult words. These useful words and phrases are colour-coded in the margins. We have avoided using a highly academic tone which is often found in many textbooks in order to make the text more accessible to students whose first language is not English. However, at the same time we have ensured that the complexity of the content is at the level required by successful Diploma students, and so the key subject-specific vocabulary needed is highlighted in a separate box.

Glossary

non-localized **not in one place/spread out**

child rearing **looking after a child until fully grown**

to inherit/inheritance **to receive traits/characteristics passed on from parents/grandparents**

Internal Assessment section: This is intended to help you design, write, and independently mark your own work. It is organized around the key phrases of the IB markscheme, in order to help you see what is required to achieve the top marks. Example sentences and sections are included.

Extended Essay section: This section contains examples from essays which have achieved high grades. You can use these to help prepare your own essays. They show you key sources and research. We have also included a list of suggested extended essay titles.

eBook and audio: In the accompanying eBook you will find a complete digital version of the book with interactive audio glossary, along with links to spoken audio files of opening sentences, model sentences, and hints for success to help with comprehension and pronunciation.

In addition, all the vocabulary lists are located together as downloadable files.

Above all, we hope this book helps you to understand, consolidate, and revise your course content more easily than ever, helping you to achieve the highest possible result in your exams.

Christian Bryan (EdD)
April 2013, Budapest

How to use your enhanced eBook

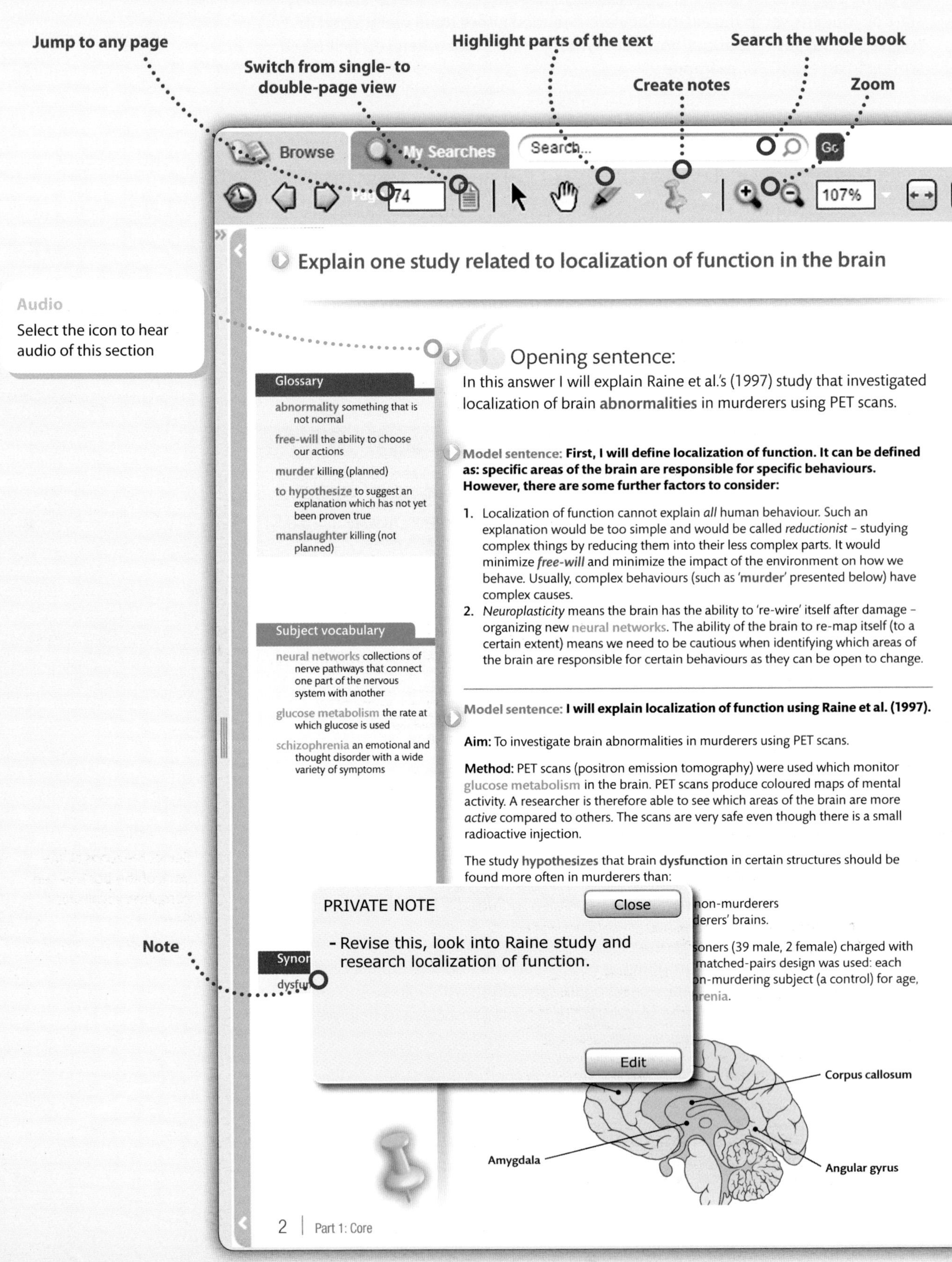

Create a bookmark

Switch to whiteboard view

Model sentence: **The results of the study clearly link specific areas of the brain with specific functions and behaviour, such as:**

There was lower activity than with controls in the prefrontal cortex which has been linked to a loss of self-control and altered emotion.

There was lower activity than with controls in the corpus callosum (which connects the two brain hemispheres) which may suggest less communication between the two hemispheres.

There was lower activity than with controls in the amygdala which is thought to control emotional expression.

There was lower activity than with controls in the angular gyrus which have been linked with **verbal** ability and educational success.

Problems with these structures may cause a lack of inhibition for violent behaviour and greater fearlessness.

Model sentence: **There are some factors to consider with this study such as:**

Gender: An effort was made to have gender balance but the number of females who took part was low. However, some generalizations can be made to both females and males.

Methodologically: A large sample was used with many controls to rule out other effects on brain activity. The matched-pairs design is a real strength of the study as drug use, age, sex, and other mental factors were taken into consideration with the control group. Therefore, any brain differences can be linked with some confidence to murderous behaviour. However, the findings apply only to a sub-group of violent offenders (not to other types of violence or crime). Furthermore, some were murderers and some were manslaughterers so caution should remain when generalizing their specific brain abnormalities to specific behaviour.

Methodologically (flaw): The PET scan method can lack **precision** so exact brain locations for behaviours are difficult to confirm.

Model sentence: **Caution should be used when assuming specific areas of the brain are responsible for specific behaviours. For example:**

The findings do not mean violence originates in these areas of the brain alone. Other social, psychological, and situational factors will be involved. The findings do not demonstrate the murderers are *not* responsible for their actions. They had the option of exercising free-will although the findings may indicate they will have found it more difficult to choose a non-violent path than an individual without these brain abnormalities. The findings do not mean PET scans can diagnose murderers. The findings do not say whether the brain abnormalities are a cause or effect of behaviour. However, this is a thorough study which possibly shows a link between abnormal brain structures and extreme behaviour.

Hints for success: Your main aim is to explain Raine et al. (1997). Remember the definition of localization of function and then three areas of the brain that Raine et al. (1997) found and link them to specific behaviours.

Synonyms

verbal .... spoken/verbal

flaw .... fault

precision .... accuracy

Glossary

inhibition feeling of worry/embarrassment that stops you from doing/saying something

to generalize/generalization to comment on something very basic, based on limited facts, and apply it to other situations

offender a person who is guilty of a crime

violence using force to attack others

The biological level of analysis | 3

Glossary with audio

Click on highlighted terms to see the definition and hear the audio

Vocabulary lists

Select the icons at the back of the book to see complete vocabulary lists

Explain one study related to localization of function in the brain

Glossary

abnormality something that is not normal

free-will the ability to choose our actions

murder killing (planned)

to hypothesize to suggest an explanation which has not yet been proven true

manslaughter killing (not planned)

Subject vocabulary

neural networks collections of nerve pathways that connect one part of the nervous system with another

glucose metabolism the rate at which glucose is used

schizophrenia an emotional and thought disorder with a wide variety of symptoms

Synonyms

dysfunction......... abnormality

Opening sentence:

In this answer I will explain Raine et al.'s (1997) study that investigated localization of brain **abnormalities** in murderers using PET scans.

Model sentence: **First, I will define localization of function. It can be defined as: specific areas of the brain are responsible for specific behaviours. However, there are some further factors to consider:**

1. Localization of function cannot explain *all* human behaviour. Such an explanation would be too simple and would be called *reductionist* – studying complex things by reducing them into their less complex parts. It would minimize ***free-will*** and minimize the impact of the environment on how we behave. Usually, complex behaviours (such as '**murder**' presented below) have complex causes.
2. *Neuroplasticity* means the brain has the ability to 're-wire' itself after damage – organizing new **neural networks**. The ability of the brain to re-map itself (to a certain extent) means we need to be cautious when identifying which areas of the brain are responsible for certain behaviours as they can be open to change.

Model sentence: **I will explain localization of function using Raine et al. (1997).**

Aim: To investigate brain abnormalities in murderers using PET scans.

Method: PET scans (positron emission tomography) were used which monitor **glucose metabolism** in the brain. PET scans produce coloured maps of mental activity. A researcher is therefore able to see which areas of the brain are more *active* compared to others. The scans are very safe even though there is a small radioactive injection.

The study **hypothesizes** that brain **dysfunction** in certain structures should be found more often in murderers than:

1. dysfunction in the same structures of non-murderers
2. dysfunction in other areas of the murderers' brains.

Participants: The 'murderers' were 41 prisoners (39 male, 2 female) charged with murder or **manslaughter** in California. A matched-pairs design was used: each murderer was matched with a 'normal' non-murdering subject (a control) for age, sex, and absence or presence of **schizophrenia**.

Results:

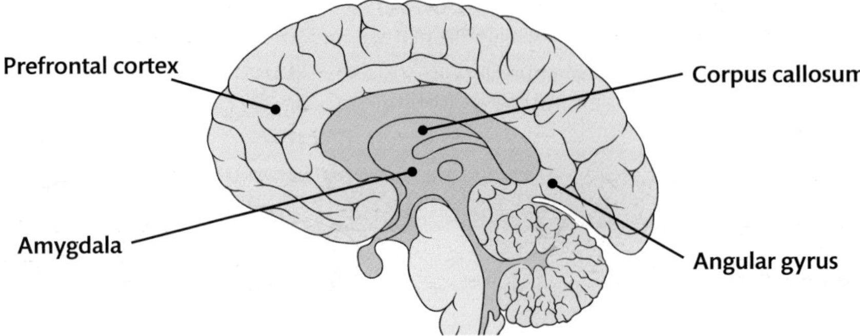

Model sentence: The results of the study clearly link specific areas of the brain with specific functions and behaviour, such as:

There was lower activity than with controls in the prefrontal cortex which has been linked to a loss of self-control and altered emotion.

There was lower activity than with controls in the corpus callosum (which connects the two brain hemispheres) which may suggest less communication between the two hemispheres.

There was lower activity than with controls in the amygdala which is thought to control emotional expression.

There was lower activity than with controls in the angular gyrus which have been linked with **verbal** ability and educational success.

Problems with these structures may cause a lack of **inhibition** for violent behaviour and greater fearlessness.

Model sentence: There are some factors to consider with this study such as:

Gender: An effort was made to have gender balance but the number of females who took part was low. However, some **generalizations** can be made to both females and males.

Methodologically: A large sample was used with many controls to rule out other effects on brain activity. The matched-pairs design is a real strength of the study as drug use, age, sex, and other mental factors were taken into consideration with the control group. Therefore, any brain differences can be linked with some confidence to murderous behaviour. However, the findings apply only to a sub-group of violent **offenders** (not to other types of **violence** or crime). Furthermore, some were murderers and some were manslaughterers so caution should remain when generalizing their specific brain abnormalities to specific behaviour.

Methodologically (flaw): The PET scan method can lack **precision** so exact brain locations for behaviours are difficult to confirm.

Model sentence: Caution should be used when assuming specific areas of the brain are responsible for specific behaviours. For example:

The findings do not mean violence originates in these areas of the brain alone. Other social, psychological, and situational factors will be involved. The findings do not demonstrate the murderers are *not* responsible for their actions. They had the option of exercising free-will although the findings may indicate they will have found it more difficult to choose a non-violent path than an individual without these brain abnormalities. The findings do not mean PET scans can diagnose murderers. The findings do not say whether the brain abnormalities are a cause or effect of behaviour. However, this is a thorough study which possibly shows a link between abnormal brain structures and extreme behaviour.

Hints for success: Your main aim is to explain Raine et al. (1997). Remember the definition of localization of function and then three areas of the brain that Raine et al. (1997) found and link them to specific behaviours.

Synonyms

verbal .... spoken/verbal

flaw .... fault

precision............. accuracy

Glossary

inhibition feeling of worry/embarrassment that stops you from doing/saying something

to generalize/generalization to comment on something very basic, based on limited facts, and apply it to other situations

offender a person who is guilty of a crime

violence using force to attack others

Using one or more examples, explain the effects of neurotransmission on human behaviour

→ Nerve cells → building block of behaviour
→ Method by which messages are sent → Neurotransmission
→ Neurotransmitters
Body's natural messengers
→ Transmits info from one Neuron to another.
→ They have range of effects on human behaviour

Opening sentence:

In this answer I will explain the effects of neurotransmission on human behaviour using examples.

Model sentence: I will first explain what neurotransmission is:

Nerve cells, called neurons, are one of the building blocks of behaviour. Neurons send electrochemical messages to the brain so people can respond to **stimuli** either from the environment or from changes in the body. The method by which these messages are sent is called *neurotransmission*. Neurotransmitters cross the gap (the synapse) between two neurons. Therefore, neurotransmitters are the body's natural chemical messengers which **transmit** information from one neuron to another. Neurotransmitters have been shown to have a range of different effects on human behaviour. For example: norepinephrine (noradrenaline) is associated with **arousal** and being **alert**; serotonin is associated with sleep, arousal levels, and emotion.

①

Example 1: Japanese monks on a mountain (Kasamatsu and Hirai, 1999)

Model sentence: One example of how the neurotransmitter serotonin can affect behaviour can be seen in the following deprivation study:

Aim: To investigate how sensory deprivation affects the brain.

Method: The researchers studied a group of Buddhist monks who went on a 72-hour **pilgrimage** to a holy mountain in Japan. During their stay on the mountain, the monks did not eat food or drink water, they did not speak, and they were not protected from the cold weather. After about 48 hours, they began to have **hallucinations**, often seeing ancient ancestors or feeling a presence by their sides. The researchers took blood samples before the monks went up the mountain, and then again immediately after the monks reported having hallucinations.

Results: Serotonin levels had increased in the monks' brains.

Conclusion: Sensory deprivation caused the release of serotonin, which actually changed the way that the monks experienced the world. The higher levels of serotonin activated the parts of the brain called the hypothalamus and the frontal cortex, resulting in the hallucinations.

Evaluation:

- **Gender:** Only men were used so caution should be used when **generalizing** to women.
- **Cultural:** Very specific (Japanese monks), caution should be used when generalizing to other cultures.

Example 2: Serotonin, OCD and lovers (Marazziti, 1999)

Model sentence: A second example of how the neurotransmitter serotonin can affect behaviour can be seen in the following study:

Aim: To investigate the effect of serotonin on attraction and obsessive compulsive disorder (OCD).

Glossary

stimulus something that makes you or your body react

transmit pass/send something along

alert able to think quickly and clearly

pilgrimage a religious journey

hallucination seeing, feeling or hearing something that is not really there

to generalize/generalization to comment on something very basic, based on limited facts, and apply it to other situations

Synonyms

arousal .... stimulation

serotonin (Neurotransmitter)
→ affects sleep, arousal levels and emotion

Subject vocabulary

sensory deprivation taking away sight, hearing, smell, taste or touch

hypothalamus a small portion of the brain with many functions including having links with the wider nervous system

frontal cortex area at the front of the brain concerned with (among many things) emotional expression

obsessive compulsive disorder (OCD) a mental disturbance where people feel the need to do things over and over again

Method: Marazziti (1999) advertised for 20 couples who had been in love for less than 6 months. She wanted to see if the brain mechanisms associated with attraction were related to the brain mechanisms of OCD. The team of researchers found 17 female and three male volunteer students who had recently fallen in love, and obsessed about a new love, for at least 4 hours every day. A separate group of people with OCD was studied at the same time, in addition to a control group.

Results: By analysing blood samples from the lovers, Marazziti discovered that serotonin levels of new lovers were equivalent to the low serotonin levels of OCD patients.

Conclusion: From a purely biological point of view, the act of falling in love resembles OCD (low levels of serotonin).

Evaluation:

- **Methodological:** This was a correlational study so caution should be used when assuming low levels of serotonin *caused* either OCD or 'in love' type behaviour. Low levels of serotonin may be the *consequence* of the behaviour and not the cause.
- **Cultural:** This is a very culturally specific study (Italy) and so caution should be used when generalizing to other cultures.

Example 3: Acetylcholine on memory (Martinez and Kesner, 1991)

Model sentence: **A third example of how neurotransmitters can affect behaviour can be seen in the following study with acetylcholine and memory:**

Aim: To investigate the role of acetylcholine on memory.

Method: Acetylcholine is believed to play a role in memory formation. Rats were trained to go through a maze and get to the end, where they received food. Once the rats were able to do this, they injected one group of rats with an acetylcholine-blocking substance which decreased available acetylcholine. They also injected a second group of rats with a substance that prevented the 'clean-up' of acetylcholine from the synapse and returns the neuron to its 'resting state' – allowing the second group to have a higher level of acetylcholine than usual. The third group was a control group and was not given any injections. The independent variable in this study was the level of acetylcholine. One group had a greater amount of acetylcholine than the other. The dependent variable was memory and this was measured by seeing how fast the rats could run the maze.

A summary of the method:

- IV: Level of acetylcholine – one group had a greater amount of acetylcholine than the other.
- DV: Memory – measured by how fast the rats could run a maze.

Results: Rats who had lower levels of acetylcholine were slower at finding their way round the maze and made more errors than the control and the higher acetylcholine group. The higher acetylcholine group ran through the maze and found the food more quickly than the other two groups and took fewer wrong turns.

Conclusion: Acetylcholine played an important role in creating a memory of the maze. When acetylcholine levels are down, memory ability levels are down. When acetylcholine levels are up, memory ability levels are up.

Evaluation: It is questionable to what extent these findings can be generalized to humans. However, recent research has shown that acetylcholine-producing cells in the forebrain are damaged in the early stages of Alzheimer's disease.

Subject vocabulary

correlational study looking at how one variable relates to/ affects another

independent variable (IV) the variable an experimenter controls or changes

dependent variable (DV) the variable an experimenter measures

Alzheimer's disease an incurable illness characterized by brain deterioration. Memory loss is a common symptom

Hints for success: Do not spend too long evaluating studies; the focus should be on explaining how neurotransmitters affect behaviour.

Using one or more examples, explain functions of two hormones in human behaviour

Opening sentence:

In this answer I will use examples to explain the functions of two hormones in human behaviour. The two hormones are oxytocin and testosterone.

A hormone is similar to a neurotransmitter because it is a chemical messenger that carries a signal from one cell to another. Hormones differ from neurotransmitters as they travel through the blood stream while neurotransmitters travel across synapses (the gaps) between neurons.

Oxytocin

Oxytocin is a hormone that is produced by the **hypothalamus** after being **stimulated** by the **pituitary gland**. If oxytocin is given to healthy individuals it seems there is an increase in trust and generosity.

Study 1:

Model sentence: **A study showing the *positive* effects of oxytocin was conducted by Guastella et al. (2008).**

Method: Oxytocin or a **placebo** was given to 69 healthy human male volunteers. They were then shown 36 happy, angry, or neutral human faces. Participants returned the following day to make 'remember' and 'know' judgements for a mixture of 72 new and the previously seen faces.

Results: Participants given oxytocin were more likely to make 'remember' and 'know' judgements for previously seen happy faces compared with angry and neutral human faces. In contrast, oxytocin did not influence judgements for faces that had not been seen previously.

Conclusions: This study shows that giving oxytocin to male humans **enhances** the **encoding** of positive social information to make it more **memorable**.

Study 2:

Model sentence: **A study showing the *negative* effects of oxytocin was conducted by Shamay-Tsoory et al. (2009).**

The researchers argued that humans have a strong social tendency to compare themselves with others and they tend to feel jealous when they receive less valuable rewards. They also tend to be happy when their own rewards are higher than others in the same situation. Jealousy and 'schadenfreude' (enjoyment over other's misfortune) are social emotions widely agreed to be a symptom of the human social tendency to compare one's rewards with those of others. They speculated that oxytocin may have a **moderating** effect on the intensity of these emotions.

Method: 56 participants were either given **nasal** doses of oxytocin or a placebo. They played a game of chance with another (fake) participant who either won more money (jealousy **manipulation**), lost more money ('schadenfreude' manipulation), or won/lost equal amounts of money.

Subject vocabulary

hypothalamus a small portion of the brain with many functions including having links with the wider nervous system

pituitary gland an offshoot of the brain that releases many hormones

placebo a fake treatment that can often have an effect. Researchers compare their effects with the real treatment

encoding labelling

Synonyms

stimulated .... activated

conducted .... carried out

enhance .... improve/increase

Glossary

memorable likely to be remembered

to moderate/moderation to make less extreme

nasal via the nose

to manipulate/manipulation to control something or someone to your advantage

Results: In comparison with the placebo, oxytocin increased the jealousy ratings when the (fake) participant won more money. Oxytocin also increased the ratings of 'schadenfreude' (enjoyment over other's misfortune) when the (fake) participant lost more money. However, oxytocin appeared to have no effect on the emotional ratings following equal monetary gains nor did it affect general mood ratings.

Conclusions: This study shows oxytocin is involved in increasing envy and 'schadenfreude' and not just positive pro-social behaviours.

Testosterone

Model sentence: My second example of a hormone and its functions is testosterone. I will present one study to illustrate my explanation.

Testosterone is mainly secreted in the testes of males and the ovaries of females. It is the main male sex hormone and linked with **aggression**. On average, an adult human male body produces about 40 to 60 times more testosterone than an adult human female body, but females are more sensitive to the hormone.

Study:

Model sentence: A study showing the *aggressive* effects of testosterone was conducted by Wagner and Beuving (1979).

Method: The researchers performed a laboratory experiment on rats whereby the independent variable was testosterone and this was manipulated via castration. The dependent variable was aggression and this was measured by counting bites and bite attacks.

Results: Castration reduced aggression. Injections of testosterone restored aggression in castrated mice who were previously judged to be aggressive and who had lost their aggression due to castration.

Conclusion: Testosterone has clear links with aggressive behaviour in mice.

Evaluation:

- **Methodological:** This was a very tightly controlled study with a clear independent variable (testosterone) and a clear, **quantifiable** dependent variable (number of bites shown).
- **Generalizing**: Caution should always be used when generalizing the results of animal studies to humans.

Aggression has also been linked to low levels of serotonin and monoamine oxidase. The levels of these chemicals are controlled by genes. Suomi (2005) studied wild rhesus monkeys that are closely related to humans in terms of genetic code, and found high levels of serotonin in the least aggressive animals and low levels in the most aggressive. This suggests testosterone is not the only hormone involved in aggression. It may be that serotonin acts as a 'brake' on the effects of testosterone. Furthermore, Suomi studied **rearing styles**: one group was reared in a **nurturing**, supportive environment and the other in a less supportive, non-nurturing environment (left to look after themselves with their siblings). As expected, the non-nurtured group had low levels of serotonin and high levels of aggression and the opposite was true of those reared by their mothers; they had high levels of serotonin and low levels of aggression coupled with risk-taking behaviour. Suomi argued that the environment was therefore shown to moderate the effects of hormones on behaviour.

Subject vocabulary

pro-social behaviour behaviour that is judged to be positive for society (e.g. charity work, helping neighbours)

secreted the release of chemicals

independent variable (IV) the variable an experimenter controls or changes

castration the removal of male sexual organs

dependent variable (DV) the variable an experimenter measures

Glossary

aggression/aggressive behaviing in an angry or threatening way

quantifiable can be measured using numbers

Synonyms

rearing styles ...... parenting styles

nurturing .... caring

Hints for success: Do not spend too long evaluating studies; the focus should be on explaining the functions of two hormones.

Discuss two effects of the environment on physiological processes

Brain plasticity refers to the brain's ability to rearrange the connections b/w neurons as a result of experience or learning.

Opening sentence:

In this answer I will discuss the effects of ***parental nurturing*** on the brain and the effect of a physically enriched environment on the brain.

Model sentence: **The physiological processes I will focus on are those that take place within the brain.**

[The brain is a dynamic system that interacts with the environment. Not only can the brain determine and change behaviour, but behaviour and environment can change the brain. *Brain plasticity* refers to the brain's ability to rearrange the connections between its neurons as a result of learning or experience.]

---

(6)

Effect 1: The effect of *parental nurturing* on the brain is to *increase the size of the hippocampus*

Aim: To investigate the effects nurturing mothers have on the brain development of their children.

Method: Luby (2012) used magnetic resonance imaging (MRI) to scan 92 children's brains.

An experiment was conducted when the children were aged 3 to 6 years. The children were put into a **frustrating** situation whereby they and their mothers were left in a room with a brightly wrapped package. The children were not allowed to open the package and they were told to wait while the mother filled out a number of forms. Researchers observed how the children and mothers handled this situation, which was meant to copy the usual **stressors** of daily parenting. Mothers who offered reassurance and support that helped their child control their behaviour were rated as being *nurturing*. Mothers who either ignored the child or harshly scolded the child were rated as *non-nurturing*. When the children were between 7 and 10 years old, Luby performed MRI brain scans on them.

Results: Children with the nurturing mothers had hippocampi that were 10 per cent larger than the hippocampi of children who had mothers that were non-nurturing.

Conclusion: Nurturing mothers impact on the brain development of children.

Evaluation: The study offers common-sense insight into a real-world problem. However, not all variables can be controlled. For example, non-nurturing mothers may also not feed their children healthily which may also impact on their children's brain development.

Synonyms

nurturing............ caring

Subject vocabulary

physically enriched environment providing physical stimulation (such as toys)

physiological related to the body

dynamic system active system that changes with needs and experience

hippocampus part of the brain involved with (among other things) emotions and memory

magnetic resonance imaging (MRI) a brain imaging technology that allows researchers to 'see' brain processes in action

Glossary

frustrating/frustration a feeling of being annoyed or upset because you cannot do something

stressor a situation which usually causes stress

Effect 2: The effect of a *physically enriched environment* on the brain is to increase *the thickness of the* cerebral cortex in rats

Aim: To investigate the effect of either enrichment or deprivation on the development of neurons in the cerebral cortex.

Method: Rosenzweig and Bennett (1972) performed an experiment by placing rats into either an environmentally enriched condition or an environmentally deprived condition. Therefore, the independent variable was *richness of the environment* and was operationalized by either giving the rats interesting toys to play with or not giving them interesting toys to play with. The dependent variable was the *effect of the environment on the brain* and this was operationalized by measuring the thickness of the frontal lobe. The rats spent 60 days in their respective environments and then they were sacrificed.

Results: Post-mortem studies of the rat brains showed that those that had been in the stimulating environment had an increased thickness in the cerebral cortex. The frontal lobe, which is associated with thinking, planning, and decision making, was heavier in the rats that had been in the stimulating environment.

Conclusion: Having interesting toys created the best conditions for developing the cerebral thickness of rats' brains.

Evaluation: Tightly controlled study with a clear independent variable and clear, quantifiable dependent variable. However, this is an animal study and caution should be used when generalizing the results to humans. Ethically, the experiment followed the correct guidelines for the treatment of animals. The rats were bred for experimental purposes and were used sparingly.

In sum, the two effects are:

Effect 1: The effect of parental nurturing *on the brain is to* increase the size of the hippocampus *(supported by Luby, 2012).*

Effect 2: The effect of a physically enriched environment *on the brain is to increase* the thickness of the cerebral cortex *in rats (supported by Rosenzweig and Bennet, 1972).*

Hints for success: Do not spend too long evaluating studies; the focus should be on the two effects of the environment on the brain.

Subject vocabulary

cerebral cortex brain tissue

independent variable (IV) the variable an experimenter controls or changes

operationalized *how* the IV is manipulated and *how* the DV is measured

dependent variable (DV) the variable an experimenter measures

frontal lobes the front part of the brain associated with planning and judgement

sacrificed killed for the study

Glossary

post-mortem studies performed after death

quantifiable can be measured using numbers

sparingly as few as possible

Examine one interaction between cognition and physiology in terms of behaviour; Evaluate two relevant studies

Opening sentence:

In this answer I will examine the interaction between cognition and physiology in the context of anterograde amnesia and the hippocampus.

Anterograde amnesia means not being able to create *new* memories. Sufferers are not able to pass information from their short-term memory store to their long-term memory store. This leads to a partial or complete inability to remember the past. Clive Wearing (CW) and Henry Molaison (HM) suffer from anterograde amnesia as the result of damage to the hippocampus: HM had his hippocampus removed. CW had his damaged after having a virus. Researchers use case studies to study rare events or events that are simply interesting. Case studies are *intensive investigations of one unit (e.g. one person, group, team, or event)*. They produce rich, detailed results but the key drawback is not being able to generalize.

Study 1: The case of Henry Molaison (HM) (based on Blakemore, 1988)

Molaison had been suffering a very high number of regular epileptic fits since the age of 16. At 27 he had surgery to remove various parts of his brain including the hippocampus. The surgery cured his epilepsy but he was left with **severe** anterograde amnesia. His short-term memory was generally normal; for instance, he could **retain** verbal information for about 15 seconds without **rehearsal** and for much longer with rehearsal. However, he could not transfer information into long-term memory or, if he could, he could not **retrieve** it.

Evaluation:

Positives

The study of Molaison greatly added to the understanding of human memory. For example, he was not able to remember any new fact or event but he was able to learn and remember **motor skills** suggesting these areas are separate in the brain. He performed normally in tests of **intellectual ability**, again suggesting the separate storage of memory functions (e.g. stores for words). His case supports the general distinction between short-term memory and long-term memory stores.

Negatives

It was first thought Molaison's brain surgery allowed a good understanding of how particular areas of the brain may be linked to memory processes. However, MRI scans of Molaison's brain in the late 1990s revealed the extent of damage was more widespread than previously thought. The MRI scans showed it was not possible to identify one particular region responsible for Molaison's memory problems. This can also be seen as a strength of the case study approach as constant follow-ups using new technology allowed previous errors in theory to be corrected.

Subject vocabulary

cognition/cognitive related to mental processes (such as perception, memory, problem-solving)

physiology bodily events

hippocampus part of the brain involved with (among other things) emotions and memory

short-term memory store usually a memory storage time of a few seconds

long-term memory store usually an indefinite memory storage time within a lifetime

epileptic fit a form of brain seizure where the brain stops working normally

magnetic resonance imaging (MRI) a brain imaging technology that allows researchers to 'see' brain processes in action

Glossary

to generalize/generalization to comment on something very basic, based on limited facts, and apply it to other situations

severe very bad

motor skills skills associated with bodily movement

Synonyms

retain.................. keep/save

rehearsal .... practice

retrieve............... get back/recover

intellectual ability............ intelligence

Study 2: The case of Clive Wearing (CW) (based on Blakemore, 1988; Baddeley, 1990)

Clive Wearing was an **accomplished** musician. In March 1985 he suffered a rare brain infection caused by the cold sore virus (Herpes simplex). The virus attacked his hippocampus and destroyed it, along with other parts of his cortex. Like Molaison, he lives in a snapshot of time, constantly believing that he has just awoken from years of unconsciousness. He can read music, play the organ, and conduct music. Also like Molaison, he can learn new skills (e.g. reading some writing in the mirror or mirror-reading). Unlike Molaison, his ability to remember his earlier life was not as accurate.

Evaluation:

Positives

Clive Wearing (and his wife) have given highly detailed analysis of memory function and abilities. According to his wife, over time, Wearing developed a 'sense' of his own condition 'through a kind of interior rehabilitation'. He changed from the initial stages of his illness from endless, confused, and repeated questioning to a form of acceptance; developing a mild adaption and awareness as well as being calmer and happier. Wearing's sense of humour, intelligence, substantial musical ability, and underlying personality characteristics remain **intact**, suggesting they do not need the formation of new memories to remain active. His wife also states he has learnt new things such as where his coffee cups and milk are kept and is able to recognize the care home he lives in.

Negatives

The brain infection which caused the memory problems was too widespread for researchers to accurately locate the exact areas of the brain that might be responsible for certain aspects of memory.

Case studies are intensive investigations of one unit (e.g. one person, group, team, or event). *They produce rich, detailed results but the key drawback is not being able to generalize.*

Hints for success: CW and HM have faults as research studies. They are case studies and can be generalized but only to some extent. However, they offer clear insight into the relationship between memory and the brain.

Synonyms

accomplished ..... talented/skilful

intact .... unchanged

Subject vocabulary

cortex brain tissue

underlying personality characteristics deep-rooted personality traits (e.g. being kind and happy)

Discuss the use of brain imaging technologies in investigating the relationship between biological factors and behaviour

Opening sentence:

In this answer I will discuss the use of PET and MRI scans in investigating the relationship between brain functions and behaviour.

PET scans

PET scans (positron emission tomography) monitor **glucose metabolism** in the brain. PET scans produce coloured maps of mental activity. A researcher is therefore able to see which areas of the brain are more *active* compared to others. The scans are very safe even though there is a small radioactive injection. PET scans have been used to diagnose **abnormalities** like **tumours**, or changes caused by **Alzheimer's disease**; to compare brain differences in normal individuals and in those with **psychological disorders**; and to compare differences between males and females.

Model sentence: **I will discuss the use of PET scans to investigate the relationship between brain abnormalities and murder.**

Study 1: Raine et al. (1997)

Aim: To investigate brain abnormalities in murderers using PET scans.

Method: PET scans (positron emission tomography) were used.

The study **hypothesizes** that brain **dysfunction** in certain structures should be found more often in murderers than:

1. dysfunction in the same structures of non-murderers
2. dysfunction in other areas of the murderers' brains.

Participants: The 'murderers' were 41 prisoners (39 male, 2 female) charged with murder or **manslaughter** in California. A matched-pairs design was used; each murderer was matched with a 'normal' non-murdering subject for age, sex, and absence or presence of **schizophrenia** (known as the 'control').

Results:

Model sentence: **Using a PET scan clearly linked specific areas of the brain with specific functions and behaviour.**

Compared to the controls, there was lower activity in the:

- prefrontal cortex which has been linked to a loss of self-control and **altered** emotion
- corpus callosum (which connects the two brain hemispheres) which may suggest less communication between the two hemispheres
- amygdala which is thought to control emotional expression
- angular gyrus which have been linked with verbal ability and educational success.

Subject vocabulary

glucose metabolism the rate at which glucose is used

tumour an abnormal growth of cells/tissue

Alzheimer's disease an incurable illness characterized by brain deterioration. Memory loss is a common symptom

psychological disorders abnormal behaviour which needs treatment

schizophrenia an emotional and thought disorder with a wide variety of symptoms

Glossary

abnormality something that is not normal

murder killing (planned)

to hypothesize to suggest an explanation which has not yet been proven true

dysfunction/dysfunctional not working or behaving normally

manslaughter killing (not planned)

Synonyms

altered................ changed

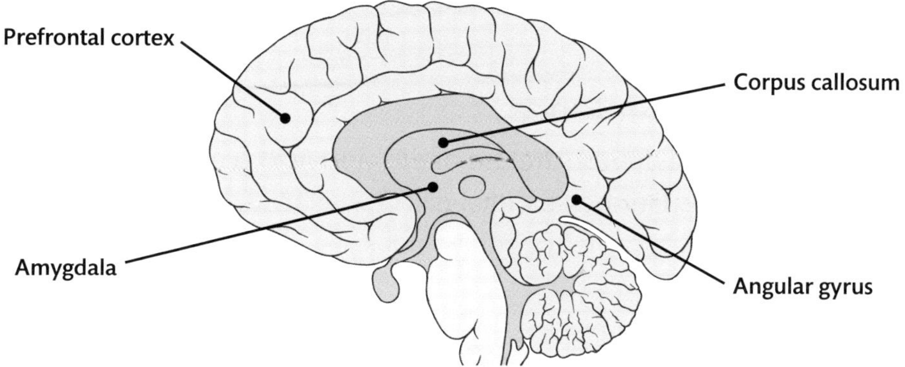

MRI scans

An MRI (magnetic resonance imaging) is a scan that studies the structure and physical functions of the brain by tracking blood oxygen levels. More active areas of the brain require more oxygen. MRIs are one of the most common brain mapping techniques because of the relatively wide availability of the machines. They have high resolution up to 1 mm and are considered more accurate than PET scans. The images produced must be interpreted carefully, since brain processes are **complex** and often **non-localized**.

Model sentence: I will discuss the use of MRI scans to investigate the relationship between nurturing mothers and hippocampus size.

Study 2: Luby (2012)

Aim: To investigate the effects nurturing mothers have on the brain development of their children.

Method: MRIs to scan 92 children's brains.

An experiment was **conducted** whereby mothers were labelled either nurturing or non-nurturing depending on how they handled a stressful task with their children. The children were aged 3 to 6 years. When the children were between 7 and 10 years old, Luby performed MRI brain scans on them.

Results:

Model sentence: MRI scans were able to show that the children with nurturing mothers had hippocampi that were 10 per cent larger than the hippocampi of children who had non-nurturing mothers. The behaviour of the mothers had affected the growth of their children's brain.

General evaluation:

Using brain imaging technology takes a *reductionist approach* to complex issues (such as murder and **child rearing**). The brain differences in the murderers (Raine et al., 1997) may have been a consequence of a violent lifestyle and not the cause. The smaller hippocampi (Luby, 2012) may have been the result of lifestyle factors such as poor diet or biological factors such as **inheritance**. However, in both examples, technology was used to show a possible link between specific brain areas and behaviour.

Subject vocabulary

resolution refers to how clear an image is

hippocampus part of the brain involved with (among other things) emotions and memory

brain imaging technologies various techniques to either directly or indirectly image the structure and function of the brain. Researchers can 'see' how the brain operates while the individual carries out basic tasks

reductionism/reductionist approach studying complex things by reducing them into their less complex parts

Synonyms

complex .... complicated

nurturing .... caring

conducted .... carried out

Glossary

non-localized not in one place/ spread out

child rearing looking after a child until fully grown

to inherit/inheritance to receive traits/characteristics passed on from parents/ grandparents

Hints for success: You do not have to know exactly how the technology works; you just have to know how it shows brain processes in action and how this helps us understand how the brain works.

With reference to relevant research studies, to what extent does genetic inheritance influence behaviour

Subject vocabulary

genetic inheritance traits/characteristics from parents/grandparents

genetic mutant mice mice that were deliberately changed (genetically) for the purposes of the experiment

serotonin a neurotransmitter related to feelings of wellbeing and happiness

receptor molecule that receives/responds to a neurotransmitter as it moves across the synaptic gap (the gap between neurons)

independent variable (IV) the variable an experimenter controls or changes

dependent variable (DV) the variable an experimenter measures

heritable behaviour behaviour that is inherited (passed down genetically)

cerebral spinal fluid clear fluid inside the brain

metabolite a product of metabolism

Synonyms

psychological...... mental/emotional

intention............ purpose

engineered......... created

correlated with ... linked to

reared .... parented

ethical .... moral

juvenile .... young

Glossary

quantifiable can be measured using numbers

to generalize/generalization to comment on something very basic, based on limited facts, and apply it to other situations

Opening sentence:

In this answer I will demonstrate the extent to which genetic inheritance influences behaviour. I will do this by using aggression and risk taking as examples of behaviour.

Model sentence: **First, I will define aggression.**

Aggression is behaviour aimed at causing pain, **psychological** harm, or physical harm. An important aspect of aggression is ***intention***. For example, a doctor who gives an injection that harms someone, but who did so with the intention of preventing the further spread of illness, is not considered to have committed an aggressive act as their intention was *not* to harm the individual.

Genetic inheritance: supporting evidence

Model sentence: **Animal studies have shown a clear link between aggression and genetic inheritance.**

Study: Mutant mice

Bock and Goode (1996) **engineered** genetic mutant mice by removing a gene that produced serotonin receptors. Fewer serotonin receptors means the effects of serotonin are felt less. While showing normal behaviour in everyday activities such as eating and exploration, the mutant male mice attacked intruders with twice the force of normal male mice.

Aim: To investigate the effects of serotonin on aggression. The independent variable was serotonin receptor sites (under genetic control) manipulated/controlled by removing the gene responsible for them. The dependent variable was the aggression of the mice, measured by counting the number of bites.

Results: Aggression can be **correlated with** genetic changes. Mice **reared** without aggressive role models were *still* showing aggressive behaviour suggesting a clear connection between the serotonin receptor site gene and aggression.

Evaluation: Tightly controlled study with clear independent variable and dependent variable - both **quantifiable**. Caution should be used when **generalizing** to humans. **Ethical** guidelines were followed as the animals were bred for experimental purposes and major insights gained into heritable behaviour.

Eventually, Suomi and Lesch (2002) identified a gene that allows serotonin to be processed efficiently or inefficiently. They took cerebral spinal fluid from 132 **juvenile** rhesus monkeys and analysed it for serotonin metabolite traces. A high level of metabolite would indicate a high level of serotonin processing. Bullying behaviour (risk-taking) was correlated with a poor level of serotonin processing. Monkeys with a gene that did not allow them to process serotonin very well were more aggressive.

Environmental considerations

Model sentence: It is reductionist and simplistic to assume genes are solely responsible for a complex behaviour such as aggression. Factors in the environment such as parenting must always be considered.

Study 1: Genes and 'good mothering' in humans

Caspie and Moffitt (2012) conducted a longitudinal case study over 26 years with 1037 children born in 1972 in New Zealand. They found children were much more likely to grow up to be aggressive and **anti-social** if they had inherited a 'short' version of a gene called MAOA. However, they noted carriers only became anti-social if they had *experienced an **abusive** upbringing*. Carriers of MAOA who experienced good mothering were usually completely normal. Therefore, the environment had a clear impact on their behaviour.

Study 2: Neurotic monkeys and 'supermoms'

Suomi (2002) wanted to see how much personalities could be influenced by the environment. He noticed bullies came from **harsh**, **stern** mothers and the neurotics came from **anxious**, shy mothers. He took neurotic babies from their neurotic mothers - babies who in newborn testing were already seen to be nervous themselves - and gave them to nurturing mothers (supermoms). He concluded the neurotic side to their personalities had a genetic cause as they were not old enough to be influenced by their mothers. However, after being raised by supermoms, the babies turned out very close to normal. Maestripieri (2009) took non-neurotic, high-scoring infants from nurturing supermoms and had them raised by abusive, non-nurturing mothers. This setting produced nervous monkeys. This study again shows the environment has a clear impact on behaviour.

Study 3: Genetic bullies and 'supermoms'

Suomi (2004) found monkeys who were genetically **predisposed** to be aggressive bullies (risk takers) but who had nurturing mothers did better at many key tasks than monkeys who were not genetically predisposed to be aggressive bullies (and were non-risk takers) but who also had nurturing mothers. For example, they had more playmates as youths and were better at sensing and responding to **conflicts**. They also rose higher in their social hierarchies. The combination of bullying (risk-taking) genes and nurturing mothers (supermoms) had made them *more successful* than any other group. This study shows how genes with a potentially negative social impact combined with an appropriate environment can mean the individual can succeed.

Caution should be used when generalizing the findings of animal studies to humans. However, animal studies allow high levels of manipulation that would not be allowed on humans. The findings help us to understand key biological mechanisms.

Subject vocabulary

reductionist/reductionist approach studying complex things by reducing them into their less complex parts

longitudinal case study research that has taken place over a long period of time, usually years

social hierarchies social organizations from the most powerful to the least powerful

Glossary

anti-social not sociable

to predispose/predisposition a tendency to behave in a particular way

Synonyms

abusive .... cruel/violent

neurotic .... nervous

harsh .... severe/strict

stern .... serious

anxious .... nervous/ worried

conflicts .... disagreements

Hints for success: Make it clear you think aggression is a complex human behaviour and unlikely to be the result of one genetic trait. It is more likely to be the result of a combination of environmental and genetic factors.

Examine one evolutionary explanation of behaviour

Opening sentence:

In this answer I will examine the Theory of Natural Selection first developed by Charles Darwin.

Model sentence: **The basic assumptions of the Theory of Natural Selection are:**

- The resources needed for survival are limited. There is a struggle to survive in an environment that presents challenges to individuals and species. Therefore, individuals and species are in competition with each other for resources and mates.
- Individuals in the population have **variations** in their traits due to genetic mutations (although Darwin did not fully understand this). Such variations in traits make the individual organism more, or less, adapted to their environment and therefore more, or less, competitive in relation to other individuals and species.
- Individuals with better adapted traits *have more chance* of surviving and passing their better adapted genes on to the next generation.
- Individuals with less well adapted traits *have less chance* of surviving and passing their less well adapted genes on to the next generation.
- Over time, genes which result in the individual being better adapted will exist in greater numbers and the successful trait will be seen more in the population.
- Over time, genes which result in the individual being less well adapted will exist in fewer numbers and the less successful trait will be seen less in the population - eventually dying out.

Basic mechanisms of natural selection case studies

Supporting evidence for the Theory of Natural Selection is **vast** and **diverse** ranging from analysis of fossils to observing organisms in their different **habitats**. The following studies show the basic mechanisms of natural selection:

1. Model sentence: **The assumption that there is a struggle to survive in an environment that presents challenges to individuals and species is shown by the effect of pollution on the development of a darker coloured peppered moth (Kettlewell and Ford, 1956).**

   Moths in certain areas have evolved darker wings as a result of pollution. Darker wings help them blend in better with the bark of the trees which were marked by pollution. As a result, moths with darker wings were eaten less than moths that were lighter in colour. Eventually, darker coloured moths became more common.

2. Model sentence: **The assumption that having innate traits that benefit the individual can be shown by the existence of fear of the snake shape in monkeys (Mineka, 1983).**

   Rhesus monkeys raised in **captivity** did not show a fear response when faced with snakes. However, when they were shown videos of other monkeys being afraid of snakes the monkeys raised in captivity quickly showed the same fear response. The response was the same for crocodiles. However, when captive-raised monkeys were shown a video of monkeys being afraid of flowers, the captive

Subject vocabulary

mates potential partners for producing children

traits characteristics

genetic mutations changes in genes

fossils remains of a creature/plant from thousands of years ago

innate traits characteristics people are born with

Synonyms

variations............ differences

vast..................... large

Glossary

diverse large differences in a population

habitat a specific place in the environment where creatures live

moth an insect similar to a butterfly

captivity not free/kept by man

monkeys did not acquire a fear response to flower pots. This lack of learned fear was the same for rabbits. The results suggest an innate pre-dispositional fear to shapes which pose a threat. Such a disposition would aid survival.

3. Model sentence: **The assumption that having innate traits that benefit the individual can be shown by the disgust response in pregnant women (Fessler, 2006).**

   Nausea experienced by women in their first trimester of pregnancy can be very serious. During this period, a combination of hormones lowers the expectant mother's immune system so it does not reject the new 'foreign' genetic material in her womb (the growing baby). Fessler hypothesized that the nausea response helps to compensate for the less effective immune system – if the mother feels disgust more easily she will stay away from material which may cause her and her baby harm. Fessler gathered 496 healthy pregnant women between the ages of 18 and 50 and asked them to consider 32 situations which could possibly cause nausea – including walking barefoot and stepping on an earthworm, someone accidentally sticking a fish hook through their finger, and **maggots** on a piece of meat in an outdoor waste bin. Women in their first trimester scored much higher in disgust sensitivity than women in the second and third trimesters. Sensitivity seems to decrease as the risk of disease and infection decreases. The results suggest disgust aids survival as a form of protection against potential sources of disease.

4. Model sentence: **Disgust responses in a large sample illustrate the cross-cultural existence of beneficial traits in humans which supports the Theory of Natural Selection (Curtis et al., 2004).**

   An online survey was designed where people could see pairs of images in which one was infectious or could be harmful to the immune system, and the other image looked similar but was non-infectious. For example, one picture was of brown **sewage** water and the other was brown coloured water. There were 77 000 participants from 165 countries. The disgust reaction was most strongly elicited for those images which actually threaten one's immune system and less so for visually similar but non-infectious substances. This suggests an innate reaction to poisonous substances which would act as an evolutionary benefit. In addition, women had higher disgust reactions than men.

Epigenetics

Model sentence: Epigenetics **supports the basic assumptions of the Theory of Natural Selection because it shows adaptations to environmental challenges.**

As an individual organism moves through its lifecycle it is affected by the environment. For example, if food sources become scarce it will need to become more **dominant** than its competitors to successfully find food. It was previously understood that genetic identity was set at birth and could not be altered. However, new evidence suggests the environment may influence and cause changes in DNA *through the lifespan of the individual* and *those changes can be passed onto the next generation and generations thereafter.*

Epigenetics is the study of how heritable traits are passed on via genes but which cannot be explained by changes in DNA sequence. Epigenetics places a focus on how changes occur (on a genetic level) *over the lifetime of the individual* and the extent to which these changes are passed on to the next generation.

Glossary

disgust thoughts/feelings of sickness

maggots fly larvae/baby flies

sewage human waste material

adaptations changes to make more suitable for a new situation

Subject vocabulary

pre-dispositional traits that exist in biology and are usually caused by genes

first trimester the first stage of pregnancy (3 months)

epigenetics the study of how heritable traits are passed on via genes but which cannot be explained by changes in DNA sequence

Synonyms

nausea .... sickness/vomiting

dominant .... stronger

Supporting evidence

Study 1: Dominant pecking in chickens

Natt et al. (2009) hypothesized that unpredictable food access would cause chickens to show a more dominant feeding strategy.

Method: The independent variable was either predictable or unpredictable feeding environment and was manipulated using light/darkness. The dependent variable was level of dominance in feeding and was measured by counting the number of pecks for food. All **offspring** were separated from their parents.

Results: Chickens adapted their feeding behaviours in response to changes in their environment. The offspring of such chickens can **retain** these adaptive behaviours despite never being directly exposed to the same environment or the parent.

Conclusion: Hormonal changes in the chickens influenced their genetic makeup and made their offspring better adapted to a problematic environment.

Study 2: Fat father rats

Fang Ng et al. (2010) hypothesized that poor diet of the father (and not the mother) over the lifetime of the individual would negatively impact on the offspring.

Method: The independent variable was *poor diet* and was manipulated by giving 40 per cent more calories to the 'study' rats than the control rats – making them fat. The dependent variable was the extent to which it would biologically affect the offspring and was measured by looking at the levels of *glucose intolerance* and *insulin secretion in both groups of rats.*

Results: The 'study' rats became **obese** and developed glucose intolerance. After the rats were mated, the researchers analysed the offspring. They noted the female offspring were more sensitive to the effects of their father's diet so the team focused on baby female rats. By 6 weeks old, the young female rats were glucose intolerant. By 12 weeks of age, they had **impaired** insulin secretion. Additional research showed their father's high-fat diet actually changed gene expression in female offspring.

Conclusion: Poor diet negatively affected the father's sperm which produced less healthy offspring.

Model sentence: **Epigenetics demonstrates how environmental changes *over the lifetime of an individual* affect their genes which then cause changes in their offspring. It presents an additional mechanism for explaining changes in individuals and species and offers new ways of approaching theory and research for the Theory of Natural Selection.**

Subject vocabulary

independent variable (IV) the variable an experimenter controls or changes

dependent variable (DV) the variable an experimenter measures

glucose intolerance too much blood sugar and is a serious health condition

insulin a hormone that lowers the level of glucose (a type of sugar) in the blood

secretion the release of chemicals

Synonyms

offspring............ young/babies

retain.................. keep/save

impaired............ damaged

Glossary

obesity being fat in an unhealthy way

Hints for success: Your role is to *examine* not *evaluate* one evolutionary explanation of behaviour. Aim to uncover the assumptions of the theory of natural selection and how new research has shown the impact of the environment and genetic inheritance.

Students should use caution when using epigenetics to answer this question. Epigenetics uncovers the basic assumptions of the Theory of Natural Selection because it shows **adaptations** to environmental challenges. However, it is very new research and can be challenging to present on an exam paper. Students should always present the basic assumptions with supporting studies before attempting to explain epigenetics. The basic assumptions are:

1. The assumption that there is a struggle to survive in an environment that presents challenges to individuals and species is shown by the effect of pollution on the development of a darker coloured peppered **moth** (Kettlewell and Ford, 1956).
2. The assumption that having innate traits that benefit the individual can be shown by the existence of fear of the snake shape in monkeys (Mineka, 1983).
3. The assumption that having innate traits that benefit the individual can be shown by the **disgust** response in pregnant women (Fessler, 2006).
4. Disgust responses in a large sample illustrate the cross-cultural existence of beneficial traits in humans, which supports the Theory of Natural Selection (Curtis et al., 2004).

Subject vocabulary

epigenetics the study of how heritable traits are passed on via genes but which cannot be explained by changes in DNA sequence

uncover to find out what is underneath the surface

innate traits characteristics people are born with

Glossary

adaptations changes to make more suitable for a new situation

moth an insect similar to a butterfly

disgust thoughts/feelings of sickness

Discuss ethical considerations in research into genetic influences on behaviour

Synonyms

ethical .... moral

procedure........... method

Subject vocabulary

ethical considerations issues about the correct/morally correct way to research

Aboriginal people the original native people of Australia

eugenics an idea that argues a population can be improved through genetic engineering. People with more 'desirable' traits reproduce while people with less 'desirable' traits reproduce less or not at all

Glossary

guidelines rules of research

true parentage who the real parents are

adoption raising/parenting a child that is not yours

confidentiality keeping information a secret

informed consent participants have full knowledge of what they are taking part in

consent to give approval or permission for something

implication an effect that an action or decision will have on possible results in the future

discrimination unfair treatment of certain people or groups

ethnic group a particular race of people

Opening sentence:

In this answer I will discuss **ethical** considerations in research into genetic influences on behaviour. I will use the ideas of *participant awareness, coding*, and ***guidelines*** *for research in animal science* to address this question.

Model sentence: **Research involving genetics needs to have clear ethical guidelines.**

Research involving genetics:

- can reveal unexpected information that may harm research participants - for example, evidence of **true parentage** or unrevealed **adoptions** within a family or when a person discovers from the study that he or she carries the gene for a particular genetic disorder causing undue stress to the participant
- can often be complex and misunderstood - careful consideration needs to be given to how participants and their families are kept informed about the nature of genetic research
- often uses animals in experimental settings to test gene theories or treatments - there are clear guidelines for researchers when they use animals in laboratory conditions.

Ethical consideration 1: Participant awareness and cultural sensitivity

Model sentence: **Participants should always know how their confidentiality will be protected, and what will happen to any genetic information obtained as part of the study.**

The aims and **procedure** of the study must be explained in plain language and participants must sign an **informed consent** paper to show they have a clear understanding of the study they are participating in, and the **implications**, including any potential harm.

Some groups, including Aboriginal people, may disagree with genetic studies as a cultural principle. Given the existence of other forms of **discrimination** against such groups, and the history of the eugenics movement, it is very important to consult with relevant community leaders and organizations. Consent is a community matter for many Aboriginal and **ethnic groups** as well as an individual concern.

Researchers should always remember that their participants are living people and should always consider their feelings with regards all aspects of the research process.

Ethical consideration 2: Coding

Model sentence: Privacy can be protected by coding information.

Codes are assigned to the research material and only a small number of researchers have access to the codes. Researchers can make the sample fully **anonymous**. In such a way researchers cannot link samples or information to particular people. This protects confidentiality from insurance companies, employers, police, and others, but it also can limit the scientific value of the study by preventing follow-up and further investigation.

Glossary

anonymous participants' personal details are not known

Ethical consideration 3: The use of animals in research

Model sentence: Animals in genetic research are particularly useful as researchers do not have the same level of moral obligation as they do towards humans. However, there are strict guidelines that have to be followed:

The British Society of Animal Science wrote a set of ethical guidelines for the use of animals in research experimentation which they refer to as the 3Rs:

- *Refinement:* Any animal science research undertaken should be as focused as possible and have *realistic and achievable aims* of increasing knowledge of the species of interest in relation to our understanding of its functioning, performance, health or welfare.
- *Replacement:* Researchers must consider all available options to *replace* animals with other techniques that will fulfil the research objectives. Researchers should always actively look for non-animal methods of investigation.
- *Reduction:* There is a scientific, moral, and legal requirement to expose as few animals to pain, suffering, and distress as possible.

The three ethical considerations are:

1. *participant awareness and cultural sensitivity*
2. *coding*
3. *the use of animals in research.*

Hints for success: Use logical sub-headings to demarcate your work. They will give clear structure and focus. In this case use the labels *participant awareness and cultural sensitivity, coding,* and *the use of animals in research* for ethical considerations.

General Learning Outcomes

Learning outcomes → important

Synonyms

demonstrated ..... shown/showed
aggressive .... angry/threatening
anti-social .... not sociable
abusive .... cruel/violent
neurotic .... nervous
mate .... breed/reproduce
modify .... change
correlated with ... linked to
manipulated .... controlled/changed

Glossary

to inherit/inheritance to receive traits/characteristics passed on from parents/grandparents

carrier a person who does not have a disease but can pass it to others

upbringing the way a parent raises/treats their young

predetermined already decided

castration removal of the external sex organs

Subject vocabulary

longitudinal case study research that has taken place over a long period of time, usually years

serotonin a neurotransmitter related to feelings of well-being and happiness

cerebral spinal fluid clear fluid inside the brain

metabolite a product of metabolism

testosterone a hormone found in large amounts in males. It is responsible for male physical characteristics (such as broad shoulders) and is thought to play a significant role in male behaviour traits

independent variable (IV) the variable an experimenter controls or changes

dependent variable (DV) the variable an experimenter measures

GLO 1: Outline principles that define the biological level of analysis

GLO 2: Explain how principles that define the biological level of analysis may be demonstrated in research (that is, theories and/or studies)

Principle 1: Patterns of behaviour can be **inherited**.

Caspie and Moffitt (2012) conducted a longitudinal case study over 26 years with 1037 children born in 1972 in New Zealand. They found children were much more likely to grow up to be **aggressive** and **anti-social** if they had inherited a 'short' version of a gene called MAOA. However, they noted **carriers** only became anti-social if they had *experienced an **abusive upbringing***. Carriers of MAOA who experienced good mothering were usually completely normal. Therefore, it shows an interaction between genes and the environment.

Suomi (1971) argued monkeys are genetically **predetermined** to engage in risk-taking and aggressive behaviour. He identified two types of rhesus monkey personality:

Personality type 1: *Neurotics* – Non-risk takers and shy. These accounted for about 20 per cent of each generation. These monkeys are slow to leave their mothers' sides when young; they are quiet and nervous and form fewer bonds with other monkeys. Despite a naturally **neurotic** personality, they slowly acquire the necessary social skills necessary for living in a group and eventually **mate**.

Personality type 2: *Bullies* – Risk takers and aggressive. These accounted for about 10 per cent of each generation. They did not know how to control their aggression *despite strong environmental cues from other monkeys to **modify** their behaviour.* For example, they could not read social signs from other monkeys to calm down and so they annoyed their peers and adult monkeys with their unacceptable behaviour. They were slowly socially rejected; they became isolated. Most died before reaching adulthood.

Principle 2: Animal research may inform our understanding of human behaviour.

Suomi and Lesch (2002) identified a gene that allows serotonin to be processed efficiently or inefficiently. They took cerebral spinal fluid from 132 juvenile rhesus monkeys and analysed it for serotonin metabolite traces. A high level of metabolite would indicate a high level of serotonin processing. Risk-taking bullying behaviour was **correlated with** a poor level of serotonin processing. Monkeys with a gene that did not allow them to process serotonin very well were more aggressive.

A study showing the *aggressive* effects of testosterone on rats was conducted by Wagner and Beuving (1979).

Method: The researchers performed a laboratory experiment on rats whereby the independent variable was testosterone and was **manipulated** via **castration**; the dependent variable was aggression and was measured by counting bites and bite attacks.

Results: Castration reduced aggression. Injections of testosterone restored aggression in castrated mice who were previously judged to be aggressive and who had lost their aggression due to castration.

Conclusion: Testosterone has clear links with aggressive behaviour in mice. Methodologically this was a very tightly controlled study with a clear independent variable (testosterone) and a clear, quantifiable dependent variable (number of bites). However, caution should always be used when generalizing the results of animal studies to humans. And testosterone did not cause previously judged non-aggressive mice to become aggressive. Therefore, caution should be used when arguing testosterone alone is enough to cause aggression.

Aggression has also been linked to low levels of serotonin and monoamine oxidase. The levels of these chemicals are controlled by genes. Suomi (2005) studied wild rhesus monkeys that are closely related to humans in terms of genetic code and found high levels of serotonin in the least aggressive animals and low levels in the most aggressive. This suggests that testosterone is not the only hormone involved in aggression. It may be that serotonin acts as a 'brake' on the effects of testosterone. Furthermore, Suomi studied **rearing** styles: one group was reared in a **nurturing**, supportive environment and the other in a less supportive, non-nurturing environment (left to look after themselves with their siblings). As expected the non-nurtured group had low levels of serotonin and high levels of aggression and the opposite was true of those reared by their mothers; they had high levels of serotonin and low aggression coupled with risk-taking behaviour. Suomi argued the environment was therefore shown to moderate the effect of hormonal **predisposition** on behaviour.

Principle 3: Cognitions, emotions, and behaviours are products of the anatomy and physiology of our nervous and endocrine systems.

Cognitions: Memory has been linked to the hippocampus in the form of anterograde amnesia which is an inability to create new memories. Sufferers do not have the ability to pass information from their short-term memory store to their long-term memory store. This leads to a partial or complete inability to recall the past. Clive Wearing and Henry Molaison suffer from anterograde amnesia as the result of damage to the hippocampus: HM had his hippocampus removed. CW had his damaged after getting a virus.

Emotions: Aggressive emotions have been linked to brain structures. Raine et al. (1991) found lower activity than in the controls in the prefrontal cortex which has been linked to a loss of self-control and altered emotion. There was lower activity than in the controls in the amygdala which is thought to control emotional expression.

Behaviours: Wagner and Beuving (1979) clearly demonstrate a link between the endocrine system (testosterone) and aggressive behaviours in mice.

Subject vocabulary

quantifiable something which can be measured exactly with numbers

hippocampus part of the brain involved with (among other things) emotions and memory

Synonyms

rearing................ parenting

nurturing............ caring

Glossary

to predispose/predisposition a tendency to behave in a particular way

GLO 3: Discuss how and why particular research methods are used at the biological level of analysis

Research method 1: Experiments

Experiments manipulate the independent variable to measure the effect on a dependent variable (while controlling other variables). A good example of an experiment was conducted on rats by Wagner and Beuving (1979) whereby the independent variable was testosterone and this was manipulated via castration and the dependent variable was aggression and this was measured by counting bites and bite attacks. Experiments are used because they show clear causation between variables. Experiments allow variables to be isolated and then studied in-depth (e.g. testosterone and aggression).

Research method 2: Case studies

The cases of Clive Wearing and Henry Molaison offer detailed **insight** into rare disorders caused by biological problems. Case studies collect detail from as many sources as possible. For example, in both cases, the families became a key part of the research process which produced richer and more personal data as they were able to interact with the subjects and offer insights as to how they behaved both before and after the memory loss. This has been particularly true with Clive Wearing: his wife has given key insights into his condition and adaption. Both of these case studies are good examples of how to conduct ethical research within a biological area of interest.

Experiments are used because they show clear causation between variables. They allow variables to be isolated and then studied in-depth (e.g. testosterone and aggression).

Case studies are used because they offer detailed insight into rare disorders caused by biological problems. They produce rich and personal data.

Subject vocabulary

glucose metabolism the rate at which glucose is used

metabolism biological activity

psychological disorders abnormal behaviour which needs treatment

biological determinism the idea that behaviour has a biological *cause*

reductionism/reductionist approach studying complex things by reducing them into their less complex parts

non-invasive when no break in the skin is created and there is no contact with an internal body space beyond a natural body orifice

Synonyms

ethical .... moral

Glossary

insight clear and/or deep information

GLO 4: Discuss ethical considerations related to research studies at the biological level of analysis

Ethical consideration 1: The use of animals in research

Animals in genetic research are particularly useful as researchers do not have the same level of moral obligation as they do towards humans. Wagner and Beuving (1979) and Suomi and Lesch (2002) made good use of their animal subjects to show how complex behaviour has biological roots (biological reductionism). However, there are strict guidelines that should be followed:

The British Society of Animal Science wrote a set of ethical guidelines for the use of animals in research experimentation which they refer to as the 3Rs:

- *Refinement:* Any animal science research undertaken should be as focused as possible and have *realistic and achievable aims* of increasing knowledge of the species of interest in relation to our understanding of its functioning, performance, health, or welfare.
- *Replacement:* Researchers must consider all available options to *replace* animals with other techniques that will fulfil the research objectives. Researchers should always actively look for non-animal methods of investigation.
- *Reduction:* There is a scientific, moral, and legal requirement to expose as few animals to pain, suffering, and distress as possible.

Ethical consideration 2: The use of non-invasive techniques (such as PET scans)

Raine et al. (1997) made good use of PET scans while preserving the **anonymity** of the human subjects they researched. Non-invasive techniques do not cause harm to subjects and still give valuable insights into links between biological factors and behaviour.

Ethical consideration 3: Informed consent

The cases of Clive Wearing and Henry Molaison offer good examples of ethical research into rare disorders caused by biological problems. Neither Wearing or Molaison could give *informed* consent as they did not have the ability to understand the research process. However, in both cases, the families became a key part of the research process and were able to give **consent *by proxy***. The researchers were careful not to be seen to be exploiting sick men for their own ends. Henry Molaison had his anonymity protected until after he died. The use of the families had research benefits as they were able to offer personal data and offer insight as to how they behaved both before and after the memory loss. This has been particularly true with Clive Wearing – his wife has given key insights into his condition and adaption. Both of these case studies are good examples of how to conduct ethical research within a biological area of interest.

Researchers should always remember their participants are living people and should always consider their feelings with regards to all aspects of the research process.

Glossary

anonymity keeping the name secret

consent by proxy to give permission on another person's behalf

Hints for success: Always use previously learned material to support a GLO answer and use examples of research to support each point you are making.

Evaluate schema theory with reference to research studies

Opening sentence:

In this answer I will evaluate schema theory with reference to research studies.

Model sentence: I will first define schema theory.

Schemas help organize information in memory. They are arranged as **hierarchies** of knowledge and characteristics. They are also *mental plans* for action as they allow us to know what to expect and how to behave in different situations.

Schemas are organized according to *fixed values* (unchangeable characteristics that *must* be present, e.g. table and chairs in a restaurant), *default values* (the most typical or probable characteristics a schema is likely to encounter, e.g. waitress and menu), and *optional values* (characteristics that may vary according to the specific memory the schema is storing, e.g. chopsticks or knives and forks).

Schemas are fairly **stable** and **resistant to** change. This means there is **continuity** in the ways we process information and the ways we act.

The content of schemas is **constructed** through personal experience and taught beliefs.

Schemas represent social norms for ways of thinking and behaving.

Evaluation:

Positives

Schema theory is well supported with empirical studies.

Model sentence: A key advantage of this theory is the amount of empirical evidence it has supporting it. For example:

Example study 1: Office schema

Brewer and Treyens (1981) tested memory for objects in an office that 30 subjects had waited in individually for 35 seconds. Their 'office schema' seemed to strongly affect their recall. Expected objects (e.g. a desk - a fixed value) that were in the room were recalled well but unexpected objects (e.g. a pair of **pliers** - optional value) were usually not. Some participants falsely recalled expected objects that were not actually in the room (e.g. books and pens - default values).

Example study 2: War of the Ghosts

Aim: To investigate the effect of schemas on memory (Bartlett, 1932).

Method: Bartlett asked English participants to read *The War of the Ghosts*, a Native American **folk tale** containing details about hunting seals in canoes.

The participants' memory for this story was tested by serial reproduction and repeated reproduction. In *serial reproduction*, the first participant reads the original story and then **reproduces** it on paper. The first participant's reproduction is read by the second participant who also reproduces it for a third participant. This procedure continues until six or seven reproductions are completed by an equal number of

Glossary

hierarchy a system based on importance

stable remains the same

to resist/be resistant to to not want to do something

continuity permanence

plier a tool

folk tale traditional story

to reproduce/reproduction to make a copy

Synonyms

constructed......... built

Subject vocabulary

social norms expected or usual ways to behave

empirical studies studies that produce testable data (usually quantitative or numbered) and are conducted with correct procedures

subjects people

participants. In *repeated reproduction*, the same participant writes all six or seven reproductions over many years.

Results: The two methods led to very similar findings; the story became increasingly shorter and changed to suit the English cultural background of the participants. For example, 'hunting seals' became 'fishing' and 'canoes' became 'boats'. What started as a very strange story to the participants became a traditional English story.

Evaluation: Methodologically this is a very **robust** study with two ways of assessing schema use (serial reproduction and repeated reproduction) and conducted over many years. Culturally this is very specific to England in the 1930s. The details cannot be generalized to modern society as most modern English people know what seals and canoes are. However, the basic principle remains **intact** and demonstrated with this research: *people change details to suit their own frame of understanding of the world (schemas).*

Negatives

Schema theory does not explain *why* information that does not quite fit our schemas, especially minor details, may be **ignored** and forgotten (selection and storage) or **distorted** (normalization) so as to make better sense to us.

Schema theory does not explain why the guesses/filling-in of memory by the default values (integration and interpretation, retrieval) may be completely **inaccurate**.

Schema theory describes but does not fully explain *how* schemas are constructed and maintained.

Schemas help organize information in memory. They are arranged as hierarchies of knowledge and characteristics. They are also mental plans for action as they allow us to know what to expect and how to behave in different situations.

Schemas are fairly stable and resistant to change. This means there is continuity in the ways we process information and the ways we act.

The content of schemas is constructed through personal experience and taught beliefs.

Schemas represent social norms for ways of thinking and behaving.

Hints for success: Use supporting studies as positive evaluation. They show a theory has support from research.

Synonyms

robust................. strong

intact.................. unchanged

distorted............ changed

inaccurate.......... wrong

Glossary

ignored not given attention to

Evaluate two models or theories of one cognitive process (for example, memory, perception, language, decision-making) with reference to research studies

Subject vocabulary

cognition/cognitive related to mental processes (such as perception, memory, problem-solving)

empirical data from standardized and properly conducted research studies

primacy first

recency last

Opening sentence:

The cognitive process I will address is *memory*. The two models I will evaluate are the multi-store model (MSM) and the Levels of Processing model (LOP).

Model 1: The multi-store model (MSM) of memory (Atkinson and Shiffrin, 1968)

According to the MSM, memory consists of three types of memory store: sensory store, short-term store (STS), and long-term store (LTS)

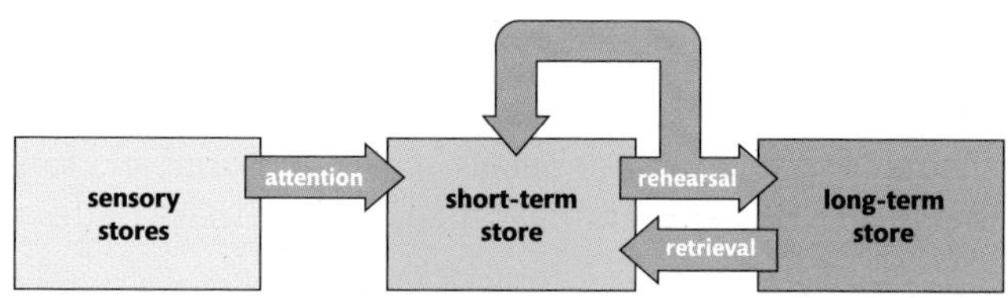

The sensory store is of unlimited capacity. It has many stores to reflect our various senses. For example, visual information enters the visual sensory store and is stored in visual form (images). Auditory information enters the auditory sensory store and is stored as a sound-based code (sounds).

The STS has an extremely limited capacity. It can store only around seven units of information at any one time. The LTS is of unlimited capacity and information stored there can last up to a lifetime. LTS uses codes *based on meaning* (known as semantic codes). Information that is remembered is retrieved from the LTS (retrieval), which brings information back to the STS.

Evaluation of the MSM

Positive evaluation

The MSM is supported by empirical evidence.

Evidence 1: Free-recall experiments and the serial position curve

Glossary

in succession one after the other

to rehearse/rehearsal to practise or repeat something

displaced replaced by another

In free-recall experiments, subjects are given a number of words (for example, 20) **in succession** to remember and are then asked to recall them in any order ('free recall'). The results reliably fall into a pattern known as the *serial position curve*. This curve consists of a primacy effect – participants tend to recall the first words of the list very well, which indicates that the first words entered the STS and had time to be **rehearsed** and passed on to the LTS. The items from the middle of the list are remembered far less well than those at the beginning and the end. This is probably because the increasing number of items fills the limited capacity of the STS and these later items are unable to be properly rehearsed and transferred to LTM before they are **displaced**. A recency effect is participants usually recall those items from the end of the list first. This is because the words are in the STS and are therefore available for immediate recall.

In sum: Words that are in a definite store (either STS or LTS) will be recalled well. Those that have not been rehearsed properly will not be recalled as well.

Evidence 2: Anterograde amnesia

Anterograde amnesia is a memory disorder where the patient is not able to create new memories. Examples are Clive Wearing and Henry Molaison.

Model sentence: **Anterograde amnesia appears to stop the rehearsal between the STS and LTS which clearly supports the basic assumptions behind the MSM of *stores* and *rehearsal*.**

Negative evaluation

- It does not account for how memories are stored based on their importance.
- It does not account for the emotional aspect of memory.
- The emphasis is on structures (the stores) and not *processing*. The MSM did make reference to a number of control processes, including attention and rehearsal, but it does not say in detail how these work or why they work.

Model 2: The Levels of Processing model/theory (LOP) of memory (Craik and Lockhart, 1972)

According to the LOP, memory is a by-product of **perception**. Memory is a direct consequence of the way information is perceived or then **encoded**. The deeper the level at which information is processed, the longer-lasting the memory trace it creates in memory. The LOP ignores the idea of different memory stores. Craik and Lockhart do not deny stores exist; they just focus on *processing of information* rather than storage.

Evaluation of the LOP approach

Positive evaluation

The LOP approach is supported by empirical evidence.

Evidence: Craik and Tulving (1975) had participants process words differently by asking them structural, phonological, and semantic questions (What does this word look like? Is the word written in capital letters? What does this word sound like? What does this word mean?). The participants were not told to memorize the target words. Following the initial task, participants were tested to see if they had learned the target words. Participants were surprised with a list of words containing words already presented to them and new words. The participants had to recognize the words already shown to them (this is called a memory recognition test).

Results: Words processed at the semantic level were the best remembered, followed by the phonologically processed words. Words processed at the structural level were the least well remembered.

Negative evaluation

- There is no *'why'* in the theory - we don't know why certain information is processed differently than others.
- The theory is too simplistic and does not address the retrieval stage of the memory process. Retrieval is a key part of memory.
- The theory lacks ecological validity. Most of the supporting studies have been conducted using words as recall items. Real life is more complex.

Subject vocabulary

attention the control process responsible for the transfer of information from the sensory store to the STS

ecological validity having realism and being able to generalize to real-life situations

Glossary

to perceive/perception to see or understand information

encoded processed

Hints for success: Only write the names of the models once. Put the initials in brackets after you have written them. Then use the initials for the rest of the answer - in this case MSM and LOP. It should be noted: all models are simplistic and can never fully show the cognitive process being represented (in this case memory).

Explain how biological factors may affect one cognitive process

Opening sentence:

The biological factors I will address in this answer are *lesions* and Alzheimer's disease (AD). The cognitive process is memory.

Biological factor 1: Lesions

A lesion is damage to brain tissue. Lesioning demonstrates that different memories are stored in different areas of the brain.

Study 1: Rats in the water maze (Clark et al., 2009)

Aim: To investigate the effect of hippocampal lesioning on spatial memory.

Method: Rats were placed in a container of water - a water maze. A platform was placed just below the surface of the water - allowing them to climb out of the water but be unable to see the platform below the surface of the water. They could only find the platform by seeing objects outside of the maze (for example, posters on the testing room wall). All rats quickly learned the platform location within the first few days of training.

One group was lesioned (experimental group); one group was not (control group). The independent variable (IV) was the lesion on the hippocampus. The dependent variable (DV) was spatial memory and was operationalized by the time taken to find where the invisible platform was in the water tank.

Results: Lesion groups could not remember where the platform was and when they did locate it they took significantly longer to re-locate it than the non-lesion group.

Conclusion: The hippocampus is responsible for spatial memory.

Study 2: The case of Henry Molaison (previously known as HM) (based on Blakemore, 1988)

Molaison had been suffering epileptic fits since the age of 16. At 27 he had surgery to remove various parts of his brain including the hippocampus. The surgery cured his epilepsy but he was left with **severe** anterograde amnesia. His short-term store (STS) was generally normal; for instance, he could retain verbal information for about 15 seconds without **rehearsal** and for much longer with rehearsal. This suggests the damage caused by his surgery meant he could not transfer information into his long-term store (LTS) or, if he could, he could not retrieve it.

A lesion is damage to brain tissue.
Lesioning demonstrates that different memories are stored in different areas of the brain.

Subject vocabulary

Alzheimer's disease an incurable illness characterized by brain deterioration. Memory loss is a common symptom

cognition/cognitive related to mental processes (such as perception, memory, problem-solving)

hippocampal lesioning damage to the hippocampus

spatial memory the ability to understand geographical spaces and remember where objects are placed

independent variable (IV) the variable an experimenter controls or changes

hippocampus part of the brain involved with (among other things) emotions and memory

dependent variable (DV) the variable an experimenter measures

operationalized *how* the IV is manipulated and *how* the DV is measured

epileptic fit a form of brain seizure where the brain stops working normally

Glossary

maze a puzzle where a correct route has to be found

to rehearse/rehearsal to practise or repeat something

Synonyms

severe................. very bad/serious

Biological factor 2: Alzheimer's disease (AD)

Alzheimer's disease (AD) is a serious **degenerative** brain disease affecting memory.

Causes:

- **Tau protein:** Tau protein normally forms part of the support structure of neurons. In Alzheimer's disease, the tau protein is abnormal and, as a result, the structural support of neurons collapses.
- **Amyloid protein:** Amyloid protein forms into amyloid plaques and damages the membranes of neurons (Lorenzo et al., 2000). Most AD patients develop amyloid plaques before the **onset** of AD (Selco, 1990).

Amyloid plaques and abnormal proteins lead to the **degradation** of brain tissue.

AD does not influence every memory system equally.

Episodic memory

Episodic memory is the most severely affected. Episodic memory is memory for events and personal experiences (autobiographical memory) that occurred in a given place at a particular time. An analysis by Salthouse and Becker (1998), of data from 180 AD patients and over 1000 normal elderly individuals, found that AD was mainly a disorder of episodic memory.

Semantic memory

Semantic memory stores general knowledge about the world, concepts, and language. There is a steady decline in semantic memory.

Procedural memory

Procedural memory is memory for the performance of particular types of action such as riding a bike. Procedural memory is less affected by AD.

Supporting study

Aim: To investigate early detection of Alzheimer's (Mosconi, 2005).

Method: A longitudinal study followed a sample of 53 normal and healthy participants between 9 years and 24 years. PET scans were used together with a computer program to measure hippocampus metabolism.

Results: Individuals who showed early signs of reduced metabolism in the hippocampus were associated with later development of AD.

Conclusion: The hippocampus is a central part of memory processes and reduced metabolism may be a sign of AD.

Conclusions from studying AD

AD develops through a series of stages through the medial and temporal lobe structures (MTLs). The MTLs are important for episodic and semantic memory.

The two biological factors are lesions and Alzheimer's disease.

The cognitive process is memory.

Glossary

degenerative cannot be reversed/only gets worse

degradation breaking down/wasting away

Subject vocabulary

amyloid plaques tangles of protein in nerve tissue that cause damage

longitudinal study research that has taken place over a long period of time, usually years

positron emission tomography (PET) (positron emission tomography) monitors glucose metabolism in the brain. PET scans produce coloured maps of mental activity to show where the brain is using energy

metabolism biological activity

Synonyms

onset .... start

Hints for success: Use logical sub-headings to separate your answers. They will give a clear structure and focus. In this case use: *Biological factor 1: Lesions* and *Biological factor 2: AD.*

Discuss how social or cultural factors affect one cognitive process

Opening sentence:

The cognitive process I will address in this answer is memory. The social factor I will discuss is *schooling*. The cultural factor is *cultural schemas*.

Schooling and memory storage

Aim: To investigate the effect of schooling on memory (Cole and Scribner, 1974).

Method 1: They gave free-recall word tasks to children in the USA and children from the Kpelle people of **rural Liberia**. The researchers did not use the same list of words in the two countries. They used local college-educated people in Liberia to help develop the word lists to make sure the words used in the memory tests were familiar to the participants.

Result 1: Older children did *not* recall more items after practice. This was *unexpected* because usually older children remember more. This was only the case if the children had attended school.

Result 2: The non-schooled children did not improve their performance on free-recall tasks after the age of 10. They remembered around ten items the first time. After 15 practice trials they remembered only two more items.

Result 3: Children who had attended school in Liberia learned the lists just as well as children in the USA.

Conclusion: Schooling improves ability on free-recall memory tests. Schooling forces students to **rehearse** information. It forces students to learn large amounts of information in a short space of time.

Method 2: The recall task was now presented as part of a story rather than a list of words. This is called a *narrative*.

Result: The **illiterate** children recalled the objects easily and organized them according to the roles they played in the story.

Conclusion: The use of narrative/stories appears to be a more natural method for memory. Children from rural backgrounds are more likely to grow up learning via stories. Therefore, their preferred method of memory will be by stories.

Evaluation:

- **Ethics:** The study paid close attention to which types of words would be familiar to the participants. This was to make the study fair.
- **Culture:** The study used local people to help **construct** the memory tests. The study is quite old so there is limited cultural generalizability to today but the basic idea has common sense value - schooling forces children to remember large amounts of information (usually words) in a very particular way. This will be shown in free-recall tasks with words.

Subject vocabulary

cognition/cognitive related to mental processes (such as perception, memory, problem-solving)

schema a frame for understanding the world

free-recall a method used to study memory. Participants study a list of items and then are asked to recall the items in any order.

Synonyms

rural .... countryside

ethics.................. morals

construct .... build

Glossary

Liberia a country in Africa

to rehearse/rehearsal to practise or repeat something

illiterate cannot read

Cultural schemas

The War of the Ghosts

Aim: To investigate the effect of cultural schemas on memory (Bartlett, 1932).

Method: Bartlett asked English participants to read *The War of the Ghosts*, a Native American **folk tale** containing details about hunting seals in canoes.

The participants' memory for this story was tested by serial **reproduction** and repeated reproduction. In serial reproduction, the first participant reads the original story and then reproduces it on paper. The first participant's reproduction is read by the second participant who also reproduces it for a third participant. This procedure continues until six or seven reproductions are completed by an equal number of participants. In repeated reproduction, the same participant writes all six or seven reproductions over many years.

Results: The two methods led to very similar findings; the story became increasingly shorter and changed to suit the English cultural background of the participants. For example, 'hunting seals' became 'fishing' and 'canoes' became 'boats'. What started as a very strange story to the participants became a traditional English story.

Evaluation: Methodologically this is a very **robust** study with two ways of assessing schema use (serial reproduction and repeated reproduction) and conducted over many years. Culturally this is very specific to England in the 1930s. The details cannot be **generalized** to modern society as most modern English people know what seals and canoes are. However, the basic principle remains **intact** and demonstrated with this research - people's memory is affected by their own frame of understanding of the world (cultural schemas).

Culture affects memory *through schemas, demonstrated by* The War of the Ghosts.

Schooling affects memory *by improving ability on free-recall memory tests. Schooling forces students to rehearse information. It forces students to learn large amounts of information in a short space of time.*

Hints for success: You can evaluate studies but do not dismiss them. They are reasonable support for the **phenomena**.

Glossary

folk tale traditional story

to reproduce/reproduction to make a copy

to generalize/generalization to comment on something very basic, based on limited facts, and apply it to other situations

Synonyms

robust................ strong

intact.................. unchanged

phenomena........ events/happenings

With reference to relevant research studies, to what extent is one cognitive process reliable?

Synonyms

reliable .... unfailing

altered .... changed

robust .... strong

intact .... unchanged

recall .... remember

Subject vocabulary

cognition/cognitive related to mental processes (such as perception, memory, problem-solving)

schema a frame for understanding the world

independent variable (IV) the variable an experimenter controls or changes

dependent variable (DV) the variable an experimenter measures

operationalized *how* the IV is manipulated and *how* the DV is measured

Glossary

verb word used to describe an action

folk tale traditional story

to reproduce/reproduction to make a copy

to generalize/generalization to comment on something very basic, based on limited facts, and apply it to other situations

(eye)witness a person who sees something, usually a crime

testimony statement of what is true

Opening sentence:

The cognitive process I will address in this answer is memory. I will show how memory can be **altered** by *cultural schemas*, *leading verbs*, and *age-related schemas*.

Evidence 1: Cultural schemas affect memory

Aim: To investigate the effect of cultural schemas on memory (Bartlett, 1932).

Method: Bartlett asked English participants to read The War of the Ghosts, a Native American **folk tale** containing details about hunting seals in canoes.

The participants' memory for this story was tested by serial **reproduction** and repeated reproduction. In serial reproduction, the first participant reads the original story and then reproduces it on paper. The first participant's reproduction is read by the second participant who also reproduces it for a third participant. This procedure continues until six or seven reproductions are completed by an equal number of participants. In repeated reproduction, the same participant writes all six or seven reproductions over many years.

Results: The two methods led to very similar findings; the story became increasingly shorter and changed to suit the English cultural background of the participants. For example, 'hunting seals' became 'fishing' and 'canoes' became 'boats'. What started as a very strange story to the participants became a traditional English story.

Evaluation: Methodologically this is a very **robust** study with two ways of assessing schema use (serial reproduction and repeated reproduction) and conducted over many years. Culturally this is very specific to England in the 1930s. The details cannot be **generalized** to modern society as most modern English people know what seals and canoes are. However, the basic principle remains **intact** and demonstrated with this research - people's memory is affected by their own frame of understanding of the world (cultural schemas).

Evidence 2: Verbs affect memory of false objects

Aim: To investigate how leading verbs can change **eyewitness testimony** with **recall** of objects (Loftus and Palmer, 1974).

Method: Participants were presented with a one-minute film showing a car accident. The independent variable (IV) was the presence of a leading verb (either hit or smashed). The dependent variable (DV) was recall of false objects and was operationalized by asking whether the participants saw any *broken glass* a week after seeing the film. In reality there was no broken glass.

Results: 32 per cent of those who had been asked about the cars' speed with the verb smash claimed they had seen broken glass compared to only 14 per cent of the participants in the hit group.

Conclusion: Verbs can change memory and cause objects to be remembered that were not present.

Evidence 3: The effect of age-related schemas on eyewitness testimony

Aim: To investigate the effects of age of witness and age of **suspect** on eyewitness testimony (Parker and Carranza, 2005).

Method: 48 elementary school children and 48 college students viewed a slide sequence of a **mock** crime. This was followed by showing photos with either the **criminal** present or absent within them. The IV was age and the DV was accuracy of memory.

Results: Younger child witnesses had a higher rate of choosing the correct criminal than adult witnesses.

Conclusion: Older people have more fixed expectations or schemas over what a criminal should look like. Therefore they made more mistakes if the criminal who committed the crime did not fit their existing schemas. They tried to fit what they remembered with their existing schema.

Concluding comments

Memory is not a straightforward recall. Memory is an active reconstructive process rather than a passive reproductive one. It should be noted in all of these studies the '**gist**' of the situation (e.g. hunting trips, car crashes, and crimes taking place) was recalled correctly. Memory of specific details was influenced when researchers deliberately set out to influence it. Investigating memory is important because of the influence eyewitness testimonies have on legal trials.

Verbs affect memory by changing memory and causing objects to be remembered that were not present.

Age affects memory as older people have more fixed expectations or schemas over what a criminal should look like. Therefore they made more mistakes if the criminal who committed the crime did not fit their existing schemas. They tried to fit what they remembered with their existing schema.

Memory is an active reconstructive process rather than a passive reproductive one.

Glossary

suspect a person who may have committed a crime

mock not real

criminal a person who commits a crime

gist main idea

Subject vocabulary

active reconstructive process a process that builds knowledge rather than receives it and is therefore open to change

passive reproductive process a process that receives knowledge and does not add to it. This extreme view of memory is no longer considered realistic

Hints for success: Use logical sub-headings with clear labels to separate your answers. They will give a clear structure and focus. In this case: *Evidence 1, 2, 3,* and *4*.

Discuss the use of technology in investigating cognitive processes

Opening sentence:

The technologies I will discuss are PET scans and MRI scans with memory.

PET scans

PET (positron emission tomography) is a scanning method that measures glucose use and blood flow. Therefore, it is possible to see which parts of the brain are more active during certain tasks.

Key study 1

Aim: To investigate early **detection** of Alzheimer's disease (AD) (Mosconi, 2005).

Method: A longitudinal study, which followed a sample of 53 normal and healthy participants between 9 years and 24 years. PET scans were used together with a computer program to measure hippocampus activity.

Results: Individuals who showed early signs of reduced activity in the hippocampus were associated with later development of AD.

Conclusion: The hippocampus is a central part of memory processes and reduced activity may be a sign of AD.

Key study 2

Aim: To investigate if the hippocampus is involved with spatial memory (Maguire et al., 1997).

Method: An observational study in which PET scans were given to London taxi drivers who were asked to **recall complex** routes around London. They were then asked to recall famous landmarks that were not on taxi routes.

Results: When they were asked to recall complex routes around London the hippocampus was shown to be **activated**. When they were asked to recall famous landmarks the hippocampus was not activated.

Conclusion: The hippocampus is involved in spatial memory.

Discussion of PET scans to investigate memory

PET scan research with humans can be used in combination with animal research (such as the *rats in the water maze* by Clark et al., 2009). Experiments on living human brains for social science research purposes are not permitted for **ethical** reasons. However, conclusions can still be drawn. For example: the hippocampus is a key part of spatial memory and is shown by experimental evidence with lesioning on rats and observational evidence with PET scans on London taxi drivers.

Subject vocabulary

glucose blood sugar

longitudinal study research that has taken place over a long period of time, usually years

spatial memory the ability to understand geographical spaces and remember where objects are placed

observational study a method where the researcher has very little control over the variables; they are useful for real-life situations

social science academic disciplines that study the human condition such as sociology (with the focus on society) and psychology (with the focus on the individual)

lesioning damage to brain tissue

Synonyms

detection .... discovery/finding

recall .... remember

complex .... complicated

ethical .... moral

Glossary

to activate/activated to make something work or switch something on

MRI scans

MRI (magnetic resonance imaging) provides a three-dimensional picture of brain structures. They work by detecting changes in the use of oxygen in the blood. When an area in the brain is more active, it uses more oxygen.

Key study

The case of Henry Molaison (previously known as HM; based on Blakemore, 1988).

Molaison had been suffering epileptic fits since the age of 16. At 27 he had surgery to remove various parts of his brain including the hippocampus. The surgery cured his epilepsy but he was left with **severe** anterograde amnesia. His short-term store (STS) was generally normal; for instance, he could **retain verbal** information for about 15 seconds without **rehearsal** and for much longer with rehearsal. However, he could not transfer information into his long-term store (LTS) or, if he could, he could not **retrieve** it.

Discussion of MRI scans to investigate memory

It was first thought Molaison's brain surgery allowed a good understanding of how particular areas of the brain may be linked to memory processes. However, MRI scans of Molaison's brain in the late 1990s revealed the extent of damage was more widespread than previously thought. The MRI scans showed it was not possible to identify one particular region responsible for Molaison's memory problems.

Concluding comments

Brain technologies are used to investigate the relationship between a brain area and cognitive processes. This is known as *localization of function*: specific areas of the brain are responsible for specific behaviours. However, there are some further factors to consider:

1. Using technologies such as PET and MRI scans means there is a temptation to use localization of function to explain all human behaviour. They give clear imagery that can be linked to specific behaviour. However, such an explanation would be too simple and would be called reductionist - studying complex things by reducing them into their less complex parts.
2. Neuroplasticity means the brain has the ability to 'rewire' itself after damage - organizing new neural networks. The ability of the brain to re-map itself (to a certain extent) means we need to be cautious when using technologies such as PET and MRI scans to identify which areas of the brain are responsible for certain cognitive processes as they can be open to change.

Subject vocabulary

epilepsy a brain disorder that can cause seizures

anterograde amnesia the inability to create new memories. Information cannot be transferred from the STS to the LTS

short-term store (STS) of limited capacity and can only store around seven units of information at any one time. The STS can store information from a few seconds to half a minute

long-term store (LTS) of unlimited capacity and information stored there can last up to a lifetime. LTS uses codes *based on meaning* (known as semantic codes)

cognition/cognitive related to mental processes (such as perception, memory, problem-solving)

Synonyms

severe .... very bad/ serious

retain .... keep/save

verbal .... spoken/oral

Glossary

to rehearse/rehearsal to practise or repeat something

to retrieve to get back

Hints for success: Use logical sub-headings to separate your answers - in this case *PET scans* and *MRI scans*. They will give a clear structure and focus. You can use the abbreviations and not the full labels for the technology.

To what extent do cognitive and biological factors interact in emotion

Subject vocabulary

cognition/cognitive related to mental processes (such as perception, memory, problem-solving)

autonomic nervous system the system that controls vital processes away from conscious awareness, e.g. breathing, swallowing, and heart rate

endocrine system the system that delivers hormones to the body. Hormones are chemicals which influence the body (e.g. testosterone)

neurotransmitters chemicals in the brain that are involved with communication

Glossary

to interpret to give meaning to something

to moderate/moderation to make less extreme

Synonyms

arousal	stimulation
deficits	shortages
aggression	anger/ violence
neurons	nerves
rage	anger

Opening sentence:

In this answer I will demonstrate how cognitive and biological factors are involved in emotion. I will use theories and studies to support my answer and evaluate where appropriate.

Model sentence: **I will first define emotion:**

Emotion is a physiological or bodily change, **interpreted** by an individual who then decides on an appropriate behavioural response. It consists of three basic components.

- Physiological or bodily change: such as **arousal** of the autonomic nervous system and the endocrine system that are not conscious.
- Subjective interpretation: the person's own interpretation of an emotion (e.g. happiness). This is a cognitive process and may or may not be conscious.
- Behavioural display: such as smiling, showing anger, or running away.

Therefore, physiology and emotion are linked by *cognition* (thought processes). There is an *appraisal* process that considers the bodily reaction to a stimulus and what behaviour should then follow.

Physiological factors

Model sentence: **There are many physiological factors involved in emotion. Here I present two:**

1. **The brain stem**

   The brain stem connects the brain to the spinal cord. It contains structures responsible for releasing brain neurotransmitters, including:

   Noradrenaline – involved in pleasurable sensations while **deficits** are thought to be involved in depression.

   Dopamine – involved in the control of emotion and **aggression**.

   Endorphins – released by many **neurons** throughout the nervous system. They play a vital role in **moderating** the experience of pain, fear, and anxiety.

2. **The neocortex and sham rage**

   The neocortex is part of the cerebral cortex but it is the newest part to evolve (hence the term *neo*). Bard (1934) showed that the removal of the neocortex in cats and dogs produced sham rage. Sham rage can be defined as rage reactions triggered by unthreatening stimuli. Bard was able to establish unthreatening stimuli by using a repeated measures design (e.g. touching the same cats' tails before and after surgery). Sham rage symptoms are normal anger and defence reactions the animals would usually display. The key finding is the animals showing rage to previously non-rage-inducing stimuli. The behaviour of each animal was observed before the surgery was performed, noting how calm and friendly the animal was with humans and other animals, as well as their reactions to being handled. After the surgery, Bard observed that the animals would have an extreme rage reaction to stimuli that had previously produced little to no response, like touching the tail. He concluded the reason for this might be that the removal of the neocortex causes a loss of **inhibition** of the areas involved in the rage reaction, causing those areas to become **hyperactive**.

Cognitive factors

Model sentence: I will now focus on the cognitive factor of appraisal.

Study: The adrenaline and the stooge experiment

Individuals interpret signals being sent to them and then give them meaning (appraisal). Schachter and Singer (1962) conducted a laboratory experiment whereby they injected participants with either a placebo substance or adrenaline (adrenaline is known as epinephrine in the USA) and then put them in a room with either a happy or angry stooge. A stooge is an individual who was part of the experiment but whose real role was not explained to the participants.

Their main results were:

- *Adrenaline informed group:* Participants who were told of the real side effects of adrenaline (general arousal of the sympathetic nervous system causing accelerated heartbeat/breathing, etc.) reported no significant increase in happiness or anger. Why? Because they had an explanation for their physiological arousal and did not need to appraise (give meaning to) their new-found physiological state.
- *Adrenaline ignorant:* Participants who were told of no side effects reported being happier/angrier. Why? They needed an external explanation for their new-found aroused state. They now needed to appraise the situation when they found their bodies reacting (accelerated heartbeat, etc.). They could not 'blame' the substance they had been injected with as they had been told it would *not* give them side effects. Therefore they had to look for an explanation. They found the 'cause' of their new-found aroused state in the form of the angry or happy stooge. This mistaken appraisal had led to the emotion being *felt* as either happy or angry depending on which stooge they were exposed to.
- *Control ignorant:* Participants who were given a placebo (a saline solution which has no direct effect on arousal of their nervous system) and told there would be no side effects at all were found to be slightly happier/angrier. Although they did not experience physiological arousal and did not need an external explanation for their aroused state as they did not have one, they *still* felt happier/angrier being in the same room as a happy or angry stooge. This means an external, non-biological event (a stooge) had an impact on their emotions.

Emotion consists of three basic components:

- *physiological or bodily change*
- *subjective interpretation*
- *behavioural display.*

Glossary

inhibition feeling of worry/embarrassment that stops you from doing/saying something

Synonyms

hyperactive......... overactive

Subject vocabulary

adrenaline hormone secreted by the adrenal glands in response to stress and leads to increased heart rate, pulse rate, and blood pressure

placebo a fake treatment that can often have an effect. Researchers compare their effects with the real treatment

Hints for success:
The emphasis is on demonstrating the extent cognitive and biological factors are involved in emotion. While evaluating theories and studies is important do not focus your answer too heavily on this area of evaluation. Make sure you address *both* cognitive and biological factors as evenly as possible in terms of space on the exam paper.

Evaluate one theory of how emotion may affect one cognitive process

Subject vocabulary

cognition/cognitive related to mental processes (such as perception, memory, problem-solving)

empirical data from standardized and properly conducted research studies

Glossary

to encounter to come across

to rehearse/rehearsal to practise or repeat something

to ruminate to think over and over

civil rights movements groups fighting for legal rights for citizens

Synonyms

vivid .... clear

assassinations ..... killings

recalled .... remembered

Opening sentence:

The theory I will evaluate is flashbulb memory (FBM) by Brown and Kulik (1977).

A flashbulb memory is a highly detailed, exceptionally clear 'snapshot' of a moment in which a piece of surprising and emotional news was heard.

They usually:

- form in situations where we **encounter** *surprising* and highly *emotional* information
- are maintained by means of overt **rehearsal** (involving discussion with others) and covert rehearsal (private rehearsing or **ruminating**)
- differ from other memories in that they are more **vivid**, last longer, and are more consistent and accurate.

Flashbulb memories have six characteristic features: place (where the event happened), ongoing activity (what the person was doing), informant (who broke the news), own affect (how did I feel?), other affect (how did other people feel?), and aftermath (what did I do next? what happened in the long run?).

Positive evaluation

Flashbulb theory supports the underlying assumptions of Levels of Processing by Craik and Lockhart (1972): Emotional events are more likely to be processed more deeply and therefore remembered. It has common-sense value.

Model sentence: There is empirical evidence for the existence of FBM.

Study 1

Aim: To investigate flashbulb memory (Brown and Kulik, 1977).

Method: Brown and Kulik (1977) asked 80 American participants (40 white and 40 black) to answer questions about ten events. Nine of the events were mostly **assassinations** or attempted assassinations of well-known American personalities (e.g. JF Kennedy, Martin Luther King). The tenth event was a self-selected event of personal relevance and involving unexpected shock. Examples included the death of a friend or relative or a serious accident. Participants were asked to recall the circumstances they found themselves in when they first heard the news about the ten events.

Result 1: 90 per cent of the participants **recalled** the assassination of JF Kennedy in 1963 and where they were in vivid detail.

Result 2: African-Americans reported more FBMs for leaders of **civil rights movements** (e.g. the assassination of Martin Luther King) than white Americans.

Result 3: Most participants recalled a personal FBM which tended to be related to learning about the death of a parent.

Conclusion: Surprising information is likely to be remembered. Events which have high personal and emotional relevance are likely to be remembered. This is shown by the African-Americans having FBMs for civil rights leader assassinations.

Model sentence: **There is physiological evidence for the existence of FBM.**

Study 2

Aim: To investigate the role of the amygdala in memory formation.

Method: Meta-analysis of literature from animal lesion studies and human brain imaging studies (McGaugh, 2004).

Results: The amygdala plays an important role in **regulating** the effects of adrenaline (caused by emotional events) and memory formation. The findings of human brain imaging studies show the activation of the amygdala influences long-term memory. The degree of emotional activation of the amygdala **correlates** highly with memory ability. It is thought it is influenced by the presence of adrenaline.

Conclusion: Emotions are biological events and these influence memory formation via the amygdala.

Negative evaluation

Neisser (1982) suggests memories are so clear because the event itself is rehearsed and *reconsidered* after the event. What is actually being remembered is not a memory of an event but a memory of a story about an event: people remember their **reconstruction** rather than the actual event. For example: flashbulb memories usually appear in the form of stories with a storytelling structure, such as place (Where were we?), activity (What were we doing?), a character (Who told us?), and affect (How did we feel about it?).

Emotions force us to make sense of the event. The use of stories/narratives ('I was sitting on the floor when I heard...') helps us deal with the emotional situation we found ourselves in but not remember the actual information accurately.

FBMs usually produce a great deal of confidence from the individual that their memories are accurate but the levels of inaccuracy are so high it is possible to argue that FBM could not actually be considered as a 'memory'.

Neisser and Harsch (1992) investigated people's memory accuracy of the Space Shuttle Challenger crash. It was a televised event and many people watched it. They questioned people 24 hours after the accident, and then again 2 years later. The participants were very confident their memories were correct, but the researchers found that 40 per cent of the participants had inaccurate memories. Conclusion: Emotions create inaccuracy in memory.

Flashbulb memory theory is built on memory research from public events (e.g. assassinations and national tragedies). There is a shortage of studies regarding personal events such as accidents or trauma because the accuracy of these details is difficult to **verify**.

A flashbulb memory is a highly detailed, exceptionally clear 'snapshot' of a moment in which a piece of surprising and emotional news was heard.

Subject vocabulary

amygdala a part of the brain associated with memory

meta-analysis a review of many studies into the same phenomena to see what broad conclusions can be made

lesion brain damage

Synonyms

regulating .... controlling

correlates .... with links to

reconstruction .... rebuilding

verify .... check/ confirm

Hints for success: *Evaluate* means positive *and* negative things. Try and remember a balance of each.

Subject vocabulary

schema a frame for understanding the world

Synonyms

recalled .... remembered

robust................. strong

intact.................. unchanged

Glossary

plier a tool

folk tale traditional story

to reproduce/reproduction to make a copy

GLO 1: Outline principles that define the cognitive level of analysis

GLO 2: Explain how principles that define the cognitive level of analysis may be demonstrated in research (that is, theories and/or studies)

Principle 1: *Mental representations guide behaviour.*

Model sentence: Schemas **are mental representations. They guide behaviour by *creating expectations* and this influences memory.**

Example 1: Office schema

Brewer and Treyens (1981) tested memory for objects in an office that 30 subjects had waited in individually for 35 seconds. Their 'office schema' seemed to strongly affect their **recall**. Expected objects (e.g. a desk - a fixed value) that were in the room were recalled well but unexpected objects (e.g. a pair of **pliers** - optional value) were usually not. Some subjects falsely recalled expected objects that were not actually in the room (e.g. books and pens - default values).

Example 2: *The War of the Ghosts*

Aim: To investigate the effect of schemas on memory (Bartlett, 1932).

Method: Bartlett asked English participants to read *The War of the Ghosts*, a Native American **folk tale** containing details about hunting seals in canoes.

The participants' memory for this story was tested by serial **reproduction** and repeated reproduction. In serial reproduction, the first participant reads the original story and then reproduces it on paper. The first participant's reproduction is read by the second participant who also reproduces it for a third participant. This procedure continues until six or seven reproductions are completed by an equal number of participants. In repeated reproduction, the same participant writes all six or seven reproductions over many years.

Results: The two methods led to very similar findings; the story became increasingly shorter and changed to suit the English cultural background of the participants. For example, 'hunting seals' became 'fishing' and 'canoes' became 'boats'. What started as a very strange story to the participants became a traditional English story.

Evaluation: Methodologically this is a very **robust** study with two ways of assessing schema use (serial reproduction and repeated reproduction) and conducted over many years. Culturally this is very specific to England in the 1930s. The details cannot be generalized to modern society as most modern English people know what seals and canoes are. However, the basic principle remains **intact** and demonstrated with this research - people change details to suit their own frame of understanding of the world (schemas).

Principle 2: *Mental processes can be scientifically investigated.*

Model sentence: **Memory is a mental process. It has been scientifically investigated by using free-recall experiments where variables are controlled**

and the focus is on remembering impersonal material that can be tested on many subjects.

Example of an experiment: Verbs affect speed estimates

Aim: To investigate how leading verbs can change **eyewitness testimony** with speed estimates (Loftus and Palmer, 1974).

Method: Participants watched seven film clips of different car accidents. The independent variable (IV) was the verb used to ask the question about the cars' speed: About how fast were the cars going when they hit each other? For the other conditions the verb hit was replaced with contacted, collided, bumped, and smashed into. The dependent variable (DV) was memory and was operationalized by average speed estimates.

Results:

Verb	*Speed estimate*
Contacted	31.8 mph
Hit	34 mph
Bumped	38.1 mph
Collided	39.3 mph
Smashed	40.8 mph.

Conclusion: Memory is an active reconstructive process that can be easily **manipulated** by a **subtle** change of words.

GLO 3: Discuss how and why particular research methods are used at the cognitive level of analysis

Research method 1: Observational study using PET scans (positron emission tomography)

PET scans monitor glucose metabolism in the brain. PET scans produce coloured maps of mental activity.

Example 1

Aim: To investigate if the hippocampus is involved with spatial memory (Maguire et al., 1997).

Method: An observational study in which PET scans were given to London taxi drivers who were asked to recall **complex** routes around London. They were then asked to recall famous landmarks that were not on taxi routes.

Results: When they were asked to recall complex routes around London the hippocampus was shown to be activated. When they were asked to recall famous landmarks the hippocampus was not activated.

Conclusion: The hippocampus is involved in spatial memory.

Model sentence: Using an observational method, researchers are able to link cognitive processes (such as memory) with areas of the brain in a real-life situation (taxi drivers). This helps understanding in terms of *where* cognitive processes are located, and means the findings can be generalized to real-life situations.

Subject vocabulary

independent variable (IV) the variable an experimenter controls or changes

dependent variable (DV) the variable an experimenter measures

active reconstructive process a process that builds knowledge rather than receives it, and is therefore open to change

glucose metabolism the rate at which glucose is used

hippocampus part of the brain involved with (among other things) emotions and memory

spatial memory the ability to understand geographical spaces and remember where objects are placed

observational study a method where the researcher has very little control over the variables; they are useful for real-life situations

Glossary

verb a word used to describe an action

(eye)witness a person who sees something, usually a crime

testimony a (formal) statement of what is true

Synonyms

manipulated .... controlled / changed

subtle .... small/less obvious

complex .... complicated

Research method 2: Experiments

Subject vocabulary

causation behaviour that has been caused rather than is random or left to free-will

determinism the idea that all behaviour has a *cause*

hippocampal lesioning damage to the hippocampus

Experiments manipulate the IV to measure the effect on a DV (while controlling other variables). Experiments are used because they show clear causation between variables which shows clear determinism. They are used because the cognitive process can be isolated.

Example 1: Verbs affect memory of false objects

Aim: To investigate how leading verbs can change eyewitness testimony with recall of objects (Loftus and Palmer, 1974).

Method: Participants were presented with a one-minute film showing a car accident. The IV was the presence of a leading verb (either hit or smashed). The DV was recall of false objects and was operationalized by asking whether the participants saw any broken glass a week after seeing the film. In reality there was no broken glass.

Results: 32 per cent of those who had been asked about the cars' speed with the verb smash claimed they had seen broken glass compared to only 14 per cent of the participants in the hit group.

Conclusion: Verbs can change memory and cause objects to be remembered that were not present.

Model sentence: **Experiments clearly isolate variables. In this case it is *leading verbs* (the IV) and *memory* (the DV). Therefore, causation can be established between the IV and DV.**

Example 2: Rats in the water maze (Clark et al., 2009)

Aim: To investigate the effect of hippocampal lesioning on spatial memory.

Method: Rats were placed in a container of water - a water maze. A platform was placed just below the surface of the water - allowing them to climb out of the water but be unable to see the platform below the surface of the water. They could only find the platform by seeing objects outside of the maze (for example, posters on the testing room wall). All rats quickly learned the platform location within the first few days of training.

One group was lesioned (experimental group), one group was not (control group). The independent variable (IV) was the lesion on the hippocampus. The dependent variable (DV) was spatial memory and was operationalized by the time taken to find where the invisible platform was in the water tank.

Results: Lesion groups could not remember where the platform was and when they did locate it, they took significantly longer to re-locate it than the non-lesion group.

Conclusion: The hippocampus is responsible for spatial memory.

Model sentence: **This experiment clearly isolates the variables of *lesions on the hippocampus* (the IV) and *spatial memory* (the DV). Therefore, causation can be established.**

GLO 4: Discuss ethical considerations related to research studies at the cognitive level of analysis

Ethical consideration 1: The use of animals in research

Animals in research are particularly useful as researchers do not have the same level of **moral** obligation as they do towards humans. Clark et al. (2009) made good use of their animal subjects to show a clear link between the hippocampus and spatial memory. However, there are strict guidelines that should be followed:

The British Society of Animal Science wrote a set of ethical guidelines for the use of animals in research experimentation which they refer to as the 3Rs:

- *Refinement:* Any animal science research undertaken should be as focused as possible and have *realistic and achievable aims* of increasing knowledge of the species of interest in relation to our understanding of its functioning, performance, health or welfare.
- *Replacement:* Researchers must consider all available options to *replace* animals with other techniques that will fulfil the research objectives. Researchers should always actively look for non-animal methods of investigation.
- *Reduction:* There is a scientific, moral, and legal requirement to expose as few animals to pain, suffering, and distress as possible.

Synonyms

moral.................. ethical

Ethical consideration 2: The use of non-invasive techniques (such as PET scans)

Maguire et al. (1997) made good use of PET scans while preserving the **anonymity** of the human subjects they researched. Non-invasive techniques do not cause harm to subjects and still give valuable **insights** into links between cognitive factors and behaviour.

Glossary

anonymity keeping the name secret

insights clear and/or deep information

consent by proxy to give permission on another person's behalf

adaption a change made for a new situation

Ethical consideration 3: Informed consent

The cases of Clive Wearing and Henry Molaison offer good examples of ethical research into rare disorders caused by biological problems. Neither Wearing nor Molaison could give *informed* consent as they did not have the ability to understand the research process. However, in both cases, the families became a key part of the research process and were able to give **consent by proxy**. The researchers were careful to not to be seen to be exploiting sick men for their own ends. Henry Molaison had his anonymity protected until after he died. The use of the families had research benefits as they were able to offer personal data and offer insight as to how they behaved both before and after the memory loss. This has been particularly true with Clive Wearing; his wife has given key insights into his condition and **adaption**. Both of these case studies are good examples of how to conduct ethical research within a cognitive area of interest.

Hints for success: Always use previously learned material to support a GLO answer and use examples of research to support each point you are making.

Describe the role of situational and dispositional factors in explaining behaviour

Subject vocabulary

personality a consistent pattern of emotions, thoughts, and behaviours

to attribute/attribution an explanation for the cause of behaviour

neuroticism a personality trait characterized by anxiety, moodiness, worry, envy, and jealousy

extraversion outgoing and not shy

introversion being shy

Glossary

obedience when a person does what they are told to do

bias/biased unfairly preferring one person or group over another

meta-analysis combining the results of different studies

longitudinal studies studies carried out over a long period of time

correlation a relationship between variables

participant someone who takes part in a research study

Synonyms

consistent .... the same

investigate .... find

Opening sentence:

I will use **personality** as an example of a dispositional factor to explain behaviour. I will use Milgram's **obedience** study to explain the role of situational factors in explaining behaviour.

What are attributions?

When we explain other people's behaviour we do not do so in a logical way. We give explanations (attributions) for behaviour that are **biased**. These biases fall into two broad categories: *situational* and *dispositional*.

A situational factor is: when we explain/attribute people's behaviour to external factors such as a social situation or social pressure.

A dispositional factor is: when we explain/attribute the cause of people's behaviour to their internal characteristics such as their personality.

The role of dispositional factors in explaining behaviour

Model sentence: **I will use personality as an example of a dispositional factor to explain behaviour.**

The five-factor model (FFM) of personality claims that much of what we need to know about somebody's personality is described by his or her position on five measurable personality factors (McCrae and Costa, 1999).

FFM factor	Low scorers are:	High scorers are:
Neuroticism (nervousness)	relaxed, stable, calm	emotional, moody, impulsive
Extraversion (outgoing)	reserved, serious, passive, **introverted**	outgoing, active, sociable, extraverted
Openness to experience	down-to-earth, practical	imaginative, creative
Agreeableness	hostile, selfish, cold	kind, trusting, warm, altruistic
Conscientiousness	easygoing, unreliable, sloppy	organized, tidy, striving

Some people think there may be additional factors - for example: religiousness (Almagor et al., 1995).

Is personality consistent across time?

Roberts and Del Vecchio (2000) conducted a **meta-analysis** of 152 **longitudinal studies** into personality. They found a high **correlation** between measures of personality obtained for groups of **participants** and the measures obtained for the same people 7 years later.

Conclusion: Personality is consistent and measureable across time.

Is personality consistent across different situations?

Key study: Facebook personalities.

Aim: To **investigate** the basic connections between personality and online behaviour (Gosling et al., 2010).

Method: Participants were given a questionnaire measuring their standing on the FFM of personality. They self-reported on their Facebook behaviours by answering a Likert-scale type set of questions.

Results: There are correlations between participants' FFM scores and their Facebook activities. For example:

Extraverts had a high number of Facebook friends and commented more on other pages.

Openness was related to adding and replacing photographs frequently.

Conclusion: Offline personality is consistent with online behaviour.

Model sentence: **Gosling et al. (2010) suggest that dispositional factors such as personality remain consistent across different situations. For example, offline personality characteristics such as extraversion and openness were reflected in online behaviour with Facebook.**

The role of situational factors in explaining behaviour

Model sentence: **I will use Milgram's obedience study to explain the role of situational factors in explaining behaviour.**

Study: Milgram's (1963; 1974) obedience study

Aim: To investigate the role of authority figures in explaining behaviour.

Method: An authority figure stood next to the participant (the 'teacher') in one room at Yale University. In the next room was a 'learner'. The 'teacher' asked prepared questions. When the 'learner' made a mistake a (fake) electric shock was given. The 'teacher' assumed he was hurting the 'learner'. Every time a wrong answer was given the voltage was increased. The 'learner' said he was suffering from a heart problem and banged on the wall. The participant (as the 'teacher') was encouraged by the authority figure to continue using standard instructions ('Please continue' and 'It is absolutely essential that you continue').

Obedience was objectively measured by the level of voltage the participant (teacher) was willing to use on the 'learner'. The higher the voltage, the higher the level of obedience. The higher voltages up to 450 volts were labelled 'Danger' and 'Severe shock' and 'XXX'. The participants thought they were hurting the 'learner'. When the screaming and banging stopped (at 300 volts), the participants had to conclude they had seriously hurt the 'learner'.

Results: No teacher stopped before 300 volts.

Sixty-five per cent of all participants continued past 300 volts (when the screaming and banging stopped) to the maximum 450 volts.

Variations: Yale University was replaced with less impressive locations: obedience rate dropped to 47.5 per cent.

Social support in the form of two more teachers (who were also confederates) who refused to obey: obedience rate dropped dramatically to 10 per cent.

Conclusion: The presence of an authority figure (in a white coat often worn by scientists or medical professionals) who issues instructions can lead to extreme obedience. High-status locations ('Yale University') lead to more obedience than more ordinary locations. The presence of social support in the form of people who are rebellious leads to less obedience.

Subject vocabulary

self-report method a type of data collection method (e.g. survey, questionnaire) where participants read the question and select a response by themselves without researcher interference

Likert scale a type of questionnaire that uses ratings scales to measure responses. For example, to measure a preference on a scale of 1–5

social support support from people in the environment

confederate fake participants who are pretending that they do not know about the experiment

Glossary

offline not connected to the internet

to reflect to show or be a sign of something

voltage the measurement of electricity

Synonyms

authority figure... someone in a position of power

rebellious .... going against a position of power

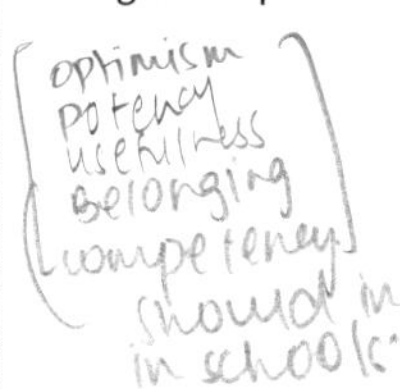

Hints for success: Use logical sub-headings to separate your work. It will give it a clear structure and focus. In this case, separate the dispositional from the situational factors.

Discuss two errors in attributions

Subject vocabulary

to attribute/attribution an explanation for the cause of behaviour

dispositional factors when we explain/attribute the cause of people's behaviour to their internal characteristics, such as their personality

personality a consistent pattern of emotions, thoughts, and behaviours

situational factors when we explain/attribute people's behaviour to external factors, such as a social situation or social pressure

linguistic to do with language

observer someone who watches a particular event but does not take part

participant someone who takes part in a research study

Synonyms

assume .... believe

challenging......... difficult

Glossary

bias/biased unfairly preferring one person or group over another

tendency the likelihood that someone will do something

stable remains the same

socioeconomic relating to the position in society and the amount of money a person earns or has

mock not real

random chosen without a definite pattern

assign to to give the role (of)

to rate to judge the level or quality of something

to reflect to show or be a sign of something

Opening sentence:

The two errors in attributions I will discuss are the Fundamental Attribution Error (FAE) and the Self-Serving **Bias** (SSB).

Model sentence: **When we explain other people's behaviour we do not do so in a logical way. We give explanations (attributions) for behaviour that will contain errors.**

The Fundamental Attribution Error (FAE)

Model sentence: **The Fundamental Attribution Error or the FAE (Ross, 1977) is the tendency people have to explain *other people's behaviour* by means of stable dispositional factors (e.g. personality) rather than situational (e.g. socioeconomic) factors.**

The more serious the consequences of the behaviour, the more likely we are to attribute this to dispositional factors.

In summary: We are fundamentally biased towards people and not towards the environment, which makes sense as we are social animals.

Why does FAE occur?

Focus of attention: Human beings are social animals who are more likely to focus on other human beings rather than on the environment.

Linguistic ease: The English language makes it easier to focus on *people* rather than situations. For example, when we talk of 'aggression' we **assume** the word refers to 'behaviour' or a 'person'; we do not assume it refers to an aggressive *situation.* This assumption is an example of linguistic FAE.

Key study 1: Mock quiz

Ross et al. (1977) set up a mock quiz. They **randomly assigned** college students to be either 'questioners' (to invent and ask **challenging** questions based on their own knowledge of a particular subject) or 'answerers' in a mock quiz. They then asked everyone taking part to **rate** the two groups as well as a group of observers. They found the 'questioners' were rated as having better general knowledge ability (despite not actually answering any questions themselves!) than the 'answerers', by both the 'answerers' and observers of the quiz. The observers paid no attention to the fact that it was a mock quiz and chose to assume that the behaviour **reflected** a dispositional factor. This was that the 'answerers' had more general knowledge.

Key study 2: Cuban essays

Jones and Harris (1967) asked participants to read essays written by fellow students. The essays were about Fidel Castro's rule in Cuba and were either supportive or critical of Castro. The participants' task was to guess what the writers of the essays really felt about Castro. Half the participants were told that the essay writers were free to choose either to take a positive view or a negative view about Castro in their essay (choice condition). The other half were told the essay writers did not have any choice and were forced to write either for or against Castro (no choice condition).

Results: Participants in the choice condition assumed the essays reflected the genuine attitudes of their writers.

Participants in the no-choice condition assumed the essays *also* reflected the genuine attitudes of their writers.

Model sentence: **It was made clear that the essay writers' behaviour was significantly changed by the situation (no-choice of essay) and yet observers *still* opted for an internal cause.**

Self-Serving Bias (SSB)

Model sentence: **The Self-Serving Bias (SSB) (Ross, 1977) is the tendency people have to explain their own successful behaviour with reference to dispositional factors (e.g. personality) and their less successful behaviour with reference to situational (e.g. socioeconomic) factors.**

Why does SSB occur?

SSB occurs to **maintain** self-esteem. If blame can be placed on events rather than on the individual, he or she will not become depressed. Abramson et al. (1989) **demonstrated** that depressed people often attribute success to external events, and failure to internal causes. In summary: depressed people do not have SSB. It **contributes** to their depression.

Key study: Teaching Maths problems to children (Johnson et al., 1964)

Aim: To investigate the effect of success and failure on SSB.

Method: Participants taught children simple Maths problems. The children were taught in a very simple way to **isolate** the variable of 'teaching Maths'. The children then took a test. Their test sheets were **altered** to either show high success rate (high score) with lots of correct answers or a poor success rate (low score) with few correct answers.

Results: Where the children's performance improved, participants explained it as showing their abilities as teachers. When the children's performance failed to improve, they explained it as showing the pupil's lack of ability.

However, this effect has not always been found with experienced teachers who tend to be more considered and confident and more able to criticize themselves. As a result, they were less likely to try to protect their self-esteem.

Glossary

to opt to choose

to isolate/isolation to separate from others

Subject vocabulary

internal cause a reason that comes from within the individual such as their personality

self-esteem how you feel about yourself

variable something that may be different in different situations

Synonyms

maintain .... keep

demonstrated ..... showed/shown

contributes .... adds

altered .... changed

Hints for success: You can evaluate studies but do not reject their conclusions. They are reasonable support for the phenomena.

Evaluate Social Identity Theory, making reference to relevant studies

Opening sentence:

In this answer I will evaluate Social Identity Theory, making reference to two studies.

Glossary

interrelated connected

categorization putting things into groups

distinctiveness what makes something stand out or unique

tendency the likelihood that someone will do something

empirical studies research which involves actual observation or experiments

notion an idea

Subject vocabulary

stereotype a perception of an individual in terms of their group membership. It is a generalization that is made about a group and then generalized to members of that group. Such a generalization may be either positive or negative

personality a consistent pattern of emotions, thoughts, and behaviours

self-esteem how you feel about yourself

Synonyms

traits .... characteristics

Social Identity Theory (SIT) is based on four **interrelated** concepts:

- social **categorization**
- social identity
- social comparison
- positive **distinctiveness**.

Social categorization

Social categorization divides the social environment into in-groups, to which an individual belongs (us), and out-groups, to which the individual does not belong (them).

In-groups show:

- Ethnocentrism – whereby in-groups judge out-groups by their own values.
- Stereotypical thinking – in-groupers and out-groupers are perceived according to relevant stereotypes.
- Self-serving bias – the **tendency** people have to explain their own successful behaviour with reference to dispositional factors (e.g. personality) and their less successful behaviour with reference to situational (e.g. socioeconomic) factors.

Social identity

Social identity is how we think of ourselves according to our membership of social groups. It is separate from personal identity, which is how we label our personality **traits** (Turner, 1982). When we establish relationships with members of different groups, the social identity can influence our behaviour.

Social comparison

According to SIT, our social identity influences how we feel about ourselves. We seek positive social identities to maintain and build up our self-esteem. Positive social identities may result from the process of social comparison. We continuously compare our in-groups with relevant out-groups and usually conclude that our in-group is superior.

Positive distinctiveness

When we establish the superiority of our in-group over relevant out-groups, we make sure that our social identities, and therefore our self-esteem, are positive enough. This is known as *positive distinctiveness*.

Model sentence: **SIT is well supported by empirical studies.**

Key study 1: Football supporters

Cialdini et al. (1976) observed college football supporters. After a successful football match, the supporters were more likely to be seen wearing college clothing. After a defeat, the supporters were less likely to be seen wearing college clothing.

Model sentence: **This study supports the notion of positive distinctiveness as the football supporters wanted to be associated with a positive social group (a winning team).**

Key study 2: Random groups, in-group favouritism and out-group rivalry (Tajfel et al., 1971)

Aim: To investigate how being put into groups produces in-group favouritism.

Method: British schoolboys were randomly placed into two groups. The boys thought they were being divided into groups according to whether they preferred a painting by Klee or Kandinsky. In this way they were given a *weak* social identity. The boys had to work *individually* (while knowing they belonged to either a Klee or a Kandinsky group) and had to **award** points to both in-group and out-group members. They were not allowed to give points to themselves.

Results: The boys showed a strong tendency to award more points to members of their in-group rather than members of the out-group. Sometimes the boys would give up any *gain* for their in-group just to make sure there was a difference between their in-group and out-group. For example, the boys would often give an in-group member 7 points and an out-group member 1, rather than giving them both 13 points as they could have done.

Model sentence: The study supports the notion of social identity (how we think of ourselves according to our membership of social groups) because the boys still regarded themselves as belonging to a group even when they were working individually. The study also supports the notion of in-group favouritism and positive distinctiveness as the boys awarded more points to their in-group members and tried to maintain a difference between the in-group and out-group.

Negative evaluation of SIT

- SIT should never be seen as a single and complete way to explain complex human behaviour. The theory fails to take into consideration the environment that **interacts** with the 'self'. Other factors such as poverty may play a larger role in behaviour than one's own **sense** of in-group identity.
- The increase in self-esteem associated with out-group **discrimination** is too short-lived to have long-lasting effects on how in-group members view themselves (Rubin and Hewstone, 1998).
- SIT describes but does not *predict* human behaviour.
- SIT does not explain why in some cases our personal identity is stronger than the group identity.

Social Identity Theory (SIT) is based on four interrelated concepts:

- *social categorization*
- *social identity*
- *social comparison*
- *positive distinctiveness.*

Social identity is how we think of ourselves according to our membership of social groups.

Subject vocabulary

favouritism a liking for

rivalry competition

Synonyms

award .... give

sense .... feeling

Glossary

to interact/interaction to act in close relationship with

discrimination unfair treatment of people or groups

Hints for success: Use supporting studies as positive evaluation. They show a theory has support from research.

Explain the formation of stereotypes and their effect on behaviour

Opening sentence:

In this answer I will divide my answer into two: I will explain the **formation** of stereotypes and then I will explain their effect on behaviour.

Model sentence: **A stereotype is a social perception of an individual in terms of their group membership or physical features. It is a generalization that is made about a group and then attributed to members of that group. Such a generalization may be either positive or negative.**

Stereotyping affects the behaviour of those who believe in the stereotype, and those who are labelled by a stereotype.

The formation of stereotypes

1. Social identity

Stereotype formation is based on:

Social comparison
We seek positive social identities to maintain and build up our self-esteem. Positive social identities may result from the process of social comparison. We continuously compare our in-groups with out-groups and usually conclude that our in-group is superior.

Positive distinctiveness
When we **establish** the superiority of our in-group over out-groups, we make sure that our social identities, and therefore our self-esteem, are positive enough.

Ethnocentrism – This can be defined as an in-group-serving **bias**. It is the group equivalent of Self-Serving Bias (SSB). It involves:

- positive behaviours by in-group members being attributed to dispositions
- negative behaviours of in-group members being attributed to situational factors
- positive behaviours of out-group members being attributed to situational factors
- negative behaviours by out-group members being attributed to dispositions.

In summary: If we do good things it is because we are good and if we behave badly that is due to external factors. The opposite applies to 'them'. It leads to negative views of out-group members.

---

2. Stereotypes are schemas

Stereotype formations are based on the following assumptions:

- The social world is very **complex** and provides us with too much information
- We have a limited ability to process information we need to simplify our social world.
- One of the ways in which we avoid **information overload** is to use stereotypes.
- Stereotypes have the following characteristics:
  - they are a quick way of explaining something

Synonyms

formation .... creation
establish .... create
complex .... complicated

Subject vocabulary

stereotype a perception of an individual in terms of their group membership. It is a generalization that is made about a group and then generalized to members of that group. Such a generalization may be either positive or negative

perception the process that allows people to interpret information

to attribute/attribution an explanation for the cause of behaviour

self-esteem how you feel about yourself

in-group the group we are in or we want to be in

out-group the group we are not in or we do not want to be in

schema a frame for understanding the world

Glossary

to generalize/generalization to comment on something very basic, based on limited facts, and apply it to other situations

bias/biased unfairly preferring one person or group over another

information overload having too much information to deal with

- they are stable and **resistant** to change
- they affect behaviour.

Stereotype formation begins with the learning of more basic schema elements. For example, the formation of a gender schema for 'female' begins with elements such as 'girls dress in pink' and 'girls play with dolls'. With advancing age more elements are added, such as information about gender-appropriate behaviours (e.g. it is okay for girls to cry in public but not boys). Eventually, strong **associations** form between all the various elements and a single schema **emerges**. Once formed, the schema becomes a **rigid** way to look at the world (Fiske and Dyer, 1985). It can lead to confirmation bias which means people tend to overlook information that contradicts what they already believe and pay attention to behaviours that confirm what they believe about a group.

The effects of stereotypes on behaviour

Effect 1: Stereotypes affect memory – waitresses drink beer: librarians wear glasses (Cohen, 1981)

Aim: To investigate the effect of stereotypes on memory.

Method: Participants were presented with a videotape showing a woman having dinner with her husband. Half the participants were told that the woman was a waitress and half were told she was a librarian.

Results: Participants who thought she was a waitress were more likely to remember that she drank. Participants who thought she was a librarian were more likely to remember that she wore glasses and listened to classical music.

Conclusion: Participants are more likely to notice and subsequently remember information which is **consistent with** their stereotypes.

Effect 2: Words cause stereotype activation – old people walk more slowly (Bargh et al., 1996)

Aim: To investigate if the use of words could **activate** a stereotype.

Method: Elderly participants were asked to form a grammatically correct sentence using what they believed to be random words.

Condition 1: Words related to and intending to activate the elderly stereotype (e.g. grey, retired, wise).

Condition 2: Words were unrelated to the elderly stereotype (e.g. thirsty, clean, private). After completing the experimental tasks, participants were directed towards the elevator.

Results: Participants who had their elderly stereotype activated walked significantly more slowly towards the elevator than the rest of the participants.

Conclusion: The social use of words had activated a stereotype of how elderly people behave and this had affected the speed the elderly people walked.

Evaluation: The study has a clear method that shows a cause-effect relationship. The independent variable (IV: age-related words) showed an effect on a clearly quantified dependent variable (DV: speed of walk to the elevator).

Synonyms

associations .... connections/relationships

emerges.............. appears

rigid.................... inflexible

Subject vocabulary

participant someone who takes part in a research study

independent variable (IV) the variable an experimenter controls or changes

dependent variable (DV) the variable an experimenter measures

Glossary

to resist/be resistant to to not want to do something

to be consistent/consistency to remain or always behave in the same way

to activate/activated to make something work or switch something on

Hints for success: Clearly separate your answer between formation and effects. Use the subtitles and exam sentences presented here to help you do this.

Explain Social Learning Theory, making reference to two relevant studies

Opening sentence:

In this answer I will explain Social Learning Theory, making reference to Bandura, Ross, and Ross (1961) and Wells-Wilbon and Holland (2001).

Social Learning Theory

Social Learning Theory (SLT) assumes that humans learn behaviour through observational learning (watching models and imitating their behaviour) by using:

- Attention: The person must first pay attention to the model.
- **Retention**: The observer must be able to remember the behaviour that has been observed.
- Motor **reproduction**: The observer has to be able to replicate the action.
- **Motivation**: Learners must want to show what they have learned.

Therefore, SLT is largely *cognitive*, with observers processing (attending to, retaining, and deciding to replicate behaviour) complex information.

Factors which influence whether or not the observer decides to **imitate** and learn:

- Consistency: If a model behaves in a way that is the same in all situations - for example, always being brave - then the observer will be more likely to imitate than if the model behaves in different ways depending on the situation.
- Identification with the model: We tend to imitate models who are like ourselves - for example, if they are the same age and gender.
- Rewards/punishment: Bandura states that people can learn from observing what happens to others; they don't have to experience the **consequences** themselves.

Supporting study 1: Bobo doll experiment

Aim(s): To show that learning can occur through observation alone of a model and that imitation can occur when the model is not present.

Method: 72 children, 36 boys and 36 girls, aged 37–69 months (with a mean age of 52 months) were used.

Results: Children in the aggressive model condition tended to imitate the model's physical and verbal aggression and non-aggressive verbal responses significantly more than children who saw the non-aggressive model. Children in the non-aggressive model condition showed very little aggression. Boys would imitate the physical and verbal aggression of male models significantly more than girls. Girls imitated only the verbal aggression and non-imitative aggression of female models more than boys.

Conclusion: Aggression can be learned from role models. The gender of the role model is important.

How does the study explain SLT?

The study separated key variables (types of aggression; types of model; levels of imitation) while controlling irrelevant variables (e.g. location; toys; age) and clearly

Subject vocabulary

imitation to copy

consistency behaviour is the same from one situation to the next

mean a form of central tendency usually referred to as the 'average'

aggressive/aggression behaving in an angry and threatening way

response reaction

variable something that may be different in different situations

dependent variable (DV) the variable an experimenter measures

independent variable (IV) the variable an experimenter controls or changes

Synonyms

imitate................ copy

consequences..... the results of the action

Glossary

to retain/retention to remember

to reproduce/reproduction to make a copy

to motivate/motivation a reason to want to do something

showed that aggressive behaviour (dependent variable; DV) can be learnt through imitating aggressive models (independent variable; IV).

Identification with the model: Boys and girls were more likely to imitate the model which was the same sex as they were. Bandura states that people can learn from observing what happens to others; in addition, because the models were not punished for their behaviour, this may have encouraged the children to imitate the aggressive behaviour.

Supporting study 2: 'Social learning theory and the influence of male role models on African American children' (Wells-Wilbon and Holland, 2001)

Aim: To assess the influence male role models have on the social learning of a group of 55 African-American students (5th grade) who were participants in a **mentoring programme** known as PROJECT 2000.

Participants: 55 African-American children aged between 10 and 12 years from a lower **socioeconomic** background.

Method: PROJECT 2000 was an organization providing positive educational mentoring and academic support services to young inner-city African-Americans, particularly African-American males. African-American men were Teacher Assistants (TAs) in the classrooms of the children during the school day in order to act as mentors and provide positive role models. The study used qualitative research techniques to collect data from students in their natural environment which included interviews and observation.

Results: The men had taught the youngsters about safety; **self-respect**; **discipline**; control; responsibility; **manners**; staying in school; not to do drugs; how to listen; **loyalty** and **honesty**; saying no to guns and violence. The students stated that the men had taught them decent values and important life skills, e.g. 'they make you want to do your work; and calm me down when I'm mad'.

How does the study explain SLT?

Behaviour and thought processes as well as attitudes and values can be learnt through imitation. Positive feelings can be created and strengthened and negative feelings can be discouraged and reduced.

Identification with the model: The boys felt close to the models because the Teaching Assistants were male.

Evaluation:

- **Gender:** The study was mainly focused on males. Care should be taken when generalizing to females.
- **Methodological:** (Positive): Rich qualitative data generated from large number of participants.

  (Negative): Competing factors were not controlled for, such as children's relationships with their teachers and families.
- **Cultural:** The study focused on African-American males from a lower socioeconomic background, therefore care should be taken when generalizing outside of this group.

Subject vocabulary

participant someone who takes part in a research study

qualitative (research) data that is usually in the form of *words* taken from interviews showing thoughts, feelings, and experiences of the participants

to generalize/generalization the extent to which we can apply results to other circumstances

Glossary

mentoring programme a special arrangement where more experienced people help and support less experienced ones

socioeconomic relating to the position in society and the amount of money a person earns or has

self-respect respect for yourself which shows that you value yourself

discipline controlling your behaviour and following the rules

manners socially acceptable ways of behaving

loyalty supporting your friends, family, country

honesty always telling the truth

Hints for success: You should focus on *explaining* Social Learning Theory and also refer to relevant studies. You should focus on how the theory works and use the studies to support your explanations. While evaluating studies is important, do not focus your answer too much on evaluating these studies.

Discuss the use of compliance techniques

Subject vocabulary

compliance technique a process that leads to intellectual and emotional submission on the part of the person who experiences it

submission to yield to a greater power

Glossary

technique a method for doing something

to comply/compliance to obey

petition a written request for something to change which is signed by a lot of people

commitment a promise to behave in a particular way

residents people who live in a location

Synonyms

display .... show

Opening sentence:

The two compliance **techniques** I will discuss are: *foot-in-the-door (FITD) technique* and *lowballing*.

Model sentence: Compliance is a form of social influence which refers to intellectual and emotional submission in reaction to a general request.

Foot-in-the-door (FITD) technique

Model sentence: The FITD technique aims at increasing compliance with a large request by first asking people to agree to a smaller request.

Key study 1: Ugly garden signs (Freedman and Fraser, 1966)

Aim: To demonstrate FITD technique.

Method: A researcher who pretended to be a volunteer worker asked **residents** in California to allow a big ugly public-service sign reading 'Drive Carefully' to be placed in their front gardens. Only 17 per cent of the householders complied with this request. A different set of residents was asked whether they would **display** a smaller and more attractive 'Be a Safe Driver' sign. Nearly all of those asked agreed with this request. Two weeks later these same residents were asked if they would display the much bigger and ugly 'Drive Carefully' sign in their front gardens.

Results: 76 per cent of the second residents complied with the second request. This is compared with the 17 per cent who had complied in the first situation.

Key study 2

When Freedman and Fraser (1966) asked a number of residents to sign a **petition** in favour of keeping California beautiful, nearly everybody agreed to do it. After 2 weeks, they asked these residents whether they would allow the big and ugly 'Drive Carefully' sign of the previous study to be displayed in their front gardens. 48 per cent of the homeowners agreed with the second request even though the two topics were not related.

Why? Signing the petition changed the view the homeowners had about *themselves*. As a result, they saw themselves as unselfish and so, 2 weeks later, they agreed to display the 'Drive Carefully' sign. This was so that they were consistent with their newly formed self-image.

Model sentence: FITD technique works because of our need to be consistent and show a commitment to previous statements or actions (Cialdini, 2009).

Studies have also shown the following:

- First requests should not be so large that people will refuse them (Burger, 1999).
- FITD requires a delay between the first request and the later larger one (Burger, 1999).
- When the *same* person makes both requests, it is difficult to get compliance (Chartrand et al., 1999).

Lowballing

Model sentence: Lowballing involves changing an offer to make it *less* attractive to the target person after this person has agreed to it.

Key study: Lowballing with a student scholarship fund (Burger and Cornelius, 2003)

Aim: To investigate lowballing.

Method and Results: Students were contacted by phone and asked whether they would be prepared to **donate** five dollars to a scholarship fund for poor students. There were three experimental conditions.

- The lowball condition – Students were told that those who donated would receive a **coupon** for a free **smoothie** at a local juice bar. Students who agreed were then informed that the investigator realized she had run out of coupons. The students were asked if they would still be willing to donate; 77.6 per cent agreed to make a donation in this condition.
- The **interrupt** condition – The caller made the same **initial** request as in the lowball condition. However, before the **participants** had a chance to give their answer, the caller interrupted them to let them know that there were no more coupons left. Only 16 per cent of the participants made a donation in this condition.
- The control condition – Participants were simply asked to donate the five dollars without any mention of coupons; 42 per cent made a donation in the control condition.

Conclusion: The results show lowballing also works because of *commitment*. It is effective only when individuals make an initial *public* commitment. Once they have made this commitment, individuals feel **obliged** to carry it out even when the conditions that led to them making the commitment have changed (Cialdini, 2009).

Compliance is a form of social influence which refers to intellectual and emotional submission in reaction to a general request.

Two compliance techniques are:

1. Foot-in-the-door (FITD) technique
   The FITD technique aims at increasing compliance with a large request by first asking people to agree to a smaller request, supported by 'ugly garden signs' (Freedman and Fraser, 1966).
2. Lowballing
   Lowballing involves changing an offer to make it less *attractive to the target person after this person has agreed to it, supported by 'student scholarship fund' (Burger and Cornelius, 2003).*

Glossary

scholarship fund an amount of money given to students to help pay for their studies

to donate/donation to give money to a group of people in order to help them

coupon a token given out free for buying something

smoothie fruit drink

to interrupt to stop someone from continuing to do something

initial first

to feel obliged to feel you have a duty to do something

Subject vocabulary

participant someone who takes part in a research study

Hints for success: Use logical sub-headings to separate your answers. In this case, the compliance techniques. If the question asks for one compliance technique, clearly label which one you are discussing in the form of a sub-heading.

Evaluate research on conformity to group norms

Subject vocabulary

to conform/conformity to follow what everyone else in a group is doing

ambiguous when a situation is not clear

unambiguous when a situation is clear

norm-formation norms are expected ways to behave

perception the process that allows people to interpret information

operationalized *how* the IV is changed and *how* the DV is measured.

independent variable (IV) the variable an experimenter controls or changes

dependent variable (DV) the variable an experimenter measures

to quantify to calculate the numerical value of something

cause–effect relationship where there is confidence that the effect on the dependent variable (DV) has been caused by the manipulation of the independent variable (IV)

to deceive/deception to make someone believe something that is not true

to generalize/generalization the extent to which we can apply results to other circumstances

Synonyms

stationary .... unmoving
judgements......... decisions
fluctuated .... varied
established .... set

Glossary

to yield to give way to

tendency the likelihood that someone will do something

to estimate to judge the approximate number/size of something

to deny to say something is not true

phenomenon an observable fact

Opening sentence:

I will evaluate research on conformity in an ambiguous situation. I will then evaluate research on conformity in an unambiguous situation.

Model sentence: **Conformity means yielding to group pressure. It refers to the tendency to change one's thoughts, feelings, or behaviour in ways that are in agreement with those of a particular individual, group, or situation.**

Ambiguous situation

Moving light study

Aim: To investigate norm-formation and conformity in an ambiguous situation (Sherif, 1935).

Method and Results: This study relies on the autokinetic effect – an illusion that makes a **stationary** light appear to move when seen in complete darkness. Participants thought that the experiment was investigating perception and were told that the experimenter was going to move the light, something that was never done. They had to make 100 **judgements** on how far the light, placed on the far wall of a darkened room, seemed to have moved.

Phase 1: Participants made their judgements alone. Their **estimates fluctuated** for some time before they moved towards a standard estimate. This was called a *personal norm.* Such personal norms varied considerably between participants.

Phase 2: Participants were joined by two other participants. They took turns in a random order to call out their estimates about the light's movement. In this group condition, participants' estimates soon reflected the influence of estimates from the others in the group. Eventually, an average of the individual estimates was **established**. This was called a *social norm.* Different groups had different social norms.

Phase 3: Participants then performed the same task alone. Their estimates now showed that they continued to follow the social norm established during the group sessions. Participants **denied** they had been influenced by other members of the group.

Conclusion: Social norms influence people's judgements.

Evaluation:

- **Methodological**: It is an experiment with a clearly operationalized independent variable (IV) (presence or absence of a group) and a clear dependent variable (DV) that can be quantified (estimation of light movement). A clear cause–effect relationship can be established. The qualitative element of the study provides rich **insight** into the **phenomenon** of conformity as the participants denied they have been influenced by the social norms – this suggests that conformity is personal. The study provides a **firm** experimental basis for further research.
- **Ethical**: Some deception was used but this was not harmful to the participants and it was necessary to investigate this important phenomenon.
- **Cultural**: The study was conducted in 1935. Care should be taken when generalizing to the present day particularly when research into conformity is so widely reported and more people are now aware of research into these areas.

It lacks ecological validity. Conformity in real life is the product of more **subtle cues** (such as media and advertising). It should be noted: All experiments lack ecological validity to some extent. It is a necessary weakness for such clear IVs and DVs.

Unambiguous situation

Asch Paradigm (Asch, 1951)

Aim: To investigate the effect of *group pressure* on conformity in an unambiguous situation.

Method: Participants were placed in a room where there were six men and the researcher. The men in the room were dressed like businessmen, in suits and ties. These men were confederates. They helped the researcher to deceive the participant. The group was told they were going to take part in 'a psychological experiment on visual judgement'. They were then shown the following cards:

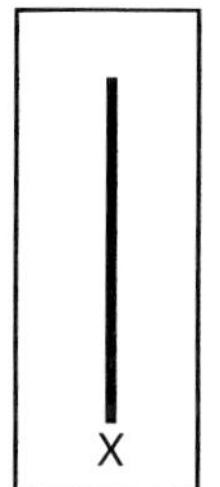

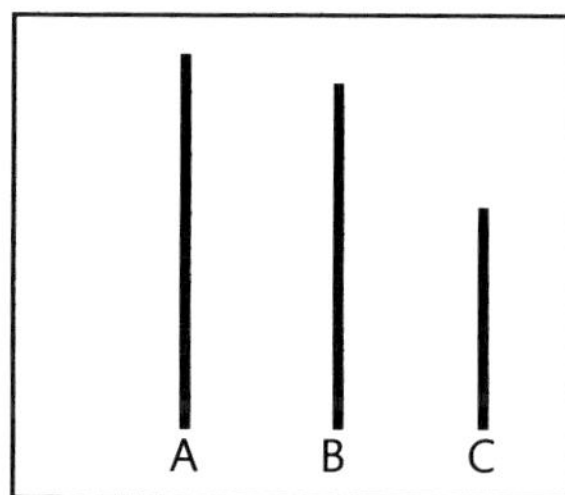

Asch's line test

The participant was asked to select the line from the second card that matched the length of the line on the first card (X). There were 18 **trials** in total. Out of these, 12 of the trials involved the confederates giving the wrong answer and these were therefore known as the 'critical trials'. The goal was to see if the participant would conform to the wrong answers given by the confederates during the critical trials, even when it was very clear that this response was incorrect.

Results:

- **Quantitative results:** About 75 per cent of the participants conformed at least once; 24 per cent never conformed.
- **Qualitative results:** The participants said they had some **self-doubt**. Others believed they suffered a distortion in their perception. They thought that perhaps they could not see the lines properly and therefore the others must be right.

Evaluation:

- **Methodological:** There is a clear independent variable (IV: presence or absence of wrong answers) and a clear dependent variable that can be quantified (DV: estimation of line size). A clear cause-effect relationship can be established.

  All experiments lack ecological validity but it is a necessary weakness for such clear IVs and DVs.

  The participants were acting in a way that they feel is required by the **features** of the experiment.

- **Cultural**: The date and place of this study should be taken into consideration. The USA in the 1950s was a very **conservative** place. It was also during the Cold War and standing out, or being an individual, was not encouraged. Care should be taken when generalizing to the present day particularly when research into conformity is so widely reported.
- **Ethical**: Some deception was used but this was not harmful to the participants and it was necessary to investigate this important phenomenon.

Subject voca[bulary]

ecological validity havi[ng] realism and being able to generalize to real-life situations

confederate fake participants who are pretending that they do not know about the experiment

Glossary

subtle not easy to notice

cue a sign

trial a test

self-doubt lacking in confidence in oneself

feature an aspect

conservative a political point of view that values tradition and tries to limit change

Synonyms

insight .... interesting new knowledge

firm .... strict

ethical .... moral

Hints for success: Clearly divide your answer into ambiguous and unambiguous and then evaluate the research.

's influencing conformity

bulary

n.
e
in ways that conform to what others expect us to do

competence how effective someone is at doing a task

social identity how we think of ourselves according to our membership of social groups

to conform/conformity to follow what everyone else in the group is doing

confederate fake participants who are pretending that they do not know about the experiment

social rejection not belonging to a group leading to social isolation which is a state whereby individuals or groups do not have contact or communication with others

unambiguous when a situation is clear

self-esteem how you feel about yourself

meta-analysis a review of many studies into the same phenomena to see what broad conclusions can be made

individualistic cultures societies in which more importance is placed on the person rather than the group

collectivist cultures societies in which more importance is placed on the group rather than the person

Glossary

to yield to give way to

tendency the likelihood that someone will do something

Synonyms

conformed.......... agreed

Opening sentence:

In this answer I will discuss *group size*, ***normative influences***, ***competence***, *culture*, and ***social identity*** factors.

Model sentence: I will first define conformity: conformity means yielding to group pressure. It refers to the tendency to change one's thoughts, feelings, or behaviour in ways that are in agreement with those of a particular individual, group, or situation.

Group size

Asch (1955) found that with only one **confederate**, just 3 per cent of the participants **conformed**; with two confederates, the rate rose to 14 per cent; and with three confederates, it rose to 32 per cent.

Normative influence

Normative influence is our need to be liked by others. It is a fear of **social rejection**. Therefore, we often behave in ways that conform to what others expect us to do.

Normative influence was the most likely cause of conformity in Asch's experiment (Asch, 1951):

- The materials (the line test) used in that experiment were **unambiguous**.
- The participants' behaviour was public – everyone could hear their answer.
- Most participants explained their conformity in terms of the fact that they wanted to be accepted by the rest of the group *and by the experimenter* (the participants said they did not want to ruin the experiment).

Competence

When individuals think they are more competent to make decisions they are *less* likely to conform. Perrin and Spencer (1988) found when they repeated Asch's study with engineers and medical students, conformity rates were almost zero. This may also be influenced by **self-esteem**: Stang (1973) found that participants with high self-esteem were less likely to conform to incorrect responses.

Culture

Smith and Bond (1993) carried out a **meta-analysis** of 31 conformity studies and found that levels of conformity (measured by the percentage of incorrect responses) ranged from 14 per cent among Belgian students to 58 per cent among Indian teachers in Fiji.

- Conformity was lower among participants from **individualistic cultures**: North America and north-west Europe (25.3 per cent) than from **collectivist cultures**: Africa, Asia, Oceania, and South America (37.1 per cent).

- Smith and Bond (1996) found that people who score high on Hofstede's collectivism scale conform more than people who score lower: this means that collectivist cultures produce more conformity.

However, care should be taken when generalizing between East and West because there is only a 12 per cent difference.

Berry (1967) used a variation of Asch's conformity paradigm and found that the Temne people of Sierra Leone conformed significantly more than the Inuit people of Canada. He explained this in terms of differences in economic practices. The Temne people have to survive on a single **crop** that is **harvested** by all the people in the community. This requires the community to co-operate and work together, and this is why Temne culture focuses strongly on social agreement. Berry found that there is less **consensus** in Inuit culture because the Inuit economy is based on continual **hunting and gathering** which is usually carried out by people on their own.

Social identity

Conformity is about **adhering** to a person's in-group norms. We conform to allow a greater sense of belongingness to our in-group. By doing this we form and maintain the social identities we want so we are more likely to conform to the norms of groups we believe we belong to. People use other people simply as a source of information about what the appropriate in-group norm is in a particular situation.

Key study: Belonging to in-groups (Abrams et al., 1990)

Aim: To investigate how in-groups cause more conformity than out-groups.

Method: A repeat of Asch's experiment with psychology students using three confederates. Depending on condition, genuine participants either thought that the confederates were, like themselves, psychology students from a neighbouring university (in-group condition), or ancient history students from the same neighbouring university (out-group condition). All group members responded publicly.

Results: 100 per cent of the participants conformed at least once when they thought the confederates belonged to their in-group. The percentage for those participants who thought the confederates belonged to the out-group was only 50 per cent.

Conclusion: We are far more influenced by groups we feel we belong to than by groups we consider as out-groups.

Subject vocabulary

Hofstede's collectivism scale a way to measure how individualistic or collectivist cultures are

to generalize/generalization the extent to which we can apply results to other circumstances

paradigm a pattern or mode of thought that encourages a particular way of looking at a phenomenon

norms expected or usual ways to behave

Glossary

crop a plant which is grown by farmers to produce food

to harvest to cut the plants grown by farmers to produce food

hunting and gathering killing wild animals and searching for wild plants to use as food

to adhere (to) to follow the rules of

Synonyms

consensus........... general agreement

Hints for success: Use logical sub-headings to demarcate your work. It will give it a clear structure and focus. In this case, use the factors listed here.

...e the terms 'culture' and 'cultural norms'

Synonyms

set .... group/collection

Subject vocabulary

stereotype a perception of an individual in terms of their group membership. It is a generalization that is made about a group and then generalized to members of that group. Such a generalization may be either positive or negative

norms expected or usual ways to behave

Glossary

symbol a picture, shape or person that has a particular meaning for a group of people

superstition a belief that certain objects, or actions, are lucky or unlucky

Culture

'A ***set*** *of attitudes, behaviours and* ***symbols*** *shared by a large group of people and usually communicated from one generation to the next' (Shiraev and Levy, 2004).*

This definition refers to (cultural) attitudes, behaviours, and symbols, terms which they explain as follows.

- Attitudes include beliefs (for example, political, religious, and moral beliefs), values, **superstitions**, and stereotypes.
- Behaviours include norms, customs, traditions, and fashions.
- Symbols can be words, gestures, pictures, or objects that carry a meaning which is recognized only by those who share a particular culture.

Cultural norms

Cultural norms are the norms of an established group which are passed on across generations and control behaviour in accordance with the group's beliefs about acceptable and unacceptable ways of thinking, feeling, and behaving.

Examine the role of two cultural dimensions on behaviour

Synonyms

dimensions......... aspects

unique................ one of a kind

Subject vocabulary

philosophical continuum a way to represent extremes. It shows the changes in between. An academic way to say this is: *A philosophical continuum presents extremes and the nuanced gradations in between*

autonomy how much power or control someone has over his or her life

to generalize/generalization the extent to which we can apply results to other circumstances

Glossary

continuum scale

extremes two things which are as different from each other as they can possibly be

self-expression what you say or write about how you feel about something

meta-analysis combining the results of different studies

Opening sentence:

Cultural **dimensions** are factors that can be placed on a philosophical **continuum**.

Dimension 1: Individualism/collectivism

Individualism ——————————————— **Collectivism**

In individualistic cultures:

- The personal is given greater focus than the social.
- Individual autonomy and **self-expression** are encouraged and people are viewed as **unique**.

In collectivist cultures:

- The social is given greater focus than the personal.
- Individual autonomy and self-expression are not encouraged.

How does this affect behaviour?

Model sentence: **Individualism/collectivism is reflected in studies on conformity.**

Smith and Bond (1993) carried out a **meta-analysis** of 31 conformity studies and found that conformity was lower among participants from individualist cultures: North America and north-west Europe (25.3 per cent) than from collectivist cultures: Africa, Asia, Oceania, and South America (37.1 per cent).

However, care should be taken when generalizing between East and West because there is only a 12 per cent difference.

Why does this affect behaviour?

Berry (1967) used a **variation** of Asch's conformity paradigm and found that the Temne people of Sierra Leone conformed significantly more than the Inuit people of Canada. The Temne people have to survive on a single crop. It requires the community to co-operate. Therefore, social agreement is very important. The Inuit economy is based on continual hunting and gathering which is usually carried out by people on their own or in very small groups.

Dimension 2: Masculinity/femininity

Masculinity ——————————————— **Femininity**

Gender identity is usually linked to biological sex organs. *Gender role* refers to the **sets** of behaviours, rights, and duties of being male or female (Bee, 1995). But the masculinity/femininity dimension refers to society not the individual. Therefore:

- Masculine societies: Men are supposed to be **assertive**, **tough**, and focused on achieving **material success**; women are supposed to be more **modest**, **tender**, and concerned with the quality of life.
- Female societies: Gender roles **overlap** - both men and women are supposed to be modest, tender, and concerned with the quality of life.

How does this affect behaviour?

Hofstede (1980) has identified some consequences for society as a whole.

For feminine societies: belief in gender equality, less male/female division of jobs, both genders can be **breadwinners**.

For masculine societies: belief in gender inequality, some **occupations** considered typically male whilst others are considered female, only men are breadwinners.

Agoraphobia

Model sentence: Masculine vs. feminine societies can show different levels of *agoraphobia*.

Agoraphobia is an anxiety about being in public places where it might be difficult (or embarrassing) to escape from and which results in panic-like symptoms (heaving breathing, sweating, etc.).

Fodor (1974) stated that agoraphobia is more common in females from masculine societies. In a more modern study, Arrindell et al. (2003) supported this view. A positive correlation was found between national masculinity levels and national agoraphobic fear levels. For example, Japan (masculine society) had the highest national agoraphobic fear scores whereas Sweden (feminine society) had the lowest scores.

Why does this affect behaviour?

In masculine societies, girls are brought up to be dependent, 'super-helpless' and lacking in autonomy. They expect to be protected and guided.

Boys are brought up to be independent and assertive. They expect to protect and guide. Fodor (1974) notes that when the stresses of adult life and marriage become too great, **passive** and helpless women become anxious and dream of becoming more independent or of being rescued. They ultimately develop a phobia.

Subject vocabulary

paradigm a pattern or mode of thought that encourages a particular way of looking at a phenomenon

gender identity whether you see yourself as a boy or as a girl

positive correlation as one variable increases (such as masculinity) so does another (such as agoraphobia)

phobia an intense fear

Glossary

variation a slightly different version

assertive having a confident and forceful personality

material success owning items such as a house, car, and household items

to overlap to contain some but not all of the same things

breadwinner the member of the family who provides the money to support the others

passive not taking any action, accepting things as they happen

Synonyms

tough .... hard

modest .... humble

tender .... soft and gentle

occupations .... jobs

Hints for success: Give the basic characteristics of the dimensions and then focus your answer on *how* and *why* they affect behaviour.

Subject vocabulary

depression an affective disorder characterized by extreme unhappiness

diagnostic scheme a set of standards to identify a behaviour

symptoms signs of an illness

anxiety a state of fear and uncertainty

somatic complaints physical illness

obsession the control of one's thoughts or feelings by a persistent idea

guilt a feeling where the person feels they have done something wrong

Glossary

phenomenon an observable fact

worthlessness not feeling useful

participant someone who takes part in a research study

Synonyms

distinctive........... typical/ particular

characteristics..... traits/ features

heartbroken........ extremely sad

Opening sentence:

I will explain emic and etic concepts using the example of depression.

Model sentence: First I will define etic and emic concepts:

Etic approaches aim to discover what all humans have in common. It looks at human behaviour which is the same all over the world (etics). Etic approaches have been used in many cross-cultural studies. In such studies theories developed in one particular culture (usually Western) are tested in other cultures.

Emic approaches are not interested in making cross-cultural comparisons but rather in discovering **phenomena** which are unique to a culture. A culture's uniqueness is explored through studies which aim to discover **distinctive** behaviours (or emics). It is assumed that a particular behaviour can only be found in the culture which is being studied.

Approaches to the study of depression

Etic approaches

The World Health Organization (WHO, 1983) used a standard diagnostic scheme to investigate the symptoms of depression of 573 patients in Switzerland, Canada, Japan, and Iran to discover if they had **characteristics** in common. It was found that most patients experienced several symptoms that were the same in all four countries. For example, 76 per cent of patients reported sadness, joylessness, and anxiety.

However, 40 per cent of patients in the WHO project showed symptoms such as somatic complaints and obsessions that were not included in the symptoms measured by the diagnostic scheme that was being used. Marsella et al. (1985) interpreted these findings as a strong demonstration of cultural factors. For example, patients in some cultures (e.g. Nigerians) are highly unlikely to report feelings of **worthlessness** or symptoms associated with guilt.

Emic approaches

Manson et al. (1985) investigated culture-specific characteristics of depression. They developed the *American Indian Depression Scale*. Through interviews with American Indians, they identified the following five categories used by the Hopi to describe illness related to depression:

- worry sickness
- unhappiness
- **heartbroken**
- drunken-like craziness
- disappointment.

Most Hopi **participants** said they could not find a word in the Hopi language that was the same as the Western word *depression*. However, they were all familiar with all five of the Hopi illness categories.

Some of the characteristics identified by Manson et al. (e.g. unhappiness) were similar to Western ways of looking at depression. Others were entirely different. The category of heartbroken, for example, included weight loss and not being likeable. In terms of categories, these symptoms are not found in any Western diagnostic schemes.

Combining etic and emic approaches

Research suggests that although depression is a **universal** illness, the way it shows itself is **culturally determined**. It would seem that the best approach would involve both etic and emic approaches. Marsella et al. (2002) state that the way depression shows itself in a particular culture depends on where the culture is located on the individualism/collectivism **continuum**. In individualistic cultures, feelings of loneliness and isolation are common. In collectivistic cultures, somatic symptoms such as headaches are more often reported.

There are two ways to study culture and cultural norms:

- *Etic approaches to studying culture aim to discover what all humans have in common.*
- *Emic approaches to studying culture aim to discover phenomena which are unique to individual cultures.*

Hints for success: Avoid suggesting there is *one* correct way to research phenomena. Combining etic and emic approaches is almost always better than using only one approach.

Glossary

universal the same everywhere

continuum scale

Subject vocabulary

culturally determined influenced/decided by culture

General Learning Outcomes

GLO 1: Outline principles that define the sociocultural level of analysis

GLO 2: Explain how principles that define the sociocultural level of analysis may be **demonstrated** in research (that is, theories and/or studies)

Principle 1: *The social and cultural environment influences individual behaviour.*

Social

Social Learning Theory (SLT) assumes humans learn behaviour through observational learning (watching models and **imitating** their behaviour).

According to Bandura, social learning involves the following factors:

- Attention: The person must first pay attention to the model;
- **Retention**: The observer must be able to remember the behaviour that has been observed;
- Motor **reproduction**: The observer has to be able to **replicate** the action;
- **Motivation**: Learners must want to show what they have learned.

Therefore, SLT is largely *cognitive* with observers processing (attending to, retaining, and deciding to replicate behaviour) complex information.

Factors which influence whether or not the observer decides to imitate and learn:

- **Consistency**: If a model behaves in a way that is the same in all situations - for example, always being brave - then the observer will be more likely to imitate than if the model behaves in different ways depending on the situation.
- Identification with the model: We tend to imitate models who are like ourselves - for example, if they are the same age and gender.
- Rewards/punishment: Bandura states that people can learn from observing what happens to others; they don't have to experience the consequences themselves. This is called vicarious reinforcement in Bandura's theory and happens when we watch people around us - both in real life or in movies.

Cultural

- Masculine societies: Men are supposed to be **assertive**, tough, and focused on **material success**; women are supposed to be more **modest**, **tender**, and concerned with the quality of life.
- Female societies: Gender roles **overlap** - both men and women are supposed to be modest, tender, and concerned with the quality of life. Consequently, masculine and feminine societies can show different levels of behaviour. An example is agoraphobia. Agoraphobia is an **anxiety** about being in places or situations where it might be difficult (or embarrassing) to escape from and which results in panic-like symptoms (heaving breathing, sweating, etc.). Fodor (1974) stated that agoraphobia is more common in females from masculine societies. In a more modern study, Arrindell et al. (2003) supported this view. It was found that there was a positive correlation between national masculinity levels and national agoraphobic fear levels. For example, Japan (masculine society) had the highest national agoraphobic fear scores whereas Sweden (feminine society) had the lowest scores.

Subject vocabulary

principle like an assumption it is an underlying idea that a theory is built on

cognition/cognitive related to mental processes (such as perception, memory, problem-solving)

correlation a relationship between variables

Synonyms

demonstrated ..... shown/showed

imitating .... copying

replicate .... repeat

modest .... humble

tender .... soft and gentle

anxiety .... nervousness/fear

Glossary

to be consistent/consistency to remain or always behave in the same way

to overlap to contain some but not all of the same things

to retain/retention to remember

to reproduce/reproduction to make a copy

to motivate/motivation a reason to want to do something

assertive having a confident and forceful personality

material success owning items such as a house, car, and household items

Principle 2: *We want connectedness with and a sense of belonging to others.*

Conformity is about **adhering** to a person's in-group norms. We conform out of a sense of belongingness to our in-group. In doing so we form and maintain the social identities we want so we are more likely to conform to the norms of groups we believe we belong to. People use other people simply as a source of information about what the appropriate in-group norm is in a particular situation.

Key study: Belonging to in-groups (Abrams et al., 1990).

Aim: To investigate how in-groups cause more conformity than out-groups.

Method: A repeat of Asch's experiment with psychology students using three confederates. Depending on condition, genuine participants either thought that the confederates were, like themselves, psychology students from a neighbouring university (in-group condition), or ancient history students from the same neighbouring university (out-group condition). All group members responded publicly.

Results: 100 per cent of the participants conformed at least once when they thought the confederates belonged to their in-group. The percentage for those participants who thought the confederates belonged to the out-group was only 50 per cent.

Conclusion: We are far more influenced by groups we feel we belong to than by groups we consider as out-groups.

Principle 3: *We construct our conceptions of the individual and social self.*

Aim: To investigate how being put into groups produces in-group favouritism (Tajfel et al., 1971).

Method: British schoolboys were randomly placed into two groups. The boys thought they were being divided into groups according to whether they preferred a painting by Klee or Kandinsky. In this way they were given a *weak* social identity. The boys had to work *individually* (while knowing they belonged to either a Klee or a Kandinsky group) and had to award points to both in-group and out-group members. They were not allowed to give points to themselves.

Results: The boys showed a strong tendency to award more points to members of their in-group rather than members of the out-group. Sometimes the boys would give up any *gain* for their in-group just to make sure there was a difference between their in-group and out-group. For example, the boys would often give an in-group member 7 points and an out-group member 1, rather than giving them both 13 points as they could have done.

Model sentence: The study supports the notion of social identity (how we think of ourselves according to our membership of social groups) because the boys still regarded themselves as belonging to a group even when they were working individually. The study also supports the notion of in-group favouritism and positive distinctiveness as the boys awarded more points to their in-group members and tried to maintain a difference between the in-group and out-group.

Subject vocabulary

connectedness interacting with other people

to conform/conformity to follow what everyone else in the group is doing

norms expected or usual ways to behave

experiment a method where the independent variable is manipulated to measure the effect on the dependent variable while controlling for other variables

confederate fake participants who are pretending to not know about the experiment

conceptions how we view something as a *whole* (e.g. an individual)

social self social identity is how we think of ourselves according to our membership of social groups. It is separate from personal identity, which is how we think of ourselves according to our personality traits (Turner, 1982)

favouritism a liking for

tendency likelihood that someone will do something

positive distinctiveness when we establish the superiority of our in-group over relevant out-groups, we make sure that our social identities, and therefore our self-esteem, are positive enough

Glossary

to adhere (to) to follow the rules of

Subject vocabulary

personality a consistent pattern of emotions, thoughts, and behaviours

self-report method a type of data collection method (e.g. survey, questionnaire) where participants read the question and select a response by themselves without researcher interference

Likert scale a type of questionnaire that uses ratings scales to measure responses - for example, to measure a preference on a scale of 1-5

extraversion outgoing and not shy

independent variable (IV) the variable an experimenter controls or changes

dependent variable (DV) the variable an experimenter measures

causation behaviour that has been caused rather than is random or left to free will

ethical relating to the idea of right or wrong behaviour

to deceive/deception to make someone believe something that is not true

phenomenon a fact or situation that is observed to exist or happen

Glossary

online connected to the internet

offline not connected to the internet

to reflect to show or be a sign of

obedience when a person does what they are told to do

to justify to give an acceptable explanation

Synonyms

characteristics..... traits/features

GLO 3: Discuss how and why particular research methods are used at the sociocultural level of analysis

Research method 1: Questionnaires

Sociocultural factors are often personal and difficult to separate from other factors. Questionnaires can be used to report on personal experiences and habits. For example:

Key study: Facebook personalities.

Aim: To investigate the basic connections between personality and **online** behaviour (Gosling et al., 2010).

Method: Participants were given a questionnaire measuring their position on the FFM of personality. They self-reported on their Facebook behaviours by answering a Likert-scale type set of questions.

Results: There are correlations between participants' FFM scores and their Facebook activities. For example, extraverts had a high number of Facebook friends and commented more on other pages.

Openness was related to adding and replacing photographs frequently.

Conclusion: Offline personalities are consistent with online behaviour.

Model sentence: Gosling et al. (2010) used a questionnaire to show how personal characteristics such as extraversion and openness were reflected in online behaviour with their personal spaces on Facebook.

Research method 2: Experiments

Experiments manipulate the independent variable (IV) to measure the effect on a dependent variable (DV) (while controlling for other variables). It is possible to establish causation with an experiment.

Milgram's **obedience** study explains behaviour by demonstrating how the situational factors of an authority figure, a high status location and the presence of social support affect obedience. He was able to clearly link the variable of 'obedience' with the presence of an authority figure. The experimental conditions allowed complete control of the variables (such as the location; the instructions) and allowed a clear link to be made.

Another good example of a controlled experiment is the 'Transmission of aggression through imitation of aggressive models' (Bandura, Ross, and Ross, 1961).

GLO 4: Discuss ethical considerations related to research studies at the sociocultural level of analysis

Ethical consideration 1: Deception

Deception is acceptable as long as it does not lead to long-term harm and can be **justified** for research purposes. Many phenomena in psychology would not be able to be researched if deception was not allowed because people would guess the nature of the experiment and this would influence the results. What has to be considered is how much the deception causes stress. For example, Milgram was able find a clear link between the variable of 'obedience' and the presence of an authority figure by deceiving the participants and allowing them to believe they were really giving electric shocks to the 'learners'. As a consequence of this they reported high levels of stress as a result of the study. Milgram also reports they *thanked* him for being allowed to take part in the study.

Ethical consideration 2: Working with children

The use of children in social science studies requires their parents to agree. It also requires researchers who are sensitive to the needs of children. For example, Bandura, Ross, and Ross (1961) can be criticized not for their use of violence (which was **mild** and within acceptable norms of how children play with those toys) but for their use of very strange role models. For example, adults hitting dolls with aggressive statements such as '**sock him on the nose**' is not usual for children to witness and probably influenced the results. Wells-Wilbon and Holland (2001) and their study 'Social Learning Theory and the influence of male role models on African American children' used qualitative research techniques in which they were able to talk to the children at length and in-depth to gain **insight** into how they saw the role models. This approach produced rich data as the method was deliberately designed for dealing with children – they were not given questionnaires but spoken to.

Hints for success: Always use previously learnt material to support a GLO answer and use examples of research to support each point you are making.

Synonyms

mild.................... gentle

sock him on the nose .... hit him on the nose

Subject vocabulary

qualitative (research) data that is usually in the form of *words* taken from interviews showing thoughts, feelings, and experiences of the participants

Glossary

insight clear and/or deep information

Examine the concepts of normality and abnormality

Opening sentence:

In this answer I will examine the **concepts** of 'normality' and 'abnormality'. The concept of normality assumes that there is a most appropriate behaviour that is healthy. The concept of abnormality assumes that **deviation** from what is normal is a sign of problems.

Model sentence: First I will discuss four different ways to explain what abnormal means.

1. **Deviation from statistical norms:** Statistical abnormal behaviour is behaviour that is different from what is average – for example, having very low **IQ** or having much higher than average **body mass**.

   Assumption 1: Behaviours which are statistically 'normal' are less likely to cause problems for people. However, statistically normal behaviours *can* cause problems for people. For example: obesity.

   Assumption 2: It is possible to use statistics to decide what is normal and abnormal. However, this is difficult in real-world situations where people show **complex** behaviours that change over time. And using statistics does not pass judgement on the behaviours – being a genius is statistically rare but possibly desirable.

2. **Deviation from social norms:** This is behaviour that is different from what is expected. For example: talking to oneself in public.

   Assumption: There are socially *correct* ways to behave. This may be true in a mono-cultural society but many Western cultures are becoming multi-cultural.

3. **Suffering:** If a person has a **psychological disorder**, they often experience suffering.

   Assumption: People who are suffering are suffering *because* they have a disorder. However, it is not always true that everyone with a disorder experiences or reports suffering.

4. **Abnormality via mental illness criteria (The Medical Model):** An attempt to be **objective** and an attempt to **standardize diagnosis** and treatment.

   Assumption: This definition assumes a reductionist position as it reduces complex behaviour to a list of symptoms that do not suit every individual. It often reduces the treatment of behaviour to the use of drugs.

Synonyms

concepts .... ideas
deviation .... difference
complex .... complicated
disorder............. illness

Glossary

intelligence quotient (IQ) a measure of someone's intelligence found from special tests

body mass the amount of fat and muscle a person has

objective free from personal opinion

to standardize to make the same

diagnosis giving a medical name to an illness

Subject vocabulary

psychological relating to thoughts, feelings, and behaviour

Model sentence: It is difficult to decide what is normal and abnormal.

Example 1: People do not have an accurate perception of themselves.

Aim: To see if 'normal' people have more of an accurate perception of themselves than people with a psychological disorder (Taylor and Brown, 1988).

Method: The researchers conducted a **literature review** from studies about the attitudes and beliefs of people with a psychological disorder.

Results: 'Normal' people have an unrealistically *positive view* of themselves. For example: it is typical in happiness research that 60 per cent of people report that they are happier than average. Normal people describe themselves using more positive words than other people use when they describe them.

Conclusion: Positive words are used to protect self-esteem. To be normal means to **overemphasize** positive **traits**. People with low self-esteem and moderate depression are more likely to be aware of their negative traits.

Example 2: It is very difficult for experts to judge what is normal and what is abnormal behaviour.

Aim: To test whether hospitals can detect whether a person really is mentally ill or not, and then to observe how patients are treated in hospitals (Rosenhan, 1973).

Method: Rosenhan organized for colleagues and friends without any diagnosed psychological disorders to go to psychiatric hospitals and report that they had been hearing voices. These people were 'pseudopatients'. Apart from questions relating to these experiences, they answered all questions honestly.

Results: Most of them were admitted to the hospital and were given a diagnosis of schizophrenia. After that, most of their behaviour was considered abnormal. For example, when taking notes about what happened in the hospital, hospital staff recorded that this patient's writing was **excessive** and abnormal; when they walked the corridors because they were bored they were accused of *obsessive pacing*.

Conclusion: The difference between normal and abnormal is very difficult for experts to judge.

There are four ways to explain what abnormal means:

1. *Deviation from statistical norms*
2. *Deviation from social norms*
3. *Suffering*
4. *Abnormality via mental illness criteria (The Medical Model).*

Synonyms

perception .... opinion/understanding

traits .... characteristics

Glossary

literature review a review of journals/studies/writings about a particular topic

to overemphasize to highlight/stress more than normal

excessive too much

Subject vocabulary

psychiatric hospital a hospital that treats abnormal behaviours

pseudopatients fake patients

schizophrenia an emotional and thought disorder with a wide variety of symptoms

obsessive pacing non-stop walking

Hints for success: Your main aim here is to show that you understand that there are different ways to understand the meaning of abnormal and normal, and that it is very difficult even for experts to decide what is normal and what is a problem. Make sure that as well as explaining these concepts, you refer to research that shows how complicated these concepts are.

Discuss validity and reliability of diagnosis

Glossary

diagnosis giving a medical name to an illness

excessive too much

Subject vocabulary

psychiatrist a medical professional who treats abnormal behaviours

diagnostic system a system that is used to diagnose disorders - for example, DSM-IV

psychological relating to thoughts, feelings, and behaviour

psychiatric hospital a hospital that treats abnormal behaviours

pseudopatients fake patients

schizophrenia an emotional and thought disorder with a wide variety of symptoms

obsessive pacing non-stop walking

Synonyms

disorder.............. illness

detect................. spot/see

ethically.............. morally

odd .... strange

faking................. pretending

genuine............. real/true

Opening sentence:

In this answer I will discuss the validity and reliability of **diagnosis** in abnormal psychology.

Diagnosis

Psychiatrists use diagnostic systems to identify what **disorder** their clients have. Two common systems are the Diagnostic and Statistical Manual (DSM) from the United States, and the International Classification of Diseases (ICD) from the World Health Organization.

Validity

Validity refers to the *correctness* of a diagnosis - does a person really have the disorder?

Validity is achieved by checking if doctors can identify the difference between someone who has a particular disorder and someone who does not.

Model sentence: **Rosenhan (1973) demonstrates validity is difficult to achieve.**

Study 1

Aim: To test whether hospitals can **detect** whether a person really is mentally ill or not, and then to observe how patients are treated in hospitals (Rosenhan, 1973).

Method: Rosenhan organized for colleagues and friends without any diagnosed psychological disorders to go to psychiatric hospitals and report that they had been hearing voices. These people were 'pseudopatients'. Apart from questions relating to these experiences, they answered all questions honestly.

Results: Most of them were admitted to the hospital and were given a diagnosis of schizophrenia. After that, most of their behaviour was considered abnormal. For example, when taking notes about what happened in the hospital, hospital staff recorded that this patient's writing was **excessive** and abnormal; when they walked the corridors because they were bored they were accused of *obsessive pacing*.

Conclusion: The difference between normal and abnormal is very difficult for experts to judge. Achieving a valid diagnosis is also difficult but **ethically** necessary.

In defence of the diagnosis process

Hospitals have an ethical responsibility to investigate **odd** behaviour. Hearing voices is odd behaviour. Even if the hospital staff thought they were **faking**, they still had an ethical responsibility to investigate. As doctors they had a duty to admit the pseudopatients in order to protect the community and protect the people from themselves. Even if the doctors did not believe hearing voices was **genuine**, walking into a hospital and lying about hearing voices is still abnormal behaviour.

Study 2

Staff were told at a psychiatric hospital that pseudopatients would try to gain **admittance**. No pseudopatients actually appeared, but 41 *real* patients were judged with great confidence to be pseudopatients by at least one member of staff.

Conclusion: There is a lack of scientific evidence on which medical diagnoses can be made.

In defence of the diagnosis process

Many real **dysfunctional** patients fake their symptoms. People who fake their symptoms can *still* be considered dysfunctional and need investigation. For example: a non-depressed person who fakes being depressed can be considered to be dysfunctional.

Reliability

Reliability refers to how stable the diagnosis is – do different doctors agree about the diagnosis and does the diagnosis stay the same? Reliability is achieved by: Asking several doctors to make a diagnosis for the one patient and calculating how often they agree and by checking to see if a patient's diagnosis stays the same for a period of time.

Model sentence: **Nicholls et al. (1999) demonstrate reliability is difficult to achieve.**

Aim: To compare the reliability of three diagnostic systems.

Method: Researchers asked several doctors to diagnose children with eating disorders using either the DSM, the ICD, or the Great Ormond St. Hospital system. The researchers were able to see how *often* the doctors agreed when they were using each system. A high percentage of agreement should indicate a good system.

Results: The ICD system was the least reliable in this study: the doctors agreed only 36 per cent of the time. DSM was slightly better with 64 per cent agreement, but the Great Ormond St. system was much better with 88 per cent agreement.

Conclusion: Whether the diagnosis is reliable or not will depend not only on the doctors, but also how good the system is that they are using. In this case the most reliable system was designed for use with children.

Validity refers to the correctness of a diagnosis.

Reliability refers to how stable a diagnosis is between psychiatrists.

Hints for success: Give a definition of validity and reliability and clearly use the studies to support your discussion. If you use the studies as suggested above, you are using critical thinking skills, and you do not need to spend time evaluating the studies in detail.

Glossary

dysfunction/dysfunctional not working or behaving normally

Synonyms

admittance .... entry

Discuss cultural and ethical considerations in diagnosis

Synonyms

ethical .... moral

variations............ differences

disorder.............. illness

Glossary

diagnosis giving a medical name to an illness

semi-structured something that is only partly planned or organized

bilingual speaking two languages

prevalence how common something is

alcoholism addiction to alcohol

Subject vocabulary

depression an affective disorder characterized by extreme unhappiness

DSM-IV a diagnostic system

diagnostic system a system that is used to diagnose disorders – for example, DSM-IV

psychological relating to thoughts, feelings, and behaviour

Opening sentence:

In this answer I will discuss cultural and **ethical** considerations in **diagnosis**.

Cultural considerations

Model sentence: There are cultural variations in the kind of symptoms that people have and in what is considered normal.

Example 1: Depression in Hopi Indians

For example, among Hopi Indians in North America, a study was carried out to investigate what depression is (Manson et al., 1985).

Aim: To understand the meaning of depression among the Hopi Indians.

Method: Semi-structured interviews were conducted with 36 Hopi informants. The interviewer was a **bilingual** member of a Hopi community.

Results: No single translation of depression was found. Instead there were five different sicknesses that were in some way connected with the Diagnostic and Statistical Manual (DSM-IV) symptoms for depression: worry sickness, unhappiness, heartbroken, drunken-like craziness, disappointment.

Conclusion: The DSM symptoms for major depression do not match with any **disorder** that the Hopi were aware of. Instead it seems that there are different ways of responding to the problems of life among the Hopi. This may help explain differences in **prevalence**.

Example 2: Depression in American Jewish males

Aim: To see if Jewish people in the United States are more likely than other religious groups to have depression (Levav et al. 1997).

Method: The researchers reviewed statistics from two cities in the United States for rates of depression and other psychological disorders and looked for a statistical relationship with self-identified religion.

Results: There was no difference among women, but there was a significant difference among men. Jewish men had higher rates of depression and lower rates of **alcoholism** than other groups.

Conclusion: It is likely that social norms are responsible for the difference. This explanation would suggest that Jewish males are not more depressed, but that the diagnosis of alcoholism in other groups prevents many other men from getting a diagnosis of depression.

Ethical considerations

Study 1

Aim: To test whether hospitals can detect whether a person really is mentally ill or not, and then to observe how patients are really treated in hospitals (Rosenhan, 1973).

Method: Rosenhan organized for colleagues and friends without any diagnosed psychological disorders to go to psychiatric hospitals and report that they had been hearing voices. These people were 'pseudopatients'. Apart from questions relating to these experiences, they answered all questions honestly.

Results: Most of them were admitted to the hospital and were given a diagnosis of schizophrenia.

Conclusion: The difference between normal and abnormal is very difficult for experts to judge. Achieving a valid diagnosis is also difficult but ethically necessary.

Study 2

Staff were told at a psychiatric hospital that pseudopatients would try to gain admittance. No pseudopatients actually appeared, but 41 *real* patients were judged with great confidence to be pseudopatients by at least one member of staff.

Conclusion: There is a lack of scientific evidence on which medical diagnoses can be made.

Model sentence: **The Rosenhan studies demonstrate a number of ethical dilemmas.**

1. Labelling: The patients were labelled as abnormal and this affected how the staff saw them. For example, when taking notes about what happened in the hospital, hospital staff recorded that this patient's writing was excessive and abnormal; when they walked the corridors because they were bored they were accused of obsessive pacing.

2. The need to protect the community: Hospitals have an ethical responsibility to investigate odd behaviour. Hearing voices is odd behaviour. Even if the hospital staff thought they were faking, they still had an ethical responsibility to investigate. As doctors they had a duty to admit the pseudopatients in order to protect the community and protect the people from themselves. Even if the doctors did not believe hearing voices was genuine, walking into a hospital and lying about hearing voices is still abnormal behaviour.

3. The lack of certainty in diagnosis: Many real dysfunctional patients fake their symptoms. People who fake their symptoms can *still* be considered dysfunctional and need investigation. For example: a non-depressed person who fakes being depressed can be considered to be dysfunctional.

4. Warehousing: Rosenhan (1973) noted the experience of hospitalization for the pseudopatients was one of depersonalization and powerlessness. The lack of eye-contact and normal human contact and interaction led to feelings of isolation, alienation, and abandonment.

Subject vocabulary

psychiatric hospital a hospital that treats abnormal behaviours

pseudopatients fake patients

schizophrenia an emotional and thought disorder with a wide variety of symptoms

obsessive pacing non-stop walking

warehousing storing people like objects without proper human contact or care

Glossary

admitted allowed to enter

excessive too much

dysfunction/dysfunctional not working or behaving normally

fake not real

depersonalization not being allowed to be yourself

powerlessness having no control over your life

to interact/interaction to act in close relationship with

to isolate/isolation to separate from others

alienation not being part of a group

abandonment left alone/not taken care of

Synonyms

valid .... correct/reasonable

admittance .... entry

odd .... strange

faking .... pretending

genuine .... real/true

Hints for success: Use logical sub-headings to separate your answers. They will give a clear structure and focus. In this case *cultural considerations* and *ethical considerations*.

Describe symptoms and prevalence of one disorder from two of the following groups: anxiety disorders, affective disorders, eating disorders

Glossary

symptoms characteristics of an illness

prevalence how common something is

phobia strong/unreasonable fear of something

diagnosis giving a medical name to an illness

terror extreme fear

disproportionate too large or too small in comparison to something else

irrational/irrationality not based on facts or reality, but on emotions

Synonyms

anxiety .... nervousness/ fear

disorder.............. illness

Subject vocabulary

affective related to emotions

cognition/cognitive related to mental processes (such as perception, memory, problem-solving)

somatic related to the body

substance abuse also known as drug abuse. A consistent use of a substance (drug) which leads to emotional, physical, and/or psychological damage

Opening sentence:

In this answer I will describe the **symptoms** and **prevalence** of *specific phobia* (**anxiety disorder**) and *major depression* (affective disorder).

Specific phobia: symptoms

Model sentence: A person can be diagnosed with a phobia if they have a combination of symptoms from four main groups: affective, behavioural, cognitive, and somatic.

- The main affective symptom is a feeling of **terror**.
- The main behavioural symptom is trying to avoid the thing the person is scared of.
- The main cognitive symptoms are thoughts about losing control and death.
- The somatic symptoms include sweating, shaking, and increased heart rate.
- The person usually knows that their fear is **disproportionate** and **irrational**.
- There are many things and situations that people can have a phobia for. The most common ones are fears about animals and the natural environment, blood and injuries, and situations like flying or being in a closed space like an elevator.

Specific phobia: prevalence

Model sentence: Specific phobia is the most commonly diagnosed of the anxiety disorders in the USA and one of the most common in many other countries around the world.

1. It is overall third among all disorders, behind major depression and substance abuse disorders. Between 10 per cent and 20 per cent of people are diagnosed with a phobia at some time in their life.
2. Prevalence rates are lower in other countries, for example just 0.63 per cent reported in Florence, Italy.
3. More women than men have phobias, and they usually begin during childhood.

Major depression: symptoms

Model sentence: A person can be diagnosed with major depression if they have a combination of at least five symptoms from a list of affective, behavioural, cognitive, and somatic symptoms.

- The main affective symptom is a loss of interest or pleasure in daily activities, extreme low mood/unhappiness.
- The main behavioural symptoms are **agitated** movements.
- The main cognitive symptoms are problems concentrating, thoughts of death, or plans to commit suicide.
- The somatic symptoms include weight loss or weight gain and tiredness.

If a psychiatrist is using DSM-IV to diagnose the person, he or she should not give a diagnosis of depression if the person is **grieving** after a close family member or friend has recently died. In DSM-IV this means the psychiatrist should allow two months for grieving.

Major depression: prevalence

Model sentence: Major depression is the most commonly diagnosed disorder in the United States and it also has a very high prevalence in other countries.

1. Estimates of the prevalence of depression are usually between 10 per cent and 20 per cent.
2. Most of the people who get a diagnosis of depression are women, and the depression usually starts during **adolescence**.
3. There are cultural differences in the diagnosis of depression, for example in the United States, Jewish men are more likely than other men to have a diagnosis, possibly because they are more likely to see a psychiatrist when they are feeling **distressed** (Levav et al., 1997).

Symptoms refers to the characteristics of an illness.

Prevalence refers to how common something is.

Hints for success: For this learning outcome you do not need to refer to research in detail: a simple description of the symptoms and prevalence is sufficient. However, the question cannot be asked by itself: it will always be asked together with another learning outcome. Also be prepared for a question asking you about only *one* disorder and therefore only include one disorder in your answer.

Synonyms

agitated .... troubled/restless

distressed .... very upset/worried

Subject vocabulary

psychiatrist a medical professional who treats abnormal behaviours

DSM-IV a diagnostic system

Glossary

to grieve/grief to feel extremely sad (usually after a death)

adolescence teenage years

Analyse etiologies (in terms of biological, cognitive, and/or sociocultural factors) of one disorder from two of the following groups: anxiety disorders, affective disorders, eating disorders

Opening sentence:

In this answer I will analyse **etiologies** for *specific* ***phobia*** (**anxiety disorder**) and *major depression* (affective disorder).

Specific phobia: biological causes

The role of the amygdala

Aim: To compare the activity of the amygdala in people with snake and spider phobias (Åhs et al., 2009).

Method: The researchers took PET scans of participants while they viewed pictures, including pictures of spiders and snakes. They also recorded participants' self-reports of **distress** while they viewed the pictures.

Results: There was a strong **correlation** between levels of distress and activity in the amygdala in the right hemisphere of the brain.

Conclusion: The amygdala plays a role in the activation of a fear response. In people with a phobia, this part of the brain is *over-active.*

Evaluation: The study does not clearly show the *cause* of the phobia. It shows correlations between brain activity and emotional experience.

Specific phobia: sociocultural causes

Cultural **dimensions** are factors that can be placed on a philosophical **continuum**. Hofstede (1980) stated societies can be described by placing them on a masculine versus feminine continuum.

Masculine societies: Men are supposed to be **assertive**, tough, and focused on **material** success; women are supposed to be more modest, tender, and concerned with the quality of life. Female societies: Gender roles overlap – *both* men and women are supposed to be modest, tender, and concerned with the quality of life.

Key study: The importance of masculine culture in Israel.

Model sentence: Israel has been reported to be high on masculinity in other research.

Aim: To investigate the effects of culture on the **incidence** of anxiety disorders among young Israeli people in a school for military medicine and a school for **mechanics** (Iancu et al., 2007).

Method: The researchers looked for a relationship between having an anxiety disorder and several **demographic** variables like gender and age.

Results: Males were more likely to have a phobia, especially if they were at the school for mechanics, had few friends and no romantic relationship.

Conclusion: In a country high on masculinity, young males are more likely to develop an anxiety disorder unless they have appropriate social support.

Subject vocabulary

cognition/cognitive related to mental processes (such as perception, memory, problem-solving)

sociocultural (factors) relating to social and cultural issues

depression an affective disorder characterized by extreme unhappiness

affective related to emotions

amygdala a part of the brain associated with memory

positron emission tomography (PET) (positron emission tomography) monitors glucose metabolism in the brain. PET scans produce coloured maps of mental activity to show where the brain is using energy

philosophical relating to the nature of knowledge

Synonyms

etiologies	causes
anxiety	nervousness/fear
disorder	illness
distress	extreme unhappiness
dimensions	aspects
continuum	range/scale
assertive	confident/determined

Glossary

phobia a strong/unreasonable fear of something

correlation a relationship between variables

material relating to physical objects or money rather than emotions or the spiritual world

masculinity qualities typical of a man

incidence how often something occurs

mechanic a person who fixes vehicles/machinery

demographic a part/group of the population

Major depression: biological causes

Example 1: The monoamine hypothesis

This states that there is a lack of certain neurotransmitters which are responsible for depression. For example: a lack of serotonin may be related to anxiety, **obsessions**, and **compulsions**. A lack of dopamine maybe related to attention, motivation, pleasure, and reward, as well as interest in life (Nutt, 2008). Evidence comes from certain drugs which raise the levels of serotonin and dopamine and improve the mood of sufferers. However, they do not work with all people and when monoamines are reduced in healthy non-depressed people they do not become depressed.

Example 2: The role of genes

Aim: To compare the incidence of the **symptoms** of depression among identical and non-identical **twins** (Kendler et al., 2006).

Method: The researchers used telephone interviews to ask 42 000 twins if they and their family members had symptoms of depression.

Results: When one twin had symptoms of depression, the other twin also had depression more often if they were identical twins.

Conclusion: There is some evidence for the role of genes, because identical twins are more likely to both have symptoms than non-identical twins. However, they are also more likely to share the same environment which may have been the reason for their depression.

Major depression: sociocultural causes

Nicholson et al. (2008) found men who were in the lowest socioeconomic groups in Poland, Russia, and the Czech Republic were five times more likely to have depression.

Wu and Anthony (2000) found **Hispanic** communities in the USA have lower levels of depression than other communities, probably because of stronger extended family connections.

Gabilondo et al. (2010) found depression is less common in Spain than in northern European countries, probably because family connections and traditions are considered more important.

Etiologies means 'causes' of an illness.

Subject vocabulary

monoamine neurotransmitters a group of neurotransmitters. Examples include serotonin and dopamine

neurotransmitters chemicals in the brain that are involved with communication

serotonin a neurotransmitter related to feelings of wellbeing and happiness

dopamine a neurotransmitter related to attention, motivation, pleasure, and reward

genes molecular units which are the building blocks for characteristics

socioeconomic relating to social and economic issues

Glossary

obsession thinking about something all the time

compulsion a strong desire/need to do something

symptoms characteristics of an illness

twins two children born at the same time, by the same mother

Synonyms

Hispanic .... Spanish

Hints for success: For this learning outcome you do not need to refer to research in detail; linking the explanations of the disorders to the underlying assumptions is more important. Also be prepared for a question asking you about only *one* disorder.

Discuss cultural and gender variations in prevalence of disorders

Synonyms

variations.......... differences

disorder............ illness

anxiety .... nervousness/ fear

translation .... interpretation

notions............. thoughts/ ideas

Glossary

prevalence how common something is

diagnosis giving a medical name to an illness

semi-structured something that is only partly planned or organized

bilingual speaking two languages

alcoholism addiction to alcohol

Subject vocabulary

psychological relating to thoughts, feelings, and behaviour

affective relating to emotions

depression an affective disorder characterized by extreme unhappiness

DSM-IV a diagnostic system

Opening sentence:

In this answer I will discuss cultural and gender **variations** in the **prevalence** of psychological **disorders**, with a focus on **anxiety** and affective disorders.

Culture

Model sentence: Culture affects which disorders are diagnosed.

Example 1: Depression in Hopi Indians

For example, among Hopi Indians in North America, a study was carried out to investigate what depression is (Manson et al., 1985).

Aim: To understand the meaning of depression among the Hopi Indians.

Method: Semi-structured interviews were conducted with 36 Hopi informants. The interviewer was a **bilingual** member of a Hopi community.

Results: No single **translation** of depression was found. Instead there were five different sicknesses that were in some way connected with the DSM symptoms for depression: worry sickness, unhappiness, heartbroken, drunken-like craziness, disappointment.

Conclusion: The DSM symptoms for major depression do not match with any disorder that the Hopi were aware of.

Model sentence: Different cultures have different notions of psychological illness. For example, there are different ways of responding to the problems of life among the Hopi. This explains differences in prevalence.

Example 2: Depression in American Jewish males

Aim: To see if Jewish people in the United States are more likely than other religious groups to have depression (Levav et al., 1997).

Method: The researchers reviewed statistics from two cities in the United States for rates of depression and other psychological disorders and looked for a statistical relationship with self-identified religion.

Results: There was no difference among women, but there was a significant difference among men. Jewish men had higher rates of depression and lower rates of **alcoholism** than other groups.

Conclusion: It is likely that social norms are responsible for the difference. This explanation would suggest that Jewish males are not more depressed, but that the diagnosis of alcoholism in other groups prevents many other men from getting a diagnosis of depression.

Model sentence: Jewish men are less likely to be alcoholic. Therefore, alcoholism is not seen by doctors as the cause of their depressions. Therefore, they are more likely to be diagnosed with depression rather than alcoholism.

Gender

Model sentence: Gender affects how disorders manifest themselves.

Example 1: Phobias and women

The prevalence of specific phobias is higher among women (Kessler and Merikangas, 2004). It is possible there is an evolutionary advantage for women to develop anxiety disorders. For example, Davey et al. (1998) compared reactions to animals across cultures and found that women have stronger **disgust** reactions than men. More disgust could be an evolutionary advantage that helps women avoid danger from animals and infections while they are pregnant.

Example 2: Culture and gender

Cultural **dimensions** are factors that can be placed on a **philosophical** **continuum**. Hofstede (1980) stated that societies can be described by placing them on a masculine versus feminine continuum. Masculine societies: Men are supposed to be **assertive**, tough, and focused on **material** success; women are supposed to be more modest, tender, and concerned with the quality of life. Female societies: Gender roles overlap - *both* men and women are supposed to be modest, tender, and concerned with the quality of life.

Key study: The importance of masculine culture in Israel.

Model sentence: Israel has been reported to be high on masculinity in other research.

Aim: To investigate the effects of culture on the **incidence** of anxiety disorders among young Israeli people in a school for military medicine and a school for **mechanics** (Iancu et al., 2007).

Method: The researchers looked for a relationship between having an anxiety disorder and several **demographic** variables like gender and age.

Results: Males were more likely to have a phobia, especially if they were at the school for mechanics, had few friends, and no romantic relationship.

Conclusion: In a country high on masculinity, young males are more likely to develop an anxiety disorder unless they have appropriate social support.

Culture affects which disorders are diagnosed.

Gender affects how disorders manifest themselves.

Hints for success: Remember to use research to support your ideas here and remember to be balanced when writing about other cultures. There may be differences, but it is not clear that one culture is 'correct'.

Synonyms

manifest .... show

dimensions .... aspects

continuum .... range/scale

assertive .... confident/determined

Subject vocabulary

philosophical relating to the nature of knowledge

Glossary

disgust thoughts/feelings of sickness

material relating to physical objects or money rather than emotions or the spiritual world

masculinity qualities typical of a man

incidence how many times something occurs

mechanic a person who fixes vehicles/machinery

demographic a part/group of the population

Examine biomedical, individual, and group approaches to treatment

Opening sentence:

In this answer I will examine biomedical, individual, and group approaches to treatment for psychological **disorders**.

Biomedical approaches

Biomedical approaches to treatment usually use medications to **alter** the activity of neurotransmitters in the brain.

- Biomedical approaches assume by using medical treatments to affect a person biologically, doctors can improve a person's condition.
- Biomedical approaches assume there is an underlying assumption that the cause of the problem is biological and therefore the solution should also be biological.

Example: Selective serotonin reuptake inhibitors (SSRIs) are an antidepressant. These drugs work by altering the amount of serotonin in the brain.

Aim: To compare the effectiveness of SSRIs to placebos (Kirsch et al., 2008).

Method: A meta-analysis of trials submitted to the US Food and Drug Administration (FDA) for new SSRIs.

Results: Virtually no difference at moderate levels of depression between placebos and SSRIs. Significant difference at severe levels of depression between placebos and SSRIs.

Conclusion: SSRIs are effective but only for severe depression. They should also be used with other forms of therapy such as cognitive-behavioural therapy (CBT).

Individual approaches

Model sentence: I will now explain individual psychotherapy and its main assumptions.

An individual approach to therapy is when a client meets alone with a therapist and the therapist uses psychological techniques to help the person with their **symptoms**.

- Individual approaches assume the cause of a person's disorder is not biological, but is connected with learning experiences or information processing styles.
- Individual approaches assume if a person can go through individual therapy successfully, they will very often not need to be treated any more and a full recovery is possible.
- Individual approaches assume the problems are psychological and not biological. A person will be able to improve with practice.

Subject vocabulary

biomedical treatment/approach relating to the body

psychological relating to thoughts, feelings, and behaviour

neurotransmitters chemicals in the brain that are involved with communication

serotonin a neurotransmitter related to feelings of wellbeing and happiness

placebo a fake treatment that can often have an effect. Researchers compare their effects with the real treatment

meta-analysis a review of many studies into the same phenomena to see what broad conclusions can be made

cognitive-behavioural therapy (CBT) a form of therapy which focuses on changing the way patients think

psychotherapy therapy that focus on thoughts and feelings rather than purely biological causes

Synonyms

disorder.............. illness

alter.................... change

Glossary

symptoms characteristics of an illness

Example: Cognitive-behavioural therapy (CBT) for depression

CBT is when a psychological therapist talks with their client and tries to identify problems with their thinking and how they process information about the world. They do this with the client to help them identify their problems themselves.

Aim: To compare the effectiveness of CBT and a drug *fluoxetine* **longitudinally** (March et al., 2007).

Method: 327 teenagers with depression were divided into four groups: fluoxetine only, CBT only, a combination of fluoxetine and CBT, and placebo only. After 12, 18, and 36 weeks of treatment, the researchers compared doctors' ratings of the **severity** of the teenagers' depression from before and after the treatment.

Results: Many more teenagers receiving the combination therapy showed some improvement after 12 weeks. Fluoxetine alone worked faster than CBT alone but after 18 weeks they were having approximately the same effect. By 36 weeks, all three groups were approximately equally effective. There were more **suicidal** thoughts among the teenagers receiving *only* fluoxetine than the groups receiving CBT.

Conclusion: For fast treatment, fluoxetine is more effective than CBT alone, but it may increase suicide risk when it is used alone. CBT is effective at preventing suicidal thoughts and therefore the authors recommend that a combination of different therapy types is more appropriate.

Group approaches

Group therapy occurs when a therapist works with several clients at the same time, encouraging them to talk to and help each other.

- Group approaches assume that **interpersonal** contact with people who are going through similar troubles can improve the symptoms of their disorders. People can learn from each other and help each other.
- Group approaches assume that when people are surrounded by others with similar emotional experiences, they may be encouraged to talk more about them than when they are alone with a therapist.
- Group approaches assume that groups create new skills (such as personal skills) that clients can use outside therapy in daily life.

Example: Group CBT for depression

Aim: To test if group CBT could reduce the depressive symptoms and improve **self-esteem** among runaway teenagers (Hyun et al., 2005).

Method: 27 male teenage runaways in Seoul, South Korea, were **randomly** placed in a group that received CBT or a group that received no treatment.

Results: The experimental group improved significantly in symptoms of depression.

Conclusion: CBT is a cost-effective treatment that works well.

Subject vocabulary

longitudinal research that has taken place over a long period of time, usually years

Synonyms

severity.............. seriousness

Glossary

suicide killing yourself

interpersonal related to relationships between people

self-esteem confident in your own abilities

random chosen without a definite pattern

Hints for success: It is unlikely you will need to write about all three forms of treatment but make sure you know the assumptions of each, and that you use the studies to support your ideas.

Evaluate the use of biomedical, individual, and group approaches to the treatment of one disorder

Opening sentence:

In this answer I will evaluate the use of biomedical, individual, and group approaches to the treatment of major depression (affective **disorder**).

Major depression

- The main affective **symptom** is a loss of interest or pleasure in daily activities.
- The main cognitive symptoms are problems concentrating, thoughts of death, or plans to commit suicide.
- The somatic symptoms include weight loss or weight gain and tiredness.

Biomedical approaches

Biomedical approaches to treatment usually use medications to **alter** the activity of neurotransmitters in the brain.

- Biomedical approaches assume by using medical treatments to affect a person biologically, doctors can improve a person's condition.
- Biomedical approaches assume there is an underlying assumption that the cause of the problem is biological and therefore the solution should also be biological.

Model sentence: **An example of a biomedical approach is selective serotonin reuptake inhibitors (SSRIs) for the treatment of depression.**

Strengths

- They often work very quickly.
- They are efficient in terms of time and cost as the person does not need long sessions with a therapist.

Limitations

- They do not treat the cause of the problem; they only reduce the symptoms.
- The effects are usually short-term only, and the person needs to continue taking the medication to prevent **anxiety**.
- They can have side effects, for example sleepiness, weight gain and sexual problems, which may lead to other problems such as increased anxiety.
- Patients develop a tolerance for them which means they need to take more of the medication to get the same benefits.
- SSRIs have no advantage over placebos in the treatment of *short-term mild* depression. SSRIs are effective but only for severe depression. They should also be used with other forms of therapy such as cognitive-behavioural therapy (CBT).

Individual approaches

An individual approach to therapy is when a client meets alone with a therapist and the therapist uses psychological techniques to help the person deal with their symptoms.

Subject vocabulary

biomedical treatment/approach relating to the body

affective relating to emotions

cognition/cognitive related to mental processes (such as perception, memory, problem-solving)

somatic relating to the body

neurotransmitters chemicals in the brain that are involved with communication

cognitive-behavioural therapy (CBT) a form of therapy which focuses on changing the way patients think

psychological relating to thoughts, feelings, and behavioural

Synonyms

disorder.............. illness

alter..................... change

anxiety .... nervousness/fear

Glossary

symptoms characteristics of an illness

- Individual approaches assume the cause of a person's disorder is not biological, but is connected with learning experiences or information processing styles.
- Individual approaches assume if a person can go through individual therapy successfully, they will very often not need to be treated any more and a full recovery is possible.
- Individual approaches assume the problems are *psychological* and not biological. A person will be able to improve with practice.

Model sentence: **An example of individual approaches is cognitive-behavioural therapy (CBT).**

Cognitive-behavioural therapy is when a therapist talks with their client and tries to identify problems with their thinking and how they process information about the world. This process is known as *cognitive restructuring* and it means patients recognize the **irrationality** of many thoughts.

Strengths

- During CBT, a person learns to have *more control* of their thoughts and they are able to control their own recovery.
- CBT lasts for a long time, either because the person has learned how to deal with depression by themselves, or because the therapy has caused permanent changes in the way a person thinks about the world.

Limitations

- It is **costly** in terms of time and money.
- Improvements are not immediate and drugs (e.g. *fluoxetine*) may be needed to stabilize the patient.

Group approaches

Group therapy occurs when a therapist works with several clients at the same time, encouraging them to talk to and help each other.

- Group approaches assume **interpersonal** contact with people who are going through similar troubles can improve the symptoms of their disorders.
- Group approaches assume when people are surrounded by others with similar emotional experiences, they may be encouraged to talk more about them than when they are alone with a therapist.

Model sentence: **An example of group CBT for treating depression has been conducted with South Korean teenagers (Hyun et al., 2005).**

Strengths

- Groups create new skills (such as personal skills) that clients can use outside therapy in daily life.
- Group members can learn from other people's experience.
- Group members can see each other improve, acting as a motivator.
- Group therapy is cheap as many people can be treated at once.

Limitations

- People get less individual attention and therefore take longer to improve.
- Talking about personal issues in groups takes confidence. People can **drop out** because they do not feel as confident as other members of the group.
- People can learn bad habits from other members such as using alcohol and hiding it from the therapist.

Glossary

irrational/irrationality not based on facts or reality, but on emotions

interpersonal related to relationships between people

to drop out to stop attending

Synonyms

costly................. expensive

Hints for success: You need to give a balanced account including both strengths and weaknesses.

Discuss the use of eclectic approaches to treatment

Opening sentence:

In this answer I will discuss the use of eclectic approaches to the treatment.

Major depression

- The main affective symptom is a loss of interest or pleasure in daily activities.
- The main behavioural symptom is **agitated** movements.
- The main cognitive symptoms are problems concentrating, thoughts of death, or plans to commit **suicide**.
- The somatic symptoms include weight loss or weight gain and tiredness.

Eclectic treatment

Eclectic approaches to treatment take ideas from different psychological theories or mix psychological and biomedical treatments. This is usually a positive thing because each approach to treatment has different strengths and limitations.

Combining cognitive-behavioural therapy (CBT) with SSRIs

Cognitive-behavioural therapy is when a psychological therapist talks with their client and tries to identify problems with their thinking and how they process information about the world. Selective serotonin reuptake inhibitors (SSRIs) are an antidepressant. These drugs work by **altering** the amount of serotonin in the brain.

Example 1: SSRIs are not effective for mild to moderate depression.

Aim: To compare the effectiveness of SSRIs to placebos (Kirsch et al., 2008).

Method: A meta-analysis of trials submitted to the US Food and Drug Administration (FDA) for new SSRIs.

Results: Very little difference at moderate levels of depression between placebos and SSRIs. Significant difference at **severe** levels of depression between placebos and SSRIs.

Conclusion: SSRIs are effective but only for *severe depression*. They should also be used with other forms of therapy such as CBT.

Example 2: Combining cognitive-behavioural therapy for depression with an SSRI (fluoxetine)

Aim: To compare the effectiveness of CBT and a drug *fluoxetine* longitudinally (March et al., 2007).

Subject vocabulary

- **eclectic** using a mixture/combination of treatments
- **cognition/cognitive** related to mental processes (such as perception, memory, problem-solving)
- **somatic** related to the body
- **psychological** relating to thoughts, feelings, and behaviour
- **cognitive-behavioural therapy (CBT)** a form of therapy which focuses on changing the way patients think
- **placebo** a fake treatment that can often have an effect. Researchers compare their effects with the real treatment
- **meta-analysis** a review of many studies into the same phenomena to see what broad conclusions can be made
- **longitudinal** research that has taken place over a long period of time, usually years

Synonyms

- **agitated** .... troubled/restless
- **altering** .... changing
- **severe** .... very bad/serious

Glossary

- **suicide** killing yourself

Method: 327 teenagers with depression were divided into four groups: fluoxetine only, CBT only, a combination of fluoxetine and CBT, and placebo only. After 12, 18, and 36 weeks of treatment, the researchers compared doctors' ratings of the severity of the teenagers' depression from before and after the treatment.

Results: Many more teenagers receiving the combination therapy showed some improvement after 12 weeks. Fluoxetine alone worked faster than CBT alone but after 18 weeks they were having approximately the same effect. By 36 weeks, all three groups were approximately equally effective. There were more suicidal thoughts among the teenagers receiving *only* fluoxetine than the groups receiving CBT.

Conclusion: For fast treatment, fluoxetine is more effective than CBT alone, but it may increase suicide risk when it is used alone. CBT is effective at preventing suicidal thoughts and therefore the authors recommend that a *combination* of different therapy types is more appropriate.

Example 3: Antidepressant (nortriptyline) and Inter-Personal Therapy (IPT) for depression

Aim: To test the effectiveness of combining antidepressant medication with IPT (Reynolds et al., 1999).

Method: 187 older people who had completed a first phase of treatment for **acute** depression were divided into four groups:

1. Medication only.
2. Placebo.
3. IPT and medication.
4. IPT and placebo.

These treatments were continued for up to 3 years. The dependent variable was: If treatment was needed for depression again.

Results:

1. Medication only - 43 per cent became depressed again.
2. Placebo - 64 per cent became depressed again.
3. IPT and medication - 20 per cent became depressed again.
4. IPT and placebo - 90 per cent became depressed again.

Conclusions: A combination of treatments is clearly best in this situation. The researchers said that this may be partly because people who receive IPT are more likely to take their medication.

Synonyms

acute .... very serious

Discussion

- People who receive medication and some form of therapy are more likely to take their medication.
- It is difficult to judge which treatment is more effective as they are often used at the same time. Therefore, this makes it difficult for future treatments for the patient.
- Different people respond differently to different treatments. Using an eclectic approach improves the chances of them receiving the appropriate treatment but this can take time.

Hints for success: Clearly label the individual therapies. You may address the question in the context of more than one disorder if you wish.

Discuss the relationship between etiology and therapeutic approach in relation to one disorder

Synonyms

etiology .... cause

disorder.............. illness

anxiety .... nervousness/ fear

alter.................... change

severe................. very bad/ serious

Glossary

symptoms characteristics of an illness

to commit suicide to kill yourself

obsession thinking about something all the time

compulsion a strong desire/ need to do something

Subject vocabulary

affective related to emotions

cognition/cognitive related to mental processes (such as perception, memory, problem-solving)

somatic related to the body

neurotransmitters chemicals in the brain that are involved with communication

serotonin a neurotransmitter related to feelings of wellbeing and happiness

dopamine a neurotransmitter related to attention, motivation, pleasure, and reward

placebo a fake treatment that can often have an effect. Researchers compare their effects with the real treatment

meta-analysis a review of many studies into the same phenomena to see what broad conclusions can be made

cognitive-behavioural therapy (CBT) a form of therapy which focuses on changing the way patients think

Opening sentence:

In this answer I will discuss the relationship between **etiology** and therapeutic approach in relation to major depression.

Major depression

Etiology is the cause or causes of a **disorder**. A therapeutic approach is how a therapist or doctor treats a disorder.

- The main affective **symptom** is a loss of interest or pleasure in daily activities.
- The main cognitive symptoms are problems concentrating, thoughts of death, or plans to **commit suicide**.
- The somatic symptoms include weight loss or weight gain and tiredness.

Example 1: The monoamine hypothesis

There is a lack of certain neurotransmitters which are responsible for depression. For example: a lack of serotonin may be related to **anxiety**, **obsessions**, and **compulsions**. A lack of dopamine may be related to attention, motivation, pleasure, and reward, as well as interest in life (Nutt, 2008). Evidence comes from certain drugs which raise the levels of serotonin and dopamine and improve the mood of sufferers. However, they do not work with all people and when monoamines are reduced in healthy non-depressed people they do not become depressed.

How does this affect treatment?

Biomedical approaches to treatment usually use medications to **alter** the activity of neurotransmitters in the brain.

- Biomedical approaches assume by using medical treatments to affect a person biologically doctors can improve a person's condition.
- Biomedical approaches assume there is an underlying assumption that the cause of the problem is biological and therefore the solution should also be biological.

Example: selective serotonin reuptake inhibitors (SSRIs) are an antidepressant. These drugs work by altering the amount of serotonin in the brain.

Supporting study

Aim: To compare the effectiveness of SSRIs to placebos (Kirsch et al., 2008).

Method: A meta-analysis of trials submitted to the US Food and Drug Administration (FDA) for new SSRIs.

Results: Virtually no difference at moderate levels of depression between placebos and SSRIs. Significant difference at **severe** levels of depression between placebos and SSRIs.

Conclusion: SSRIs are effective but only for severe depression. They should also be used with other forms of therapy such as cognitive-behavioural therapy (CBT).

Strengths of this approach:

- There is a clear relationship between the cause and the medication given to patients.

- Medication is cheaper than individual psychological therapy for depression, which can take a long time.

Limitations of this approach:

- Drugs treat the symptoms not the cause. For example, there is no direct evidence that a lack of certain neurotransmitters is responsible for depression.
- Different people may have different biological causes.
- Patients' neurotransmitter levels are not measured before they are given the medication and therefore it is not possible to know if the medication is really appropriate.
- There are side effects of medication. For example, when young people are given SSRIs there is often an increased chance that they will attempt to commit suicide.

Example 2: Sociocultural causes

Nicholson et al. (2008) found men who were in the lowest socioeconomic groups in Poland, Russia, and the Czech Republic were five times more likely to have depression.

Wu and Anthony (2000) found **Hispanic** communities in the USA have lower levels of depression than other communities, probably because of stronger extended family connections.

Gabilondo et al. (2010) found depression is less common in Spain than in northern European countries, probably because family connections and traditions are considered more important.

Model sentence: A lack of family connections and poverty increase the chances of developing depression.

How does this affect treatment?

Therapists may use group therapy with members of the group experiencing similar backgrounds and causes to their depression. The therapist works with several clients at the same time, encouraging them to talk to and help each other.

- Group approaches assume interpersonal contact with people who are going through similar troubles can improve the symptoms of their disorders. People can learn from each other and help each other.
- Group approaches assume when people are surrounded by others with similar emotional experiences, they may be encouraged to talk more about them than when they are alone with a therapist.
- Group approaches assume groups create new skills (such as personal skills) that clients can use outside therapy in daily life.

Supporting study

Aim: To test if group CBT could reduce the depressive symptoms and improve **self-esteem** among runaway teenagers (Hyun et al., 2005).

Method: 27 male teenage runaways in Seoul, South Korea, were **randomly** placed in a group that received CBT or a group that received no treatment.

Results: The experimental group improved significantly in symptoms of depression.

Conclusion: CBT is a cost-effective treatment that works well.

Subject vocabulary

psychological relating to thoughts, feelings, and behaviour

socioeconomic relating to social and economic issues

Synonyms

Hispanic .... Spanish

Glossary

poverty being very poor

self-esteem confident in your own abilities

random chosen without a definite pattern

Hints for success: The command term in the question is discuss. This means you must make the connection between cause and treatment very clear.

General Learning Outcomes

GLO 1: To what extent do biological, cognitive, and sociocultural factors influence abnormal behaviour?

Biological factors

Model sentence: **Biological factors can be used to explain the etiologies of abnormal behaviour.**

Major depression: biological causes

Example 1: The monoamine hypothesis

This states there is a lack of certain neurotransmitters which are responsible for depression. For example: a lack of serotonin may be related to **anxiety**, **obsessions**, and **compulsions**. A lack of dopamine maybe related to attention, motivation, pleasure, and reward, as well as interest in life (Nutt, 2008). Evidence comes from certain drugs which raise the levels of serotonin and dopamine and improve the mood of sufferers. However, they do not work with all people and when monoamines are reduced in healthy non-depressed people they do not become depressed.

Example 2: The role of genes

Aim: To compare the **incidence** of the **symptoms** of depression among identical and non-identical **twins** (Kendler et al., 2006).

Method: The researchers used telephone interviews to ask 42 000 twins if they and their family members had symptoms of depression.

Results: When one twin had symptoms of depression, the other twin also had depression more often if they were identical twins.

Conclusion: There is some evidence for the role of genes, because identical twins are more likely to both have symptoms than non-identical twins.

Cognitive factors

Model sentence: **Cognitive therapy influences how patients who suffer from an abnormal disorder think.**

Example 1

An individual approach to therapy is when a client meets alone with a therapist and the therapist uses psychological techniques to help the person deal with their symptoms.

- Individual approaches assume the cause of a person's disorder is not biological, but is connected with learning experiences or *information processing styles.*
- Individual approaches assume the problems are *psychological* and not biological. A person will be able to improve with practice.

Example 2: Cognitive-behavioural therapy (CBT) for depression

Cognitive-behavioural therapy is when a psychological therapist talks with their client and tries to identify problems with their thinking and how they process information about the world.

Subject vocabulary

cognition/cognitive related to mental processes (such as perception, memory, problem-solving)

sociocultural (factors) relating to social and cultural issues

monoamine neurotransmitters a group of neurotransmitters. Examples include serotonin and dopamine

neurotransmitters chemicals in the brain that are involved with communication

serotonin a neurotransmitter related to feelings of wellbeing and happiness

dopamine a neurotransmitter related to attention, motivation, pleasure, and reward

psychological relating to thoughts, feelings and behaviour

Synonyms

etiologies............ causes

anxiety .... nervousness/fear

disorder............. illness

Glossary

obsession thinking about something all the time

compulsion a strong desire/need to do something

incidence how often something occurs

symptoms characteristics of an illness

twins two children born at the same time, by the same mother

Aim: To compare the effectiveness of CBT and a drug *fluoxetine* longitudinally (March et al., 2007).

Method: 327 teenagers with depression were divided into four groups: fluoxetine only, CBT only, a combination of fluoxetine and CBT, and placebo only. After 12, 18, and 36 weeks of treatment, the researchers compared doctors' ratings of the **severity** of the teenagers' depression from before and after the treatment.

Results: Many more teenagers receiving the combination therapy showed some improvement after 12 weeks. Fluoxetine alone worked faster than CBT alone but after 18 weeks they were having approximately the same effect. By 36 weeks, all three groups were approximately equally effective. There were more **suicidal** thoughts among the teenagers receiving *only* fluoxetine than the groups receiving CBT.

Conclusion: For fast treatment, fluoxetine is more effective than CBT alone, but it may increase suicide risk when it is used alone. CBT is effective at preventing suicidal thoughts and therefore the authors recommend that a combination of different therapy types is more appropriate.

Model sentence: CBT changes the way people think about the world and has been shown to be very effective in preventing suicide with depressed patients.

Sociocultural factors

Model sentence: Sociocultural factors can be used to explain the etiologies of abnormal behaviour.

Specific phobia: sociocultural causes

Example 1

Cultural **dimensions** are factors that can be placed on a philosophical **continuum**. Hofstede (1980) stated societies can be described by placing them on a masculine versus feminine continuum. Masculine societies: Men are supposed to be **assertive**, tough, and focused on **material** success; women are supposed to be more modest, tender, and concerned with the quality of life. Female societies: Gender roles overlap - both men and women are supposed to be modest, tender, and concerned with the quality of life.

The importance of masculine culture in Israel. Israel has been reported to be high on masculinity in other research.

Aim: To investigate the effects of culture on the incidence of anxiety disorders among young Israeli people in a school for military medicine and a school for **mechanics** (Iancu et al., 2007).

Method: The researchers looked for a relationship between having an anxiety disorder and several **demographic** variables like gender and age.

Results: Males were more likely to have a phobia, especially if they were at the school for mechanics, had few friends, and no romantic relationship.

Conclusion: In a country high on masculinity, young males are more likely to develop an anxiety disorder unless they have appropriate social support.

Subject vocabulary

longitudinally research that has taken place over a long period of time, usually years

placebo a fake treatment

philosophical relating to the nature of knowledge

Synonyms

severity .... seriousness

dimensions .... aspects

continuum .... range/scale

assertive .... confident/determined

Glossary

suicide killing yourself

phobia a strong/unreasonable fear of something

material relating to physical objects or money rather than emotions or the spiritual world

masculinity qualities typical of a man

mechanic a person who fixes vehicles/machinery

demographic a part/group of the population

GLO 2: Evaluate psychological research (that is, theories and/or studies) relevant to the study of abnormal behaviour

Example 1: Cognitive-behavioural therapy (CBT) for depression

In cognitive-behavioural therapy a psychological therapist talks with their client and tries to identify problems with their thinking and how they process information about the world.

Aim: To compare the effectiveness of CBT and a drug *fluoxetine* longitudinally (March et al., 2007).

Method: 327 teenagers with depression were divided into four groups: fluoxetine only, CBT only, a combination of fluoxetine and CBT, and placebo only. After 12, 18, and 36 weeks of treatment, the researchers compared doctors' ratings of the severity of the teenagers' depression from before and after the treatment.

Results: Many more teenagers receiving the combination therapy showed some improvement after 12 weeks. Fluoxetine alone worked faster than CBT alone but after 18 weeks they were having approximately the same effect. By 36 weeks, all three groups were approximately equally effective. There were more suicidal thoughts among the teenagers receiving *only* fluoxetine than the groups receiving CBT.

Conclusion: For fast treatment, fluoxetine is more effective than CBT alone, but it may increase suicide risk when it is used alone. CBT is effective at preventing suicidal thoughts and therefore the authors recommend that a combination of different therapy types is more appropriate.

Subject vocabulary

independent variable (IV) the variable an experimenter controls or changes

dependent variable (DV) the variable an experimenter measures

Synonyms

denied .... not given

Glossary

validity being correct/reasonable

Evaluation:

Strengths

It is an experiment and therefore there is a cause-effect relationship. The CBT treatment (**independent variable** - IV) was the cause of the improvement in symptoms (**dependent variable** - DV).

The experiment was only carried out in one culture and so it reduces the variety of cultural factors that could have influenced results.

Limitations

One group must be **denied** treatment in order for the cause of differences to be clear. However, in this case the second group eventually received treatment, even if they had to wait.

For CBT it is difficult to design a placebo. CBT was compared with *no treatment* but there is no placebo. Therefore, it is not *entirely certain* that CBT caused the improvement. This is known as lacking in internal **validity**. Other possible explanations for the improvements could be that the teenagers made social contact with a group of people who were similar.

Example 2

Model sentence: Rosenhan (1973) demonstrates validity is difficult to achieve.

Study 1

Aim: To test whether hospitals can detect whether a person really is mentally ill or not, and then to observe how patients are really treated in hospitals (Rosenhan, 1973).

Method: Rosenhan organized for colleagues and friends without any **diagnosed** psychological disorders to go to psychiatric hospitals and report that they had been hearing voices. These people were 'pseudopatients'. Apart from questions relating to these experiences, they answered all questions honestly.

Results: Most of them were **admitted** to the hospital and were given a diagnosis of schizophrenia. After that, most of their behaviour was considered abnormal. For example, when taking notes about what happened in the hospital, hospital staff recorded that this patient's writing was **excessive** and abnormal; when they walked the corridors because they were bored they were accused of *obsessive pacing*.

Conclusion: The difference between normal and abnormal is very difficult for experts to judge. Achieving a valid diagnosis is also difficult but **ethically** necessary.

Study 2

Staff were told at a psychiatric hospital that pseudopatients would try to gain **admittance**. No pseudopatients actually appeared, but 41 *real* patients were judged with great confidence to be pseudo-patients by at least one member of staff.

Conclusion: There is a lack of scientific evidence on which medical diagnoses can be made.

Evaluation:

Strengths

The study gathered very detailed information from inside the hospital that is difficult to get any other way. This means the observations and conclusions are more valid.

The procedure was standardized because the pseudopatients all told the same story, which makes the study more reliable.

Limitations

There is a problem with ethics because Rosenhan did not seek permission from the hospital staff to observe their behaviour. However, had he done so then they may have changed their behaviour. Therefore, the use of **deception** was reasonable and makes the results more realistic.

There is a problem with the interpretation of the results:

Hospitals have an ethical responsibility to investigate **odd** behaviour. Hearing voices is odd behaviour. Even if the hospital staff thought they were **faking**, they still had an ethical responsibility to investigate. As doctors they had a duty to admit the pseudopatients in order to protect the community and protect the people from themselves. Even if the doctors did not believe hearing voices was **genuine**, walking into a hospital and lying about hearing voices is still abnormal behaviour. Therefore, admitting the pseudopatients does show diagnosing abnormal behaviour is difficult but it does not show the doctors and hospitals were **incompetent**.

Many real **dysfunctional** patients pretend or fake their symptoms. People who fake their symptoms can *still* be considered dysfunctional and need investigation. For example: a non-depressed person who fakes being depressed can be considered to be dysfunctional.

Glossary

diagnosis giving a medical name to an illness

admitted allowed to enter

excessive too much

to deceive/deception to cause someone to believe something that is not true

incompetent not having the skill/ability to do a job properly

dysfunction/dysfunctional not working or behaving normally

Subject vocabulary

psychiatric hospital a hospital that treats abnormal behaviours

pseudopatients fake patients

schizophrenia an emotional and thought disorder with a wide variety of symptoms

obsessive pacing non-stop walking

Synonyms

ethical .... moral

admittance .... entry

odd .... strange

faking .... pretending

genuine .... real/true

Hints for success: Always use previously learned material to support a GLO answer and use examples of research to support each point you are making.

Evaluate theories of cognitive development

Subject vocabulary

cognitive development the development of mental processes (such as perception, memory, problem-solving)

predetermined preplanned

self-motivated wanting or a desire to do something

schema a frame for understanding the world

egocentrism self-focused and unable to understand the world from another's point of view

Synonyms

construct .... build

changed .... altered

profound .... complete

Glossary

furry covered with fur or short hair

infant/infancy a very young child who is not yet able to walk or talk

Opening sentence:

In this answer I will evaluate Piaget's and Vygotsky's theories of cognitive development. I will describe both theories and then use positive and negative criticism to evaluate them.

Piaget's assumptions

- Intelligence is under biological control and develops in the form of predetermined stages.
- Children do not passively receive their knowledge.
- Children are curious, self-motivated, and try to find information to **construct** their own understanding of the environment.
- Children construct their view of the world through mental frameworks of understanding called *schemas*. Schemas are mental representations of the world and are **changed** as a result of:
  - *Assimilation:* Occurs when new events (such as new objects, experiences, ideas, and situations) can be fitted into existing schemas of what the child already understands about the world. An example is when a child calls the family German Shepherd a 'doggie'. He may point at the neighbours' Labrador and also call it a 'doggie'. This shows he has understood the existing schema (**furry**, playful, four legs) and fitted the image into it.
  - *Accommodation:* Occurs when new events do not fit existing schemas and so they have to be changed to allow the new world view or new schemas are created. For example, a child points at a small horse and calls it a 'doggie'. He would be corrected and told it is a 'horse'. He would then have to create a new schema for 'horses.'

Piaget's four stages of cognitive development

1. The sensorimotor stage (0–2 years)

   The **infant** has no formal schema for the world or of itself. It can only know the world through its immediate senses and the motor or movement actions it performs. An example of this stage is **profound** egocentrism as the infant cannot see the difference between itself and the environment as it has no real knowledge of the world around it. Egocentrism can be seen in a *lack of object permanence* which is if an infant cannot see an object, then it no longer exists for the child.

2. The pre-operational stage (2–7 years)

   The stage is still dominated by egocentrism as the child has a limited ability to see, think, feel, or imagine the world from another person's point of view. Egocentrism can be seen in the 'Three Mountain Experiment' (Piaget and Inhelder, 1956); when 4-year-olds were shown a mountain scene, they were generally unable to describe the same scene from a doll's point of view which was placed on the other side (of the picture).

3. The concrete operational stage (7–11 years)

   The child develops *conservation* and thinking becomes logical, clearer, and mature (or more *concrete*). Conservation is the understanding that although an object's appearance changes, it still stays the same in quantity. Changing the appearance of an object does not affect its mass, number, or volume. For example, a child who has developed conservation will understand when a liquid is poured into a different shaped glass, the *amount* of liquid stays the same.

4. The formal operational stage (11+ years)

   The child's mental structures are well developed. Problems can be dealt with mentally without the need for physical objects. Children can think about possible situations and imagine themselves in different roles without the need for dolls or play acting.

Positive evaluation

- Piaget produced the first comprehensive theory of child cognitive development which has led to debate as well as research.
- Piaget modified his theory to take account of the criticisms. He saw it as it constantly changing as new evidence came to light.
- Piaget was the first to investigate whether biological maturation drove cognitive development and his view that a child's cognitive changes are controlled by their biology is now widely accepted and supported by cross-cultural research.
- Piaget viewed children as curious, self-motivated, and trying to find information to construct their own understanding of the environment. This view was new at the time and has significantly influenced schools to create child-centred classrooms which allowed children to be more active in their learning.

Negative evaluation

- Bower (1982) showed how object permanence exists in the sensorimotor stage with 3-month-old babies. He showed them an object and then placed a screen in front of it. The object was then removed and the screen taken away. The child showed surprise. If they lacked object permanence the child would not be surprised it had been taken away.
- The pre-operational stage focuses on what the child *cannot* do rather than what they can do. For example, Field et al. (1982) found children aged 4–5 can spend as much as 20 per cent of their playtime constructing complicated roles for different objects (e.g. blocks become trucks, brooms become horses with names and personalities).
- Children are not as egocentric as the theory assumes: Taylor et al. (1993) showed how pre-operational children can develop imaginary friends with complex personalities who they talk to.
- The theory has been criticized for under-estimating the role of *social* development and the methods have been criticized as being too formal for children. For example, the 'Three Mountain Experiment' shows a social scene but Piaget uses it to focus on a mental problem. When the approach was changed to a more child-friendly format (such as the use of a policeman doll), more pre-operational children were able to understand the different views. This shows they are not as egocentric as Piaget assumed.

Glossary

screen a small movable wall

Vygotsky's assumptions

- Vygotsky focused on the importance of *social interaction and culture* in a child's cognitive development.
- Vygotsky described the importance of culture through his zone of proximal development (ZPD). Instruction from an expert (usually an adult) teaches children about the world. These abilities would not be developed if they were not taught. This shows the difference between Piaget's *individual construction* approach and the importance of *social construction* suggested by Vygotsky.
- A child makes sense of the world through *shared meaning* with others. This is different to Piaget who argued a child makes sense of the world as the result of biological processes that drive cognitive development.
- Vygotsky thought of culture as a body of knowledge which was held by persons of greater knowledge who passed on ideas through language.
  - Language drives cognitive development. For children, language is mainly a way to produce change in others. Eventually, they use language to direct and control their thinking.
  - Children develop two inner voices: One for thinking; another for communication with others.

In sum: Expert supervision and cultural knowledge through language allows cognitive development to take place.

Subject vocabulary

individual construction ways of seeing the world are the result of an individual thinking about it themselves. Piaget placed his focus here

social construction ways of seeing the world are the result of social interaction. Vygotsky placed his focus here

face validity a theory or method that appears to work or make sense. This is especially useful for *non-experts*

Vygotsky's three stages of language development

1. Pre-intellectual social speech (0–3 years), where thought is not constructed using language and speech is only used to bring about social change. For example, receiving objects from a parent.
2. Egocentric speech (3–7 years), where language helps to control the child's own behaviour and it is spoken out loud. For example, when children play games they often verbalize their actions.
3. Inner speech (7+ years), where the child uses speech silently to develop their thinking and uses it publicly for social communication.

Positive evaluation

- Vygotsky placed importance on a child's inner speech. He stated that the inner voice was a key part of learning and cognitive development. There is supporting evidence for this: Behrend et al. (1992) quantified inner speech by observing the amount of **whispering** and **lip reading** children did when given a task. They found children who used the greatest amount of inner speech tended to perform better on tasks.
- Vygotsky's ideas have face validity: The disorganized thoughts of the child are responded to with the more **systematic** and logical thinking by a more knowledgeable (usually adult) helper which helps the child cognitively develop. Conner, Knight, and Cross (1997) stated that the quality of the social support provided by a mother and father could predict the success of the child in the classroom.

Glossary

to whisper to speak very quietly

to lip read to understand what someone is saying by watching the movement of their lips

Synonyms

systematic........... organized and ordered

Negative evaluation

- There is a lack of empirical support for Vygotsky's ideas but this is probably due to the fact that he focused on *processes* rather than outcomes (such as Piaget) and processes are harder to test for. For example: How does one test for the influence of *shared meaning* on a child's cognitive development? How does one test for the influence of *culture* on a child's cognitive development?
- Vygotsky can be criticized for being too **vague** in his descriptions particularly that of *social influence*. It should be noted, however, that Vygotsky died at the age of 38; his work was still in its early stages.

Piaget's assumptions:

- *Intelligence is under biological control and develops in the form of predetermined stages.*
- *Children do not passively receive their knowledge.*
- *Children are curious, self-motivated, and try to find information to construct their own understanding of the environment.*

Vygotsky's assumptions:

- *Vygotsky focused on the importance of* social interaction and culture *in a child's cognitive development.*
- *A child makes sense of the world through* shared meaning *with others. This is different from Piaget who argued a child makes sense of the world as the result of biological processes that drive cognitive development.*
- *Vygotsky thought of culture as a body of knowledge which was held by persons of greater knowledge who passed on ideas through language.*

Hints for success: Do not present Vygotsky's and Piaget's ideas as being opposites; in many ways they **complement** each other.

Subject vocabulary

empirical support data coming from standardized and properly conducted research studies

Synonyms

vague .... unclear

Glossary

to complement to make a good combination

Discuss how social and environmental variables may affect cognitive development

Opening sentence:

Cognitive development can be defined as the increasingly advanced thought and problem-solving ability from **infancy** to adulthood. I will discuss ***socioeconomic*** *status* and *parenting.*

Socioeconomic status (environmental variable)

This is defined as the total measure of a person's social and economic position, based on income, occupation, education, and how much power they have over their own lives.

Diet

Children of a lower socioeconomic status are more likely to not have breakfast (Rose et al., 2013).

Raloff (1989) carried out a longitudinal study over the course of a year with children from lower socioeconomic backgrounds. He studied 1023 6th-grade children and found those who were given free school breakfasts improved their Maths and Science scores. A meta-analysis of breakfast programme studies by the Food Research Action Centre (FRAC) in the USA concluded:

- Children who do not have breakfast have slower **memory recall**.
- Children experiencing hunger have lower math scores.
- Children who were given free school breakfasts improved their Maths and Science scores.

Discussion: There is a correlation between the variables in the above study. Not having breakfast and being hungry are likely to be part of wider parenting problems. Parents who do not feed their children properly will not care for them in other areas and will be less likely to take an interest in their schooling.

Enriched environments

Children of a higher socioeconomic status are more likely to have an **enriched** environment (such as access to books and games). The effects of this can be shown with animal studies.

Aim: To investigate the effect of either enrichment or **deprivation** on the development of rat brains (Rosenzweig and Bennett, 1972).

Method: The independent variable (IV) was richness of the environment and was operationalized by either giving the rats interesting toys to play with or not giving them interesting toys to play with. The dependent variable (DV) was the weight of the frontal lobe.

Results: The frontal lobe was heavier in the rats that had been in the **stimulating** environment.

Conclusion: The frontal lobe is associated with thinking, planning, and decision making. Therefore, levels of enrichment in a child's environment will affect their brain development and their cognitive abilities.

Subject vocabulary

cognition/cognitive related to mental processes (such as perception, memory, problem-solving)

variable something that may be different in different situations

longitudinal study research that has taken place over a long period of time, usually years

meta-analysis a review of many studies into the same phenomena to see what broad conclusions can be made

correlation a relationship between variables

independent variable (IV) the variable an experimenter controls or changes

to operationalize *how* the IV is manipulated and *how* the DV is measured

dependent variable (DV) the variable an experimenter measures

frontal lobes the front part of the brain associated with planning and judgement

Glossary

infant/infancy a very young child who is not yet able to walk or talk

socioeconomic relating to the position in society and the amount of money a person earns or has

memory recall the ability to remember things

to enrich/enrichment to improve the quality of something

to deprive/deprivation to prevent someone from having something such as toys or love

Synonyms

stimulating.......... interesting

Evaluation: This is an animal study and care should be taken when generalizing the results to human cognition.

Model sentence: Environmental effects on the frontal lobe have been shown experimentally. This would not be possible to do with humans for ethical reasons.

Parenting (social variable)

Parents of **high-achieving students** were found to set higher standards for their children's educational activities than parents of **low-achieving students** (Michigan Department of Education (MDE), 2001). The MDE states, when parents set high **expectations**, students have higher grades and graduation rates.

The MDE found families whose children are doing well in school exhibit the following characteristics:

- They have an established daily family routine such as providing time and a quiet place to read and they are **firm** about bedtime and have dinner together.
- They *model* the importance of learning, self-discipline, and hard work. For example, they read books themselves and take an interest in what the child is reading.
- They encourage children's development/progress in school by, for example, providing a warm and supportive home, showing interest in children's progress at school, helping with homework, keeping in contact with teachers and school staff.
- They encourage reading, writing, and discussions among family members such as reading, listening to children read, and talking about what is being read.

Model sentence: The notion of parenting affecting mental processes is supported by MRI studies.

Aim: To investigate the effects that **nurturing** mothers have on brain development of their children (Luby, 2012).

Method: Mothers were tested on their nurturing abilities and were labelled either nurturing or non-nurturing. Magnetic resonance imaging (MRI) was used to scan 92 children's brains when they were between 3 and 6 years old and then again when they were between 7 and 10 years old.

Results: Children with the nurturing mothers had a hippocampus that was 10 per cent larger than the hippocampi of children who had mothers that were non-nurturing.

Conclusion: Nurturing mothers influence hippocampus development in their children.

Evaluation: This was a tightly controlled experiment offering common-sense insight into a real-world problem. However, not *all* variables can be controlled. For example, non-nurturing mothers may also not feed their children healthy food which may also influence their children's brain development.

Model sentence: The hippocampus is a key part of cognition. Squire (1992) regards the hippocampus as responsible for *general declarative memory* (information that can be explicitly verbalized and a memory for facts). It is responsible for the type of memory that makes children successful at school.

Subject vocabulary

to generalize/generalization the extent to which we can apply results to other circumstances

to model to show

magnetic resonance imaging (MRI) a brain imaging technology that allows researchers to 'see' brain processes in action

hippocampus part of the brain involved with (among other things) emotions and memory

experiment a method where the independent variable is changed to measure the effect on the dependent variable while controlling for other variables

Glossary

ethical relating to the idea of what is right and wrong behaviour

high-achieving students students who do well at school such as in examinations

low-achieving students students who do not do well as school such as in examinations

to nurture/nurturing to take care of a child in terms of education, and the physical and mental attention paid to the person

Synonyms

expectations .... targets

firm .... strict

notion .... idea

Hints for success: Use logical sub-headings to separate your answers. It will give them a clear structure and focus. In this case, separate *socioeconomic status* and *parenting*.

Examine attachment in childhood and its role in the subsequent formation of relationships

Glossary

- **underlying** be the cause of/ reason for something
- **bond** connection/link
- **separation** being apart
- **to interfere (with)** to prevent something from happening
- **expectation** what you think or hope will happen
- **to be consistent/consistency** to remain or always behave in the same way
- **to be worthy of** to deserve

Subject vocabulary

- **assumption** an underlying idea that a theory is built on
- **attachment** links between people
- **adapted** changed
- **schema** a frame for understanding the world

Synonyms

- **subsequent** .... following
- **formation** .... creation
- **distress** .... extreme unhappiness
- **expressions** .... gestures

Opening sentence:

In this answer I will examine the **underlying** assumptions of 'attachment' in childhood and then discuss their role in the **subsequent formation** of relationships.

Attachment is a long lasting, strong, and close emotional bond between people and leads to distress when separation occurs.

The key assumption of attachment theories is: the bonds created between the child and caregiver (usually the parent) will be repeated with other people into adulthood (usually the husband or wife).

Bowlby's attachment theory

Bowlby's attachment theory was first published in 1951 and has been adapted and improved many times over the years by Bowlby himself and other researchers.

The basic assumptions are:

1. Between 6 and about 30 months, children are likely to form emotional attachments to familiar caregivers - usually the mother, especially if the adults are sensitive and responsive to child communications such as facial **expressions** and hand gestures, crying, laughing, and so on.
2. The emotional attachments of children show themselves in their preferences for familiar people; they try to be close to those people, especially in times of distress, and then use the familiar adults as a place from which they explore the environment.
3. Events that **interfere** with attachment, such as separation or a carer who does not respond to the child, have short-term and long-term consequences on him or her.

How does this affect future relationships?

Model sentence: The assumption of the model is: relationships are affected by the formation of a schema known as *the internal working model.*

The internal working model gives ***expectations*** of future behaviour for both the child and caregivers. The model is a template for future relationships. It allows predictions to be made and allows a person to try out alternatives mentally, using knowledge of the past.

For example: If a child receives **consistent** love from their caregiver, they will develop a schema where they believe they are ***worthy* of** love. The child will develop confidence and be able to provide love to others in the future. If a child experiences a negative early environment they will assume they are worthy of such treatment and will not develop confidence.

The role of attachment in future relationships

Model sentence: **Research on adult attachment is guided by the assumption that attachment in childhood affects attachment in adulthood.**

'The Love Quiz'

Hazan and Shaver (1987) studied parent/child and adult **romantic** relationships through questionnaires.

Aim: To investigate how *attachment* affects future relationships.

Method: The researchers found volunteers to take part in the study which means that the sample was self-selecting.

They were given two questionnaires: one to find out about their early relationships with parents; one to find out about their adult romantic attachments.

Results: They found those who had a close warm relationship with parents had a **secure**, **stable**, and loving relationship with their adult partner.

Conclusion: Early attachments affect adult romantic attachments.

Model sentence: **There are problems with the love quiz.**

Method: The study involved a self-selecting sample which means that the participants want to take part in a study. They may have extreme opinions or may feel the need to look good or justify their parental style and adult attachments.

The researchers present a *cause and effect* by assuming the childhood experience has caused the adult attachments.

Assumptions of attachment research and models

Assumption 1: They assume attachments patterns are constant within families.

However, attachment patterns differ from one family to the next, and even within children from the same parents.

Assumption 2: A child's individual personality is not as important as an attachment.

However, Kagan (1982) states that differences in children's **temperaments** influence how people interact with them. He also states that a child's temperament is **stable** over time and can predict future behaviour.

Assumption 3: They assume circumstances remain constant within families.

However, a family is not always a stable, unchanging unit over time and situation. Events can happen such as **poverty**, deaths, and house moving, and the child may not receive the same type of support all of the time. This will affect attachment development.

Synonyms

romantic............ loving

secure................ safe

Subject vocabulary

sample the group of people who take part in a study

self-selecting participants volunteered to take part in a study. This means they want to take part in a study and this limits the generalizability of the data. People who do not want to take part in a study will not have their experiences reflected in the data

cause-effect relationship where there is confidence that the effect on the dependent variable (DV) has been caused by the manipulation of the independent variable (IV)

Glossary

stable remains the same

constant the same

temperament personality

poverty being very poor

Hints for success: Clearly identify the assumptions of the theory. Clearly identify how they are thought to affect adulthood.

Discuss potential effects of deprivation or trauma in childhood on later development

Glossary

potential likely to happen

pit of despair a place without hope

depression extreme and prolonged sadness

Rhesus monkeys a type of monkey whose genes are similar to the humans. They are therefore suitable for research and results can, to some extent, be generalized to humans

incapable not being able to do something

to isolate/isolation to separate from others

to nurture/nurturing to take care of a child in terms of education, and the physical and mental attention paid to the person

to enrich/enrichment to improve the quality of something

Subject vocabulary

to deprive/deprivation to lack something you need

trauma serious physical or mental injury

disturbed not behaving normally

independent variable (IV) the variable an experimenter controls or changes

to operationalize *how* the IV is manipulated and *how* the DV is measured

dependent variable (DV) the variable an experimenter measures

frontal lobes the front part of the brain associated with planning and judgement

Synonyms

ethical .... moral

well-adjusted...... emotionally healthy

Opening sentence:

First I will use both animal research and human research to demonstrate the effects of deprivation on later development.

Animal research

The Pit of Despair

Suomi and Harlow during the 1960s and 1970s aimed to produce **depression** in **Rhesus monkeys** and then observe their behaviour as they developed. They designed a steel cage which did not allow the monkeys to have any connection with the outside world or any other living organism. Baby monkeys were placed in these steel boxes.

Results:

- After 30 days: The monkeys were found to be disturbed.
- After 1 year: The monkeys barely moved, did not explore or play, and were **incapable** of having sexual relations. Two of them refused to eat and eventually starved to death.

Model sentence: Harlow wanted to test how deprivation would influence parenting skills.

When the **isolated** monkeys became parents they were unable to parent their young. Having no social skills themselves, they were not able to engage in positive social interaction with others – including their own children: One mother held her baby's face to the floor and chewed off his feet and fingers while another crushed her baby's head and many others simply ignored their young.

Model sentence: The pit of despair demonstrates the importance of love and nurturing on later life. The study raises serious ethical concerns and would not be allowed now.

Evaluation: Monkeys are very social animals; when placed in isolation, they become badly damaged (Blum, 2002). Harlow did nothing more than demonstrate 'common sense'. It seems reasonable to assume depriving human youngsters of a loving environment will produce adults who are also not **well-adjusted**.

Enriched and non-enriched environments

Aim: To investigate the effect of either **enrichment** or deprivation on the development of rat brains (Rosenzweig and Bennett, 1972).

Method: The independent variable (IV) was richness of the environment and was operationalized by either giving the rats interesting toys to play with or depriving them of interesting toys to play with. The dependent variable (DV) was brain development and was operationalized by the weight of the frontal lobe.

Results: The frontal lobe was heavier in the rats that had been in the interesting environment.

Conclusion: The frontal lobe is associated with thinking, planning, and decision making. Therefore, levels of enrichment in a child's environment will affect their brain development and their cognitive abilities.

Evaluation: This is an animal study and care should be taken when generalizing the results to human cognition.

Model sentence: Deprivation has been shown to affect the development of rat brains in experimental conditions. This would not be possible to do with humans for ethical reasons.

Human research

Model sentence: Depriving children of a nurturing background affects their brain and cognitive development.

Example 1: Non-nurturing mothers and brain development

Aim: To investigate the effects that nurturing mothers have on brain development of their children (Luby, 2012).

Method: Mothers were tested on their nurturing abilities and were labelled either nurturing or non-nurturing. Magnetic resonance imaging (MRI) was used to scan 92 children's brains when they were between 3 and 6 years old and then again when they were between 7 and 10 years old.

Results: Children with the nurturing mothers had a hippocampus that was 10 per cent larger than the hippocampi of children who had mothers that were non-nurturing.

Conclusion: Nurturing mothers influence hippocampus development in their children.

Evaluation: This was a tightly controlled experiment offering common-sense insight into a real-world problem. However, not *all* variables can be controlled. For example, non-nurturing mothers may also not feed their children healthy food which may also influence their children's brain development.

Model sentence: The hippocampus is a key part of cognition. Squire (1992) regards the hippocampus as responsible for *general declarative memory* (information that can be explicitly verbalized and a memory for facts). It is responsible for the type of memory that makes children successful at school.

Example 2: The Edlington Torture Case (2009)

Two brothers, aged 10 and 11, tortured two other boys over a 90-minute period which they also filmed in the North of England in 2009. They were sentenced to indefinite detention. It was noted by the judge they had grown up in a very negative environment which included poverty, extreme violence, emotional neglect, and general chaos. Britton (1997) states that such environments produce a strong need to have power and control over others to compensate for the high levels of emotional unpredictability, constant feelings of shame, and general lack of control in their own lives. In some ways, the Edlington Torture Case was demonstrated experimentally with animals in the Pit of Despair.

Model sentence: Children who suffer serious abuse and neglect often have strong desires to feel power and control and this can lead to criminal and immoral behaviour. It should be noted not all children who experience negative environments will go on to commit violent acts.

Subject vocabulary

cognition/cognitive related to mental processes (such as perception, memory, problem-solving)

to generalize/generalization the extent to which we can apply results to other circumstances

magnetic resonance imaging (MRI) a brain imaging technology that allows researchers to 'see' brain processes in action

hippocampus part of the brain involved with (among other things) emotions and memory

experiment a method where the independent variable is manipulated to measure the effect on the dependent variable while controlling for other variables

Synonyms

shame............... guilt and embarrassment

abuse................ cruel or violent treatment

Glossary

to compensate (for) to balance the effect of something

to torture to hurt someone deliberately

sentenced sent to prison

indefinite detention imprisonment without a trial, for no fixed time

poverty being very poor

to neglect to not give enough care or attention to people or things that are your responsibility

chaos a situation where nothing is organized

unpredictability unable to know what will happen

Hints for success: You do not need to distinguish between deprivation and trauma.

Define resilience

Glossary

problematic difficult problems

outcome a result

to be confronted with to have to deal with something

disadvantage having social problems such as not enough money or education which make it difficult for you to succeed in life

to exclude/exclusion to not allow someone to take part

mainstream the average or normal parts of society

Subject vocabulary

norms expected or usual ways to behave

Opening sentence:

Resilience can be defined as the process of avoiding **problematic outcomes** or doing better than expected when **confronted** with problems.

What are the problems that children experience?

1. Poverty and **disadvantage**: Growing up in poverty is associated with increased levels of family stress, less effective parenting, and higher risk of separation and divorce.
2. Social **exclusion** from the **mainstream** of society: Living in poverty does not simply mean not having enough money, it also means living in places where services are in a poor state (e.g. schools, playgrounds, housing) and the **norms** of the mainstream are missing – for example, having social skills and not committing crime.

It should be noted: Poverty does not automatically mean children will do poorly in life.

Discuss strategies to build resilience

Subject vocabulary

maternal depression a condition where mothers can be very sad and feel alone after the birth of their child

social isolation a state whereby individuals or groups do not have contact or communication with others

Synonyms

well-rounded...... complete

affordable........... inexpensive

Glossary

extended family cousins, grandparents, aunts, uncles, etc.

Model sentence: There are three main strategies that are important when it comes to building resilience.

Strategy 1: Strong community programmes

Model sentence: Parents and children should have access to a well-rounded social and educational support network in the community.

For example:

- *Home visit programmes:* Government workers (usually *social workers*) visit low-income families. They can help families to increase their access to healthcare but also lower rates of **maternal depression** and help the relationship between mother and baby. They also remind the mother that it is her job to care for the child and make her aware of the social importance of her parenting skills.
- *Teen mother parent education*: Britner et al. (1997) found that creating groups for teenage mothers provided them with support and reduced their **social isolation** and depression. The programme also involved the **extended family** in the baby's care and this provided a wider social support network for new mothers.
- *High-quality and **affordable** childcare (e.g. daycare, nursery, kindergarten)*: Allows children to develop in a social environment and not just with their parent. It also allows parents to have a job or a break from parenting.

Strategy 2: Effective schooling

According to Sagor (1996) and Wang, Haertel, and Walberg (1995), schools can build resilience by having the school culture focus on five themes:

1. Competency (feeling successful).
2. Belonging (feeling valued).
3. Usefulness (feeling needed).
4. Potency (feeling empowered).
5. Optimism (feeling encouraged and hopeful).

Model sentence: **Schools can provide after-school programmes in all high-risk communities where teachers work with students outside of school hours to complete homework and play sports.**

Mahoney et al. (2005) carried out a longitudinal study of the effect of after-school programmes on the school success and **motivation** for disadvantaged children. They found an after-school programme which took place over a year achieved better test scores, reading achievement, and overall motivation for the students who took part.

Strategy 3: Close relationships

Successful children of parents employed in **unskilled** jobs, living in rented and overcrowded conditions, were still more likely to have experienced a supportive family environment, and to have parents who showed an interest in their education. A supportive family environment was defined as: parents who read to their child, who took an active interest in their education, and who took the children out for family activities such as holidays and days out (Schoon and Bartley, 2008).

Elder and Conger (2000) looked at data in the USA after a **farm crisis** in the 1980s and 1990s. The farm crisis put people out of work and their homes. They found a large number of young people had been protected from the effects and were achieving academic success and were **law-abiding** despite the awful events they had experienced. The characteristics were: strong **bonds** between parents and children; children who were raised with non-material goals (e.g. it is better to be a good person rather than have a nice car); positive connections with the wider community (e.g. church, school, and community projects); close relationship with grandparents.

Discussion

Strategies 1 and 2 are provided by the government. However, they are part of a wider political solution. For example, an individual might want to find work but if government policies shut down factories and other places for good jobs then it will be difficult. Parents may want their children to do well in school but if the school does not have good teachers or good facilities then this will be a problem. Strategy 3 is family and individual based. People have to be willing to help themselves and get involved in the community to do well. However, it is difficult to protect children from the wider norms of the community. They may have good family values with parents who teach them right from wrong but if the local community has high crime rates, poor housing, poor schooling, and unsupportive police then it can be very difficult to succeed.

Glossary

high-risk strong possibility that something bad or unpleasant may happen

to motivate/motivation a reason to want to do something

unskilled people who have not had special training

law-abiding not breaking the law

farm crisis the price of farm produce is so low that farmers do not have enough money to pay their debts and so lose their farms

bond connection/link

Subject vocabulary

longitudinal study research that has taken place over a long period of time, usually years

Hints for success: Demarcate your answers with clearly labelled strategies.

Discuss the formation and development of gender roles

Glossary

formation creation

independent able to work on their own

dependent less able to work on their own and use others for help

split screen a screen used to show films which is divided in half and shows two things at the same time

Subject vocabulary

identity a sense of the personal, a label for who a person is

to model/modelling an example to be imitated/copied

reinforcement a positive consequence for behaviour which makes it more likely to be repeated. It can be contrasted with *punishment* which is a negative consequence for behaviour and makes it less likely to be repeated

stereotype a perception of an individual in terms of their group membership. It is a generalization that is made about a group and then generalized to members of that group. Such a generalization may be either positive or negative

to generalize/generalization the extent to which we can apply results to other circumstances

ecological validity having realism and being able to generalize to real-life situations

cognition/cognitive related to mental processes (such as perception, memory, problem-solving)

Opening sentence:

In this answer I will discuss the **formation** and development of gender roles.

Model sentence: First I will define gender.

Gender refers to the *identity* a person adopts; it is a sense of how one relates to being a man or a woman. *Gender role* refers to the sets of behaviours, rights, and duties of being male or female (Bee, 1995).

Social factors that explain the formation of gender roles

Social Learning Theory (SLT) assumes that children learn gender-appropriate and gender-inappropriate behaviour through processes in the environment such as modelling and reinforcement.

Reinforcement can be direct:

You look like a girl in that hat (said to a boy).

Girls don't wear jeans (said to a girl).

Leary et al. (1982) found children who watched a lot of television are more likely to hold stereotyped ideas about gender. This suggests the importance of modelling from the media.

Lewis (1972) observed parent–child interaction and found that boys were encouraged to be active and **independent** and girls were encouraged to be passive and **dependent**.

Model sentence: These two studies were conducted in Western cultures so care should be taken when generalizing to other cultures other than those from which the participants were selected.

Model sentence: These studies were observations and so they have a degree of ecological validity as they were carried out in real-world environments.

Cognitive factors that explain the formation of gender roles

Cognitive factor 1: Gender constancy

Understanding that gender is fixed across time and situations is called *gender constancy*. For example, a boy who wears a dress is still a boy. Gender constancy occurs between 4½ and 7 years old.

Supporting study 1

Slaby and Frey (1975) divided 2- to 5-year-olds into two groups. One group they considered to have high gender constancy; and the other group they considered to have low gender constancy. They showed a film with a **split screen**, one side had male models doing a task, the other side had female models doing a task.

Results: Children with high gender constancy watched the side of the screen more which showed models who were the same gender as they were. It shows that they had more same-sex **bias** in their attention. This shows that children actively look for then respond to the 'correct' gender models once they have achieved gender constancy.

Cognitive factor 2: Schemas and stereotypes

Gender schema theory (GST) states that children form mental guides for action and then find information that supports their schema and that they forget information that does not. Ideas become fixed and stereotypes form.

Supporting study 2: Baby toys

Aim: To investigate the effect of gender-specific baby clothing on adult schemas.

The independent variable (IV) was how the baby was dressed. It was operationalized by dressing the baby as either a boy or a girl.

The dependent variable (DV) was the behaviour of the adult and was operationalized by the type of toys the adults chose to use while playing with the baby.

Results: Adults chose 'male' toys when the baby was dressed as a boy. They chose 'female' toys when the baby was dressed like a girl.

Conclusion: The way a baby is dressed causes a male or female schema to be used.

Biological factors that explain the formation of gender roles

Biological factor 1: Hormonal differences

Model sentence: **There are hormonal differences between males and females. This affects their physical development and their behaviour.**

Rough and tumble play (R&T) is found in most male **mammals** and in particular chimpanzees, orang-utans, and humans (Braggio, Nadler, Lance, and Miseyko, 1978), and even squirrels (Biben, 1998). It involves wrestling, running, and pretend battles. R&T play is thought to be the result of hormonal changes in males. Young females tend to engage in caring and social roles when they play.

Model sentence: **The universal nature of rough and tumble play (R&T play) shows how gender-specific behaviour has biological roots.**

Biological factor 2: Brain differences

Brain differences between males and females are significant (Lenroot et al., 2007).

Example: **Infants** as young as 5 months old have differences in spatial ability. Male infants are more able to recognize familiar objects from different perspectives (as the objects were **rotated**) than female infants (Moore and Johnson, 2005). This suggests biological differences as the infants have not had time to be changed by culture or the environment. It may mean men will seek out roles for which spatial expertise is needed (and women less so). For example: Spatial awareness is important in engineering and navigation.

Model sentence: **There are brain differences between men and women. These predispose men and women to carry out different gender roles.**

Synonyms

rotated .... turned around

Subject vocabulary

schema a frame for understanding the world

independent variable (IV) the variable an experimenter controls or changes

variable something that may be different in different situations

to operationalize *how* the IV is manipulated and *how* the DV is measured

dependent variable (DV) the variable an experimenter measures

rough and tumble play play where there are no rules, usually noisy and rough behaviour

universal applicable everywhere or in all cases

predisposes innate/coming from nature

Glossary

bias/biased unfairly preferring one person or group over another

mammals a sub-group of warm blooded animals with hair, e.g. humans

infant/infancy a very young child who is not yet able to walk or talk

Hints for success: It is not realistic to explain the formation and development of gender roles in terms of either a social or a cognitive or a biological approach. Gender is probably the result of a combination of all three.

Explain cultural variations in gender roles

Opening sentence:

In this answer I will explain cultural variations in gender roles.

Model sentence: First I will define gender.

Gender identity is usually linked to biological sex organs but this is not always the case as some women adopt a masculine identity and some men adopt a feminine identity - as well as personal interpretations in between. *Gender role* refers to the sets of behaviours, **rights**, and **duties** of being male or female (Bee, 1995).

Cultural variations

New Guinea tribes

Mead (1935) studied different **tribes** from New Guinea and found:

- The Mundugumour tribe: Both males and females showed 'masculine' behaviour - aggressively sexual, **ruthless**, and **bold**.
- The Arapesh tribe: Both males and females showed 'feminine' behaviour - warm, emotional, and non-aggressive.
- The Tchambuli tribe: Men showed some 'feminine' behaviour (being passive) and then women showed some 'masculine' behaviour (being dominant).

Western schools

Thompson (2000) states that schools in Western countries (e.g. UK and USA) prevent boys from fully expressing themselves the way they naturally need to. Many teachers **overreact** to boys in classrooms, corridors, and play grounds by preventing *rough and tumble play* (R&T play). R&T play is very physical and involves wrestling, running, and pretend battles. Most rough and tumble play is non-violent and *will not lead to violence*. Jarvis (2006) argues there has been a reduction in time and space that allows boys to have R&T play because schools have become nervous about how children play in the playground. The result of this is: teachers increasingly encourage 'female' behaviours (**sedentary**, quiet, and calm) and discourage 'male' behaviour (**impulsive**, physical). As a result, boys can find school a difficult place to be and not supportive of their physical needs (Fagot, 1985).

Two-spirits

The two-spirit concept refers to *gender variance* in North American Indian tribes. It is used to describe individuals who have both male and female identities. Male and female two-spirits have been found in over 130 tribes, in North America and other tribal groups.

Subject vocabulary

- identity a sense of the personal, a label for who a person is
- New Guinea an island in the Pacific Ocean north of Australia
- aggressive/aggression behaving in an angry and threatening way
- rough and tumble play play where there are no rules, usually noisy and rough behaviour
- concept clearly defined idea
- gender variance the differences *between* genders (masculine and feminine) and the differences within genders (how much variation is there between feminine behaviours of the same tribe?)

Glossary

- **rights** rules that protect you or allow you to do something
- **duty** a role a person is expected to carry out
- **tribe** a group of people in traditional societies
- **ruthless** not having pity for others
- **bold** confident and full of courage
- **sedentary** sitting, not moving about a lot
- **impulsive** acting without considering the consequences of your action

Synonyms

overreact .... respond too strongly

Explanations

Social Learning Theory (SLT)

SLT assumes that children learn gender-appropriate and gender-inappropriate behaviour through the environment. Processes in the environment include modelling and reinforcement.

Leary et al. (1982) found children who watched television a lot are more likely to hold stereotyped ideas about gender. This suggests the importance of modelling from the media.

Lewis (1972) observed parent–child interaction and found boys were encouraged to be active and independent and girls were encouraged to be passive and dependent.

Williams and Best (1990) found male **characteristics** of aggression, strength, and cruelty were **consistent** across cultures. They found female characteristics of gentleness were consistent across cultures. However, they found strong consistency in collectivist societies – men and women became more similar the more they worked together. They found weak consistency in individualist societies – men and women remained more different the more they worked separately. This supports the SLT approach to gender roles.

Cognitive factors

Gender schema theory (GST): Gender schema theory states that children form mental guides for action and then find information that supports their schema and forget information that does not. Liben and Signorella (1993) found children who were shown pictures of adults in unusual gender roles (e.g. male nurse; female car mechanic) forgot the information. This suggests children only select information that supports their schema of gender-appropriate behaviour.

Concluding comments

The learning outcome *assumes that* there are cultural variations in gender roles. There are some cross-cultural differences in how males and females are expected to behave. However, these differences are minor. Even though there are many different cultures, there are still cross-cultural *similarities* in how males and females are expected to behave. This suggests powerful biological causes of gender role behaviour. Mead is often used to show how powerful social forces influence gender. However, Mead also found cross-cultural similarities with gender. This supports the view that they have a biological cause. There are also serious concerns about how Mead gathered her data. Gewertz (1981) followed up on Mead's research and studied the Tchambuli tribe in 1974–1975 and could not find evidence that supports Mead's work. Gewertz states Tchambuli men had always **dominated** the women and made the important decisions. According to Bamberger (1974) researchers have looked for societies where women dominate men but they have not found one.

Hints for success: Divide your answer in half. First deal with cultural variations and then deal with their explanations.

Subject vocabulary

to model/modelling an example to be imitated/copied

reinforcement a positive consequence for behaviour which makes it more likely to be repeated. It can be contrasted with *punishment* which is a negative consequence for behaviour and makes it less likely to be repeated

collectivist cultures societies in which more importance is placed on the group rather than the person

individualistic cultures societies in which more importance is placed on the person rather than the group

cognition/cognitive related to mental processes (such as perception, memory, problem-solving)

schema a frame for understanding the world

Synonyms

characteristics..... traits/features

consistent........... the same

dominated.......... had power over

Describe adolescence

Synonyms

perspective......... point of view
notion .... idea
dynamic .... active and changing

Subject vocabulary

adolescent/adolescence the period between being a young child and becoming an adult, also known as teenage years

muscle tissue the collection of fibres and cells that make up the muscles

Opening sentence:

Adolescence can be described as the **transitional** period between childhood and adulthood.

Adolescence can be described from a biological **perspective** as the period when there is a fast increase in growth (known as the *growth spurt*) and the **redistribution** of muscle tissue and body fat. The individual becomes capable of producing and caring for children.

Discuss the relationship between physical change and development of identity during adolescence

Glossary

transition/transitional changing from one process or situation to another

redistribution replacing/rearrangement

breasts the two round parts on a woman's chest which produce milk when she has a baby

challenge an activity that is difficult

norms the expected or usual ways to behave

Subject vocabulary

identity a sense of the personal, a label for who a person is

sperm the cells produced by the male sex organ

menstrual cycle period each month when a woman loses blood

puberty stage of physical development when a child changes to an adult

perception the process that allows people to interpret information

attractiveness how appealing an individual is. This word is often used to describe someone's physical appearance but it does not have to refer to this

Synonyms

appearance......... how you look

Model sentence: In this answer I will discuss the relationship between physical change and development of identity during adolescence.

Physical changes

There is a fast increase in growth (known as the *growth spurt*) and the redistribution of muscle tissue and body fat. The individual becomes capable of producing and caring for children. Boys start producing sperm (around the age of 15); girls start their menstrual cycle. These changes are known as *puberty*. The body changes shape - girls become heavier with broader hips and the development of **breasts**; boys develop greater muscle mass and their shoulders widen.

Development of identity

Model sentence: I understand there are many ways to examine identity. However, in this answer I will examine identity through the notion of body image.

Body image is the ***dynamic*** perception of one's body - how it looks, feels, and moves. The notion of it being dynamic suggests it is not fixed and can change. It can therefore be influenced (Croll, 2005).

The physical changes taking place during puberty are constant **challenges** to a teenager's identity. Body image is influenced by cultural messages and **norms** about **appearance** and *attractiveness*.

- Females are much more likely than males to think their current size is too *large*.
- Over one-third of males think their current size is too *small*, while only 10 per cent of women consider their size too small.
- 50–88 per cent of adolescent girls have negative feelings about their body shape or size.
- 49 per cent of teenage girls say they know someone with an eating disorder.
- Only 33 per cent of girls say they are at the 'right weight' - 58 per cent want to lose weight; 9 per cent want to gain weight.

Croll (2005) states that puberty for boys brings **characteristics typically** approved of by society - height, speed, broadness, and strength. Puberty for girls brings characteristics typically *disapproved* of by society - girls generally get rounder and have more body fat. These changes can result in girls having more feelings of **dissatisfaction** as they go through puberty.

In summary, girls receive messages from society and may think that the physical change of becoming larger is negative. Boys receive messages from society and may think that they are not becoming large enough.

What are the consequences for identity?

Girls are more likely to become bulimic or anorexic. According to the National Institute of Mental Health (NIMH), between 2 and 3 per cent of women and 0.02-0.03 per cent of men in the USA have been **diagnosed** with bulimia. According to Frude (1998) the female:male **ratio** is 10:1. Girls become afraid of weight gain, and their self-esteem depends on staying at a certain weight. They tend to be highly dissatisfied and have a **distorted** sense of their own body.

Boys are more likely to suffer from *reverse anorexia* (known as muscle dysmorphia). Reverse anorexia is when a person (usually a boy) becomes **obsessed with** the idea that they are not muscular enough. It can cause people to:

- constantly look at themselves in a mirror
- constantly compare themselves with others
- want to increase muscle size
- dream of **lifting weights** and exercise
- become **distressed** if they miss a **workout** session or one of their many meals a day.

In summary, the physical change of size can cause problems for the development of identity during adolescence for males and females.

Are there other explanations for the problems that sometimes develop during adolescence?

Surbey (1987) provides an evolutionary reason for anorexia in girls. Anorexia often occurs in girls who are **maturing** early and this causes stress. The *reproductive suppression model* suggests that if a person **starves** their body, the ability to reproduce is delayed until a more appropriate time. However, this does not explain why boys **underestimate** their weight and shape and develop reverse anorexia.

Hints for success: Clearly show how physical changes affect identity by using appropriate sub-headings.

Synonyms

characteristic ...... trait/feature

typically............. usually

distressed .... very upset/worried

Subject vocabulary

bulimia an eating disorder where food is eaten then thrown up

anorexia an eating disorder where very little food is eaten

self-esteem how you feel about yourself

Glossary

dissatisfaction a feeling of not being pleased or happy with the way things are

to diagnose to find out what illness you have

ratio relationship between two amounts

distorted not accurate or correct

to be obsessed with to worry about something all the time

lifting weights the sport of picking up pieces of metal that weigh a particular amount

workout a period of exercise, usually in a gym

to mature to become fully grown

to starve to not eat or have enough food to survive

to underestimate to guess the amount of something that is too low

Examine psychological research into adolescence

Subject vocabulary

adolescent/adolescence the period between being a young child and becoming an adult, also known as teenage years

assumption an underlying idea that a theory is built on

identity a sense of the personal, a label for who a person is

self-esteem how you feel about yourself

empirical data coming from standardized and properly conducted research studies

to generalize/generalization the extent to which we can apply results to other circumstances

Glossary

complexity having many parts and being complicated

crisis a situation where there are a lot of problems

intimacy closeness

commitment a promise to behave in a particular way

industry activities involved in getting something done

comic a book with a series of pictures that tell a story

firm not likely to change

to be obsessed with to worry about something all the time

disrespectful being rude or not showing care for others

productivity the amount you achieve

Synonyms

formation .... creation

stress .... anxiety

Opening sentence:

In this answer I will examine psychological research into adolescence.

Exam strategy: Demonstrate the assumptions and **complexity** of research into adolescence.

Erikson's approach (1950s)

Model sentence: Erikson researched adolescents in the 1950s. The assumptions of Erikson's approach are:

- Adolescence is a period of **stress** and uncertainty caused by physical change.
- Stress and uncertainty cause a **crisis** in identity.
- Adolescents cannot achieve a sense of identity because of the biological changes that are taking place.
- The identity crisis is normal.
- Adolescents delay the **formation** of their identities until a time when things are clearer.
- Identity crises are needed to help build **firm** identities in later adulthood.
- Adolescents have problems in four main areas:
  - **Intimacy**: Adolescents fear a **commitment** to others as it may involve a loss of identity.
  - Time: Adolescents do not believe that change will happen over time but at the same time they are afraid that this might happen. This is called *time diffusion*.
  - **Industry**: Adolescents have problems concentrating or they focus a large amount of energy on one thing (for example, being **obsessed with** a band or a **comic**). This is called *diffusion of industry*.
  - Negative identity: Adolescents are **disrespectful** towards their family and society.

Model sentence: There are some problems with the assumptions of Erikson's approach:

- Erikson suggests that adolescence is associated with low self-esteem and low **productivity** although this is not always true: adolescence can be a time when young people get involved in community projects and charity work.
- Erikson did not carry out any empirical research to support his view. He used his observations of teenagers who were having therapy in the 1940s and 1950s. Care should be taken when generalizing to a larger, less troubled group and a more modern group.
- Identities were clearer and more fixed in the 1950s than they are today. For example, women were expected to become housewives; men were expected to find a job and provide for their family; people were expected to get married earlier than today.

Marcia's approach (1966)

Marcia based his own work on Erikson's. He tested it empirically. He developed a **semi-structured** interview for research and interviewed mainly American fathers and sons in the 1960s.

The assumptions of Marcia's approach are:

- Adolescence starts as a time of crisis and **confusion**. This is known as *identity diffusion*.
- Identity is established through the choices and commitments that adolescents make as they deal with the crisis and confusion.
- Adolescence ends with a commitment to a clear identity. This is known as *identity achievement*.

Model sentence: The main assumption of Marcia's approach is: Adolescence is a time of crisis and confusion. Adolescents have to make active choices about their identity.

Model sentence: There are some problems with the assumptions of Marcia's approach:

- Marcia used mainly middle-class, white male American fathers and sons in his sample and carried out his interviews in the 1960s and 1970s, therefore care should be taken when generalizing to wider cultures today. There is also an assumption in Marcia's work that adolescents have either formed an identity, or they have not. This is a **simplistic** binary approach to a complex human process. Identity development continues into adulthood.
- Marcia's work is culturally specific to America in the 1960s: Condon (1987) studied **Inuit** in the Canadian Arctic Circle and found individuals who would be seen as adolescents in Western culture but who were actually treated as adults.

Erikson's approach:

- *The identity crisis is normal.*
- *Adolescents delay the formation of their identities until a time when things are clearer.*
- *Identity crises are needed to help build firm identities in later adulthood.*

Marcia's approach:

- *Adolescence starts as a time of crisis and confusion.*
- *Identity is established through the choices and commitments that adolescents make as they deal with the crisis and confusion.*

Glossary

semi-structured something that is only partly planned or organized

confusion not understanding something because it is not clear

simplistic something made easier to understand

Inuit American Indians of Canada

Subject vocabulary

binary approach assuming there are two extremes for a behaviour

culturally specific research findings, norms, traditions, values, and behaviours that are particular to a culture and therefore have limited generalizability elsewhere

Hints for success: Focus on the assumptions of the research. Start sentences with the model sentence: 'The assumptions of this are...'

GLO 1: To what extent do biological, cognitive, and sociocultural factors influence human development?

Biological factors

Model sentence: Biological factors can be used to explain the formation of gender roles.

The biological approach assumes that behaviour is the result of biological mechanisms.

Biological factor 1: *R&T play*

Model sentence: Rough and tumble play (R&T play) shows how gender-specific behaviour has biological origins.

Rough and tumble play is found in most male mammals, in particular in chimpanzees, orang-utans, humans (Braggio, Nadler, Lance, and Miseyko, 1978) and even squirrels (Biben, 1998). It is very physical and involves **wrestling**, running, and pretend battles. R&T play is thought to be the result of hormonal changes in males.

Jarvis (2006) observed children in a **primary school** in Northern England and concluded that boys clearly preferred to do R&T play. She explains the reason for this in evolutionary terms: boys need to learn how to compete with other boys for **resources** and access to female mates and those who are more practised are more likely to be successful. Females have a caring role and do not 'need' to do R&T play.

Marsh (2000) observed children in a **nursery** and supports Jarvis (2006). She asked them to play within a 'Batcave' based on the comic character of Batman. She told the children both boys and girls could play and be 'Batmen' or 'Batwomen'. She found 'Batwomen' were more likely to be 'caring' and rescue people in need; the Batmen chased and caught bad people.

In summary, R&T play is done almost entirely by males. It is found cross-culturally and across species suggesting a clear link between biology and gender behaviour.

Biological factor 2: *Brain differences*

Brain differences between males and females are significant (Lenroot et al., 2007).

Example 1: Infants as young as 5 months old have differences in spatial ability. Male infants are more able to recognize familiar objects from different perspectives (as the objects were rotated) more than female infants (Moore and Johnson, 2005). This suggests biological differences as the infants have not had time to be changed by culture or the environment. It may mean men will seek out roles for which spatial expertise is needed (and women less so). For example: spatial awareness is important in engineering and navigation.

Example 2: Women typically have larger *limbic systems* than men (Goldstein and Seidman, 2001). The limbic system is an area of the brain linked with feelings (internal experience) and emotions (external behaviours). It can be argued having a larger limbic system allows women to be more in touch with their feelings and better able to express them. It is likely because of this ability to connect it leads more women serve in the caring professions.

Model sentence: There are brain differences between men and women. These predispose men and women to carry out different gender roles.

Subject vocabulary

cognition/cognitive related to mental processes (such as perception, memory, problem-solving)

sociocultural relating to social and cultural issues

biological mechanisms biological systems that are linked to behaviour

gender-specific specific to a particular gender (male or female)

mammals a sub-group of warm blooded animals with hair. Humans are mammals

hormone a chemical messenger that transports a signal from one cell to another. Hormones differ from neurotransmitters as they travel through the blood stream while neurotransmitters travel across synapses (the gaps) between neurons

mates potential partners for producing children

Glossary

rough and tumble play play where they are no rules, usually noisy and rough behaviour

wrestling physical fighting where one person tries to make the other fall to the ground

resources things that are useful such as food, property, abilities

Synonyms

formation .... creation

primary school.... elementary school

nursery.............. kindergarten

Cognitive factors

Cognitive factors that explain the formation of gender roles.

Model sentence: Cognitive factors such as motivation and perception will affect how a child sees and reacts to the environment.

Cognitive factor 1: *Gender constancy*

Kohlberg stated that children acquire a concept of gender and then try to find information from members of the same gender for **clues** on how to behave. Once they understand that gender is fixed and that they will be a boy or a girl forever, they become increasingly motivated to find information on the 'correct' behaviour. Understanding that gender is fixed is called gender constancy.

Gender constancy occurs between 4½ and 7 years old and the child understands that gender is fixed and means more than differences in hair length.

Slaby and Frey (1975) divided 2- to 5-year-olds into two groups. One group they considered to have high gender constancy; and the other group they considered to have low gender constancy. They showed a film with a split screen; one side had male models doing a task, the other side had female models doing a task.

Results: Children with high gender constancy watched the same side of the screen more which showed models who were the same gender as they were. It shows they had more same-sex **bias** in their attention. This shows that children actively look for then respond to the 'correct' gender models.

Cognitive factor 2: *Schemas and stereotypes*

Gender schema theory (GST) states that children form mental guides for action and then find information that supports their schema and that they forget information that does not. Ideas become fixed and stereotypes form. Liben and Signorella (1993) found children who were shown pictures of adults in unusual gender roles (e.g. male nurse; female car mechanic) forgot the information. This suggests children only select information that supports their schema of gender-appropriate behaviour.

Sociocultural factors

Different cultures deal with gender development in different ways.

For example:

New Guinea is an island in the Pacific Ocean north of Australia. Mead (1935) studied different **tribes** and found:

- The Mundugumour tribe: Both males and females showed 'masculine' behaviour – **aggressively** sexual, **ruthless**, and **bold**.
- The Arapesh tribe: Both males and females showed 'feminine' behaviour – warm, emotional, and non-aggressive.
- The Tchambuli tribe: Men showed some 'feminine' behaviour (being passive) and then women showed some 'masculine' behaviour (being **dominant**).

Subject vocabulary

motivation wanting or a desire to do something

perception the process that allows people to interpret information

constancy the understanding that objects, people, and people's traits continue to exist and do not change even when they cannot be observed (seen, heard, touched, smelled, or sensed in any way). For example, a young child may think a man who wears a dress is a woman. They may think when water is poured into a different-shaped glass then the amount has changed. These demonstrate a lack of constancy

concept clearly defined idea

schema a frame for understanding the world

stereotype a perception of an individual in terms of their group membership. It is a generalization that is made about a group and then generalized to members of that group. Such a generalization may be either positive or negative

Glossary

clue a piece of information that helps you to understand something

bias/biased unfairly preferring one person or group over another

tribe a group of people in traditional societies

aggression/aggressive behaving in an angry or threatening way

ruthless not having pity for others

to dominate/dominant to have power or influence over other people

Synonyms

bold.................... confident/ full of courage

Western schools

Thompson (2000) states that schools in Western countries (e.g. UK and USA) prevent boys from fully expressing themselves in the way that they naturally need to. Many teachers overreact to boys in classrooms, corridors, and play grounds by preventing rough and tumble play (R&T play). R&T play is very physical and involves wrestling, running, and pretend battles. Most rough and tumble play is non-violent and will not lead to violence. Jarvis (2006) states that there has been a reduction in time and space that allows boys to have R&T play because schools have become nervous about how children play in the playground. The result of this is that teachers increasingly encourage 'female' behaviours (**sedentary**, quiet, and calm) and discourage 'male' behaviour (**impulsive**, physical). As a result, boys can find school a difficult place to be and not supportive of their physical needs (Fagot, 1985).

Glossary

sedentary sitting, not moving about a lot

impulsive acting without considering the consequences of your action

pit of despair a place without hope

depression extreme and prolonged sadness

to isolate/isolation to separate from others

to nurture/nurturing to take care of a child in terms of education, and the physical and mental attention paid to the person

stimulation an action or thing that causes someone or something to become excited

controversial causing a lot of disagreement

Subject vocabulary

Rhesus monkeys a type of monkey whose genes are similar to humans. They are therefore suitable for research and results can, to some extent be generalized to humans

disturbed not behaving normally/damaged

to deprive/deprivation to lack something you need

Synonyms

ethical .... moral

GLO 2: Evaluate psychological research (that is, theories and/or studies) relevant to developmental psychology

Study 1: The Pit of Despair

Suomi and Harlow during the 1960s and 1970s aimed to produce **depression** in Rhesus monkeys and then observe their behaviour as they developed. They designed a steel cage which did not allow the monkeys to have any connection with the outside world or any other living organism. Baby monkeys were placed in these steel boxes.

Results:

- After 30 days: The monkeys were found to be disturbed.
- After 1 year: The monkeys barely moved, did not explore or play, and were incapable of having sexual relations. Two of them refused to eat and eventually starved to death.

Model sentence: Harlow wanted to test how deprivation would influence parenting skills.

When the **isolated** monkeys became parents they were unable to parent their young. Having no social skills themselves, they were not able to engage in positive social interaction with others - including their own children: one mother held her baby's face to the floor and chewed off his feet and fingers while another crushed her baby's head and many others simply ignored their offspring.

Model sentence: The pit of despair demonstrates the importance of love and nurturing on later life.

Evaluation:

- **Cultural:** During the 1960s and 1970s it was normal in Western cultures to advise parents to limit physical contact in order to avoid giving the child too much emotional **stimulation**. It was seen as spoiling the child. Harlow clearly shows how important love is in development.
- **Ethics:** Harlow was criticized for deliberately designing the equipment so that it shocked his colleagues. He probably did this to be **controversial**. This can be seen in the name he used for the equipment (pit of despair) and that he avoided using technical language. The pit of despair is considered an extreme piece of equipment that shows nothing other than 'common-sense'. This is that monkeys are very social animals and when they are isolated from other monkeys they become badly damaged (Blum, 2002). It is not the way to carry out research with animals.

- **Method:** Care should always be taken when generalizing the results of research findings on animals to humans. However, it seems reasonable to state that depriving young humans of a loving environment will produce adults who are also not **well-adjusted**.

Study 2: 'The Love Quiz'

Hazan and Shaver (1987) studied parent/child and adult **romantic** relationships through questionnaires.

Aim: To investigate the role of attachment in future relationships.

Method: The researchers found volunteers to take part in the study which means that the sample was self-selecting.

They were given two questionnaires: one to find out about their early relationships with parents; one to find out about their adult romantic attachments.

Results: They found that there was a correlation between childhood attachment and later adult attachments.

Conclusion: Early attachments affect adult romantic attachments.

Evaluation:

The study involved a self-selecting sample which means that the participants *want* to take part in a study. They may have extreme opinions or may feel the need to look good or justify their parental style and adult attachments. This is a key **failing** with this study. Another key failing is the researchers assume that there is a cause/effect relationship. They assume that the childhood experiences *caused* the adult attachments. There is no evidence in the questionnaire to accept this claim.

Model sentence: There are general problems with the assumptions of attachment research:

Assumption 1: They assume that attachments patterns are constant within families.

However, attachment patterns are different from one family to the next, and even in children from the same parents.

Assumption 2: A child's individual personality is not as important as an attachment.

However, Kagan (1982) states differences in children's **temperaments** influence how the environment interacts with them and therefore their temperament will greatly affect how they attach to adults in their environment. He also states that a child's temperament is **stable** over time and can predict future behaviour.

Assumption 3: They assume that **circumstances** remain constant within families.

However, a family is not always a stable, unchanging unit over time and situation. Events to intervene can happen such as **poverty**, deaths, and house moving, and the child may not receive the same type of support all of the time. This will affect attachment development.

Hints for success: Always use previously learnt material to support a GLO answer and use examples of research to support each point that you make.

Subject vocabulary

to generalize/generalization the extent to which we can apply results to other circumstances

attachment links between people

self-selecting participants volunteered to take part in a study. This means they want to take part in a study and this limits the generalizability of the data. People who do not want to take part in a study will not have their experiences reflected in the data

correlation a relationship between variables

Synonyms

well-adjusted ...... emotionally healthy

failing .... fault/weakness

stable .... not changing

circumstances ..... situations

poverty .... being very poor

Glossary

romantic loving

temperament personality

Describe stressors

Glossary

subjective based on personal opinion

Synonyms

components .... parts

Subject vocabulary

physiological related to the body

cognitive related to mental processes (such as perception, memory, problem-solving)

Stress is a failure to respond appropriately to emotional or physical threats (Selye, 1956). Stress is a **subjective** experience. What is stressful for one person is not stressful for another, e.g. flying in an aeroplane can be seen as fun or stressful.

Stress has three **components**:

Physiological reaction: The body reacts (e.g. increased heart rate).

Cognitive reaction: The person has to think it is stressful (e.g. 'being on this aeroplane is making me stressed').

Behavioural expression: The person has to respond (e.g. get off the aeroplane).

Model sentence: Stressors can be described as any event that leads to stress. Events can be real or imagined (e.g. a real barking dog or an imaginary monster in a comic book), cognitive (e.g. thinking the dark can be scary), environmental (e.g. noise from a neighbour), or biological (e.g. eating hot chilli).

Discuss physiological, psychological, and social aspects of stress

Subject vocabulary

psychological relating to thoughts, feelings, and behaviour

adrenaline rush an onset of adrenaline that leads to higher arousal

antibodies proteins produced by the body to protect against illness

Synonyms

significant........... major/large

correlation.......... link

Glossary

to abuse/abusive to be physically and/or verbally violent

nasal via the nose

Physiological

Model sentence: I will now discuss physiological aspects of stress.

The different genders have different physiological aspects of stress. Boys have adrenaline rushes in exams that take longer to return to normal. Girls have a gentler, lower increase of adrenaline and return to normal much more quickly (Frankenhauser et al., 1976).

Children who have had **significant** stress in their home life (such as **abuse**) have growth problems due to low levels of growth hormones (Powell, Brasel, and Blizzard, 1967).

There is a **correlation** between a change in mood and a change in the amount of antibodies in the body – suggesting good moods contribute to a healthy immune system (Stone et al., 1987).

Gross (1996) argues people often catch colds soon after periods of high stress such as exams.

Model sentence: Gross (1996) is supported by Cohen, Tyrrell, and Smith (1991). They gave participants nasal drops containing a mild cold virus. Those who had negative life events in the weeks before were twice as likely to develop colds as those participants who reported lower levels of stress.

Goetsch and Fuller (1995) show less activity of white blood cells that fight illness among medical students during their final exams.

In sum: Positive life experiences with low stress improve physical health. Negative life experiences with high stress negatively affect physical health.

Psychological

Model sentence: I will now discuss psychological aspects of stress.

Appraisal: For a situation to be stressful, it must be appraised as such by the person who is experiencing it (Lazarus, 1966). What one person considers stressful another person might not. Therefore, psychologists must consider individual interpretations people place on what they consider to be stressors.

Expectations: **HIV**-positive men who are **bereaved** stay healthier longer if they remain happy about their own future. They argue *hope* helps survival of infected men who have lost a partner (Reed et al., 1999).

Social

Model sentence: I will now discuss social aspects of stress. I will do this by discussing the workplace.

People spend a lot of time in the workplace away from their families. Stress occurs when there is a poor match between job demands and personal skills. Coping skills are the main predictor of whether an individual will experience workplace stress. Some people are not suited to the job they have chosen, or been forced to accept (The National Institute for Occupational Safety and Health (NIOSH), 1999).

Emotional labour: There has been a move away from physical labour of the industrial revolution towards a workplace where people have to **enhance**, **suppress**, and **fake** their emotions to meet the needs of employers and customers (Hochschild, 1983). This causes stress and leads to:

- ***Alienation***: People faking their emotions and so they feel their workplace is not **genuine**.
- There is lack of *emotional autonomy:* Employers insist on certain emotions (e.g. smiles and asking 'How are you today?'). The employee feels a lack of control over their emotional lives and this leads to stress.
- ***Exploitation***: People who have to fake their emotions feel exploited. For example, employees who have to smile at customers and ask questions about them ('How are you today?') often receive unwanted attention in return.

Stress is a failure to respond appropriately to emotional or physical threats.

Stress has three components: physiological, cognitive, and behavioural.

Hints for success: Use logical sub-headings to demarcate your answers. They will give them a clear structure and focus. In this case use *physiological, psychological,* and *social* aspects of stress.

Synonyms

appraisal .... assessment/ consideration

enhance .... improve/ increase

fake .... pretend

genuine .... real/true

Glossary

HIV a serious illness that attacks the immune system

bereaved having a close friend/ relative who has just died

to suppress to control/hold back

alienation not being part of a group

exploitation treating someone unfairly

Evaluate strategies for coping with stress

Synonyms

coping with .... dealing with
regulation .... control
distinct .... separate/ clear
rehearsal .... practice
specific .... focused on/ aimed at

Glossary

stressor a situation which usually causes stress

empowering giving power to

to prevent/prevention to stop something from happening

discouraged having lost your confidence

Subject vocabulary

cognition/cognitive related to mental processes (such as perception, memory, problem-solving)

Opening sentence:

The strategies for **coping with** stress I will evaluate are: Stress Inoculation Training (SIT) and Yoga.

Strategy 1: Stress Inoculation Training (SIT)

Model sentence: The aim of SIT is to alter the way the person thinks about potential stressors. This is a cognitive approach to stress regulation.

People are seen as *clients* rather than *patients* as this is more hopeful and **empowering** and the client can be seen as equal-to-the-therapist in terms of social position.

Model sentence: SIT is seen as a prevention against stress. It is not seen as a therapy.

According to Meichenbaum (1999), there are three **distinct** phases:

- Conceptualization phase (how to view a problem): Clients are encouraged to see stressful events as problems-to-be-solved.

  Re-conceptualization then takes place (the problem is seen in a different way): During talks a new *way of looking* at the problem is agreed between client and therapist.
- **Rehearsal** phase: Skills for coping with the stress are rehearsed such as breathing techniques and relaxation training.
- Application phase: Clients imagine stressful events and apply the skills they have learned. This involves role playing/acting with the therapist.

Evaluation

Model sentence: The positive aspects of SIT are:

- SIT is **specific** to the needs of the person suffering stress.
- SIT accepts the stress an individual can experience is often unavoidable – such as a work environment. Because stress is unavoidable therefore the role of therapy is to manage it. This is more realistic.
- SIT has the active cooperation of the client themselves.
- SIT encourages equality between client and therapist and encourages the individual to take control of their stress management.

Model sentence: The negative aspects of SIT are:

- Stressor avoidance may be best for some individuals. Some people are not suited to certain work or social environments and SIT may not recognize that.
- SIT takes time and money and is not suited for everyone. It needs high levels of motivation.
- The therapy requires talks about feelings and personal thoughts. This is not suited to people from cultures where this is **discouraged**.

Strategy 2: Yoga

Yoga means to yoke, or to join two things together. The aim is to connect and then purify the mind and the body.

Yoga involves:

- *Physical positions or postures:* These help with flexibility.
- *Meditation:* A focus on inner thoughts. The person trains themselves to think hard about something so they can be more thoughtful and more **compassionate**.

Evaluation

Model sentence: Yoga is a very broad term and has many different approaches. It is difficult to give specific evaluations for the whole practice.

Model sentence: The positive aspects of Yoga are:

- Yoga can be said to improve *quality of life* (Cohen, 2006). Yoga is a **holistic** lifestyle choice. It has many sensible ways to take control of one's life. It encourages people to be more peaceful and healthy and gives them strategies to achieve this.
- Yoga provides *exercise*, there is a focus on *relaxation*, and a focus on the *self*. All of these things are good common-sense approaches to reducing stress.

Supporting study: Hartfiel et al. (2010)

Aim: To determine the **efficacy** of Yoga in stress reduction.

Method: 48 employees were placed in either a Yoga group or a control group. The independent variable (IV) was the type of group they were placed in. The Yoga group was offered 6 weeks of Yoga. This was a 1-hour-long lunchtime class per week for 6 weeks. The control group received nothing. Participants were given psychological questionnaires measuring mood (the dependent variable – DV) before and after the 6-week period.

Results: The Yoga group had **significant** improvements in mood, satisfaction, confidence, and less stress.

Evaluation: Good use of an experiment to investigate a therapy. A control group, clear IV, and clear DV were used. Mood was **quantified** with questionnaires. However, this was a relatively small group and there is an issue of *internal* ***validity*** – can the researchers really be sure Yoga caused the increase in mood? It may have been the result of doing something 'new' and 'for a study'. The long-term effects were not researched.

Model sentence: The negative aspects of Yoga are:

- Stress is very specific to the individual (e.g. an unhappy job or unhappy marriage). It cannot address these very specific problems.
- Yoga will only be of benefit for those individuals who choose to follow the teachings *completely*. This may have cultural and personal limitations for some. It may have economic problems for others. For example, classes cost money; they have to be travelled to; child care has to be arranged; support is needed from family members.

Synonyms

compassionate... sympathetic/caring

efficacy............. effectiveness

significant......... major/large

quantified......... measured/calculated

Glossary

holistic focuses on the whole thing/person

validity being correct/reasonable

Subject vocabulary

independent variable (IV) the variable an experimenter controls or changes

dependent variable (DV) the variable an experimenter measures

Hints for success: Evaluation means both positives and negatives.

Explain factors related to the development of substance abuse or addictive behaviour

Opening sentence:

In this answer I will explain factors related to the development of substance abuse with alcoholism.

What is substance abuse?

Substance abuse is the *dependence* on a drug that has negative effects on the individual's physical and mental health, or the **welfare** of others (Nutt et al., 2007).

An individual is said to be addicted when they cannot ***function*** properly such as in employment or relationships.

What is alcoholism?

Alcoholism is a ***compulsive*** need for alcohol. It leads to negative effects upon the drinker's physical and psychological health. It is seen as a treatable disease.

Physiological factors

Model sentence: Alcoholism has a clear connection to physiological factors.

- Alcoholism runs in families and is particularly common with males. This suggests a clear biological link. However, this may be due to environmental factors as well such as **modelling** from other people.
- Genes can express themselves differently in different cultures. One gene has been identified that might be responsible for a nervous personality (COMT Met158Met). For example: Native American tribes who are stressed and have COMT Met158Met are less likely to become alcoholic. European white men who are stressed and have COMT Met158Met are *more* likely to become alcoholic (Cross, 2004).
- Alcoholics have fewer GABA receptors in the frontal lobes. GABA is a neurotransmitter (gamma-aminobutyric acid) that is involved in calming the body. PET scans were used to find this. Fewer GABA receptors might suggest a greater chance of feeling **anxiety** leading to an increased likelihood for alcoholism as alcohol can be used to reduce those feelings (Lingford-Hughes, 2005). However, it is not clear if the brain differences cause alcoholism or are a **consequence** of it.

Model sentence: There is strong evidence that certain biological factors may mean an individual is more likely to be an alcoholic. They do not mean it is certain they will become one.

Synonyms

welfare .... health/ happiness

function............. behave/ perform

anxiety .... nervousness/ fear

consequence ...... result

Glossary

compulsive doing something a lot and unable to stop it

to model/modelling to provide example behaviour or copy for someone or something

Subject vocabulary

psychological relating to thoughts, feelings, and behaviour

physiological related to the body

genes molecular units which are the building blocks for characteristics

frontal lobes the front part of the brain associated with planning and judgement

neurotransmitters chemicals in the brain that are involved with communication

positron emission tomography (PET) (positron emission tomography) monitors glucose metabolism in the brain. PET scans produce coloured maps of mental activity to show where the brain is using energy

Sociocultural factors

- **Cultural norms**: Alcohol has been made for around 12 000 years. It is a widely accepted part of many cultures around the world. Pubs are a central part of many UK communities; bars are a central part of many US communities; cafes that sell alcohol are a central part of many European communities. These normalize alcohol use and make **addiction** more likely.
- Commercials by alcohol companies have a significant influence on young people. Young people who see more alcohol advertisements drink more on average (Snyder et al., 2006).
- A survey in Ireland found young people identified alcohol advertisements as their favourites and believed the advertisements were targeted at them. This was because the advertisements showed scenes **associated** with young people - dancing, clubbing, and music (Dring and Hope, 2001).
- Teenagers can **interpret** alcohol advertisements as thinking alcohol is an effective way to achieve social and sexual success (Dring and Hope, 2001). This still happens even though the rules for alcohol advertising state that it should not be associated with sexual success.

Model sentence: Western society aggressively promotes alcohol use as a cultural norm. Companies use attractive commercials to influence young people.

Concluding comments

Western society promotes alcohol use as a cultural norm. This creates an environment where alcohol is difficult to avoid. There is strong evidence certain biological factors may mean certain individuals are more likely to become an alcoholic. These factors mean certain individuals are more likely to become alcoholics than individuals who do not have the same biological factors and/or do not experience the same cultural norms.

Substance abuse is the dependence on a drug that has negative effects on the individual's physical and mental health, or the welfare of others (Nutt et al., 2007).

Alcoholism is a compulsive need for alcohol. It leads to negative effects upon the drinker's physical and psychological health. It is seen as a treatable disease.

Hints for success: *Explain factors* is a plural command. Make sure you clearly label at least two before you explain them.

Subject vocabulary

sociocultural (factors) related to social and cultural issues

Glossary

cultural norms expected/accepted ways to behave

addiction a strong desire to have/do something regularly

Synonyms

associated .... linked

interpret .... understand

aggressively .... strongly

promotes .... encourages/supports

Examine prevention strategies and treatments for substance abuse and addictive behaviour

Glossary

to prevent/prevention to stop something from happening

alcoholism addiction to alcohol

assumption something that is thought to be true without proof

addicts people who are not able to stop taking harmful substances

commercials TV advertisements

Subject vocabulary

substance abuse also known as drug abuse. A consistent use of a substance (drug) which leads to emotional, physical, and/or psychological damage

Synonyms

conflict .... disagreement/ a difference

promote .... encourage/ support

adolescent .... teenager/ young person

interpret .... understand

Opening sentence:

I will examine **prevention** strategies and treatments related to the development of general drug use and **alcoholism**.

Prevention strategies

Model sentence: I will examine two prevention strategies: education programmes and advertising rules.

Education

Groups that educate young people about the dangers of substance abuse visit schools. DARE (Drug Abuse Resistance Education program) is used in nearly 80 per cent of the school districts in the United States and in 54 other countries around the world.

Model sentence: An assumption of many education programmes is that all people who take drugs will become addicts. Therefore, all drugs are seen as bad. Some people argue this is not realistic.

Model sentence: Another assumption is that it is acceptable to teach moral values that might disagree with the moral values taught by parents.

For example: Many children will see their parents using drugs. There will be **conflict** between what they are told at school and what they see at home. DARE teaches a child 'The Three Rs: Recognize, Resist, Report', which encourages children to tell friends, teachers or police if they see drug use at home.

Advertising rules

Model sentence: In the UK, the Advertising Standards Authority (ASA) has strict guidelines for the advertising of alcohol such as:

- Advertisers are not allowed to **promote** alcohol to under-18s.
- In **commercials** promoting alcohol, none of the models should look under 25. They also cannot be seen acting '**adolescent**'.
- Pop stars and sports stars that appeal to children cannot appear in alcohol commercials even to an adult audience. For example, David Beckham or Justin Bieber cannot be paid to promote beer because they are role models of young people. They can be paid to promote junk food.

Model sentence: An assumption of these rules is that children will not be encouraged to drink alcohol if they see these advertisements. However:

- A survey in Ireland found young people identified alcohol advertisements as their favourites and believed the advertisements were targeted at them. This was because the advertisements showed scenes associated with young people - dancing, clubbing, and music (Dring and Hope, 2001).
- Commercials by alcohol companies have a significant influence on young people. Young people who see more alcohol advertisements drink more on average (Snyder et al., 2006).
- Teenagers can **interpret** alcohol advertisements as thinking alcohol is an effective way to achieve social and sexual success (Dring and Hope, 2001).

Treatments

Model sentence: I will examine two treatments: Alcoholics Anonymous (AA) and drug treatments.

Alcoholics Anonymous

Alcoholics Anonymous (AA) was founded in Ohio (USA) during the 1930s. Alcoholics Anonymous (AA) assumes alcoholics have a mental problem not a moral problem. This new **paradigm** allowed alcoholism to be treated as an illness.

Alcoholics Anonymous has a focus on **spirituality**; surrendering to the power of a ***sponsor*** (an individual, usually a former alcoholic that offers guidance and support) and some idea of a God or powerful world creator figure.

Model sentence: The assumptions of AA can be seen as:

- AA assumes group bonding and public admission of wrong doing is a good way to start treatment. However it is not suited to every personality or culture.
- AA assumes religion and spirituality are suitable ways to treat addicts. However, they are not suited to every personality or culture (Honeymar, 1997).
- AA assumes alcohol use leads to addiction. AA has a zero tolerance of alcohol use. Cutting out alcohol completely is not realistic for many, nor is it fully needed.

Drug treatment

The drug naltrexone is taken to remove the positive feelings from drinking alcohol. Some scientists think it works by affecting the neural pathways in the brain where the neurotransmitter dopamine is found. Sinclair (2001) found 27 per cent of naltrexone patients had no **relapses** to heavy drinking throughout the 32 weeks. Only 3 per cent of placebo patients had no relapses.

Model sentence: The assumptions of drug treatment can cause problems.

For example:

- Drug therapy assumes a biological link with alcohol. It cannot help with social or personality causes. Therefore, naltrexone should be used with *coping skills therapy*.
- Drug therapy assumes the individual *wants* to be free from alcohol. Drugs alone do not cure the patient.
- Drugs do not stop the negative thoughts or negative life circumstances which may lead some people to drink.
- It assumes alcoholics experience a biological reward (via endorphins) when drinking which leads to more drinking. This may not be the case with all addicts. And it will differ in degree from one addict to another.

Hints for success: Use logical sub-headings to demarcate your answers. They will give them a clear structure and focus – in this case, *prevention strategies* and *treatments.*

Synonyms

paradigm .... model/example

sponsor .... mentor/counsellor

Glossary

spirituality to do with religion/religious matters

relapse the starting of a (bad) behaviour again

Subject vocabulary

neural pathways nerve pathways that connect one part of the nervous system with another

neurotransmitters chemicals in the brain that are involved with communication

dopamine a neurotransmitter related to attention, motivation, pleasure, and reward

placebo a fake treatment that can often have an effect. Researchers compare their effects with the real treatment

coping skills therapy a therapy that teaches how to deal with anxious situations. The skills can include breathing techniques and using an inner voice to calm down or how to talk with people whom they find irritating

Discuss factors related to overeating and the development of obesity

Opening sentence:

Obesity is a medical condition in which having too much body fat has a negative effect on health. It occurs when an individual eats more food energy than they use.

Model sentence: I will discuss biological and social factors related to the development of obesity. Like many other medical conditions, obesity is the result of both genetic and environmental factors.

Biological factors

Genetic influences

Fat father rats

Fang Ng et al. (2010) **hypothesized** poor diet of the father rat (and not the mother) over the life time of the individual would negatively impact on the **offspring**.

Method: The independent variable (IV) was poor diet and was operationalized by giving 40 per cent more calories than to control rats making them fat. The dependent variable (DV) was the extent to which it would biologically affect the offspring and was operationalized by glucose intolerance and insulin **secretion**. Glucose intolerance means there is too much blood sugar and is considered a serious health condition.

Results: The rats were mated. When the pups (baby rats) were 6 weeks old, they were glucose intolerant. By 12 weeks of age, they had **impaired** insulin secretion.

Conclusion: Poor diet of father rats would affect the health of their offspring.

Evaluation: Animals were used so caution should be used when generalizing the results to humans. However, this is a tightly controlled experiment with clear IVs and DVs and a cause-effect relationship can be established (methodological evaluation). The rats were bred for research purposes and were used **sparingly** (**ethical** evaluation).

Model sentence: Poor diet negatively affected the father's sperm which produced less healthy offspring that produced less insulin. The lack of insulin is thought to contribute to the development of obesity (Kahn and Flier, 2000).

Correlational evidence

Aim: To correlate genes with obesity (Lombard et al., 2012).

Method: A longitudinal study using 990 black South Africans. Body Mass Index (BMI) was used to assess how obese the participants were. The participants had their genetic history mapped out.

Results: There was a significant **association** between four genes and obesity. Each risk gene was associated with an estimated average increase of 2.5 per cent in BMI.

Conclusion: There is a clear link between genes and obesity.

Glossary

obesity being fat in an unhealthy way

to hypothesize to suggest an explanation which has not yet been proven true

sparingly as few as possible

Subject vocabulary

genetic relating to genes which are molecular units which are the building blocks for characteristics

independent variable (IV) the variable an experimenter controls or changes

operationalized *how* the IV is manipulated and *how* the DV is measured

dependent variable (DV) the variable an experimenter measures

insulin a hormone that lowers the level of glucose (a type of sugar) in the blood

to generalize/generalization the extent to which we can apply results to other circumstances

cause-effect relationship where there is confidence that the effect on the dependent variable (DV) has been caused by the manipulation of the independent variable (IV)

longitudinal research that has taken place over a long period of time, usually years

Body Mass Index (BMI) height and weight is measured to see if a person is overweight

Synonyms

offspring............ young/babies

secretion............ production

impaired............ damaged

ethically............ morally

correlation.......... link

association.......... relationship/connection

Evaluation: This is a very culturally specific study so caution should be used when generalizing to other cultures (cultural evaluation). Correlational evidence is not cause-effect evidence so caution should be used when assuming genes *cause* the *effect* of obesity. However, the only way to be sure of a cause-effect relationship is to carry out an experiment where the genes are deliberately manipulated to see if they *cause* the *effect* of obesity. This is not ethically possible while investigating genes and obesity with humans (methodological evaluation).

Model sentence: Children are not born with a predisposition to eat poor food and avoid exercise. Therefore, genes cannot be used on their own to explain obesity.

Social factors

Model sentence: Social learning theory (SLT) assumes humans learn behaviour through observational learning (watching models and imitating their behaviour).

Factors which influence whether or not the observer decides to imitate and learn are *consistency*, *identification with the model*, and the *level of rewards/punishment*.

Consistency

If a model behaves in a way that is consistent across situations, for example, always eating healthy food, then the observer will be more likely to imitate them. Tibbs et al. (2001) gave parents questionnaires to find out how often parents model dietary behaviours for their children. They found *inconsistent* and *low levels of modelling* for healthy snacks and eating fruit and vegetables.

Identification with the model

Parental modelling of physical activity for early **adolescents** was lower than parental modelling for physical activity with younger children or older adolescents (Duncan et al. 2005). This is because early adolescents may look to their **peers** as role models rather than their parents.

Parental modelling has been shown with smoking, seatbelt use, and physical activity, and suggests that observational learning is in part responsible for the transmission of health promoting (eating healthily) or risky behaviour (eating unhealthily) in children (Tinsley, 2003).

Rewards/punishment

Encouragement, helping with transport, payment of fees, and buying equipment (for example, football boots) can be seen as rewards for physical activity. There is a correlation between parents who do this and how active their children are (Sallis et al., 2007).

Punishment can come in the form of price increases. Khan et al. (2012) looked at the correlations between fast-food consumption in kindergarten children and the price of the food. They found a 10 per cent increase in the price of fast food resulted in a 5.7 per cent reduction in children eating it. This suggests *fat-taxes* would work to a certain degree. Other studies show a high taxation rate but only a small effect on behaviour.

For example:

> $0.45 tax per soft drink led to a 26 per cent **decline** in sales. So, a 20 per cent tax on sugary drinks in the USA would reduce obesity levels by 3.5 per cent - from 33.5 per cent to 30 per cent among adults (Mytton, 2012).

Glossary

to predispose/predisposition a tendency to behave in a particular way

to model/modelling to provide example behaviour or copy for someone or something

peer a person who is the same age as you or has the same position in society

Synonyms

imitating	copying
adolescents	teenagers/ young people
decline	decrease/fall

Hints for success: Present the various factors as working *with* each other. It is unlikely obesity is caused by one factor alone.

Discuss prevention strategies and treatments for overeating and obesity

Glossary

to prevent/prevention to stop something from happening

obesity being fat in an unhealthy way

compulsory something that must be done

to model/modelling to provide example behaviour or copy for someone or something

surcharge money paid in addition to the basic price

Synonyms

properly .... correctly

consumption ...... eating

generate .... make/create

reduction .... decrease/fall

decline .... decrease/fall

Subject vocabulary

meta-analysis a review of many studies into the same phenomena to see what broad conclusions can be made

Prevention strategies

Model sentence: Prevention strategies aim to try and stop obesity before it happens. I will discuss schools and fat taxes.

Schools

- School lessons can be used to teach children how to eat **properly**. In the UK, food technology lessons teach students about food and how to cook. They were made **compulsory** in 2011 for students aged between 11 and 14 years old. However, there is no evidence as yet these lessons have changed unhealthy lifestyles.
- School meals are approximately one-third of a child's food intake. In the UK, the *School Meals Review Panel* (2005) stated:
    - Improving school food leads to better behaviour in class.
    - Schools should ***model*** good food habits by serving healthy food. However:
        - The child's home is still more important in determining a child's health.
        - Children can access high fat food outside of school and choose not to eat healthy food inside school.

Fat taxes

Model sentence: A fat tax is a surcharge for fatty or unhealthy foods.

Governments would identify certain foods and then put an extra tax on them. Mytton (2012), from the British Heart Foundation's Health Promotion Research Group, carried out a meta-analysis of 30 international studies to determine the effect that food taxes had. He concludes: fat taxes would discourage the **consumption** of fatty food but only if the taxes were high.

Arguments for:

- Fat taxes **generate** money for the government which can then be used on obesity **reduction** strategies. Seventeen US states already have special taxes on soft drinks, candy, and snack foods and it is estimated that these fat taxes already generate more than US$1 billion annually. This can be spent on health care for obese people.
- Taxes worked on tobacco. For example, from 1988 to 1993, tobacco use in California **declined** by 27 per cent after taxes were increased.

Arguments against:

- Fat taxes would punish successful businesses for providing products people want.
- It is the responsibility of the individual to take care of themselves not the government.
- The taxes would be high but the results would be small. Poor people would still buy the products; they would just have less money for other things.
- For example:
    - $0.45 tax per soft drink led to a 26 per cent decline in sales. So, a 20 per cent tax on sugary drinks in the USA would reduce obesity levels by 3.5 per cent – from 33.5 per cent to 30 per cent among adults (Mytton, 2012). This is not a large reduction.

- Taxes (such as those for cigarettes) rarely work on their own. In the case of cigarettes, taxes were used together with a ban on advertising, education programmes in schools, bans on cigarette sponsorship of sports teams, etc. Therefore, effective prevention strategies are complex and require the cooperation of business and political leaders.

Treatments

Model sentence: Treatments aim to help people lose weight after they are obese. I will discuss dieting and surgery.

Dieting

A *healthy diet* is not the same as *dieting*. Dieting refers to a food programme that limits energy intake to less than the person uses. Obesity occurs when an individual eats more energy from food than they **expend**.

According to Geissler and Powers (2005), dieting only works in the long term if:

- The patient is willing to accept a new lifestyle which involves healthy food and exercise.
- Consideration is given to a patient's food likes and dislikes
- Consideration is given to a patient's socioeconomic circumstances. How rich or poor are they? Can they afford to join a gym? Can they travel to good shops that sell healthy food?
- The patient is willing to think differently about food (cognitive change) and not see it as a source of emotional comfort.

Surgery

Gastric bypass procedures (GBP) are surgeries that make the stomach smaller so less food can be eaten.

Livhits et al. (2012) carried out a literature search of US medical databases between 1998 and 2010. They found the behaviour of the patient *before* surgery (such as forcing patients to lose weight) had a significant impact on whether the patient was able to maintain weight loss *after* surgery. They also found people who were *super-obese* before surgery are more likely to become **binge eaters** *after* surgery - suggesting negative behaviour is difficult to change.

Advantages:

- Not being able to eat what they want means patients have to take control of their lives. As they lose weight, they are able to take part in other activities - this improves **self-esteem**.

Disadvantages:

- Many who have had the surgery suffer from depression in the following month as a result of a change in the role food plays in their emotions (Elkins et al., 2005).
- The change in food absorption areas can slow the absorption of some essential nutrients - therefore the patient has to have a carefully designed diet for the rest of his/her life. The question should be asked: if a patient can be **disciplined** enough to eat properly *after* surgery why can't they be disciplined in their diets *before* they need surgery?

Synonyms

expend .... use

disciplined .... controlled

Subject vocabulary

socioeconomic relating to social and economic issues

absorption uptake of substances by the body

Glossary

binge eater a person who eats too much in short periods of time

self-esteem confident in your own abilities

Hints for success: Overeating and obesity can be treated as the same. Demarcate your answer according to prevention strategies and treatments.

Examine models and theories of health promotion

Subject vocabulary

model a representation of behaviour or an idea. They allow predictions to be made about behaviour

HIV (human immunodeficiency virus) the virus that causes AIDS. This virus is passed from one person to another through blood-to-blood and sexual contact

AIDS a serious illness of the immune system that leads to death

Synonyms

promotion ...... encouragement/ support

rational .... logical

optimistic .... positive

perceptions .... opinions/ understandings

Glossary

assumption something that is thought to be true without proof

obesity being fat in an unhealthy way

to engage in/engaged to take part in

Opening sentence:

The two **models** of health **promotion** I will examine are *The Health Belief Model* and the *Theory of Reasoned Action.*

Model 1: The Health Belief Model (HBM)

The Health Belief Model (HBM) was first developed by Rosenstock (1966). The HBM proposes that people will respond best to messages about health promotion when they *believe* they are at serious risk and the risk can be reduced with behaviour change.

Assumption 1: The HBM assumes people are rational.

People *know* fast food causes **obesity** and still eat it. People *know* cigarettes cause cancer and still smoke. Therefore, it could be assumed people are not as rational as the model assumes. This may be partly due to *positive illusions* (Taylor and Brown, 1988): People want to be **optimistic** about the world rather than negative. Positive illusions are an example of *optimism bias* where people are over-optimistic about their health-risking behaviour.

Assumption 2: HBM assumes people care about their health or the health of those they care for.

People have *health apathy* (they don't care about their health or not as much as they need to). *Health apathy* is a lack of concern towards their personal health or to the personal health of people they are responsible for. This would explain why people still **engage in** unhealthy behaviour such as eating unhealthy food when they are obese and feeding it to those who are also obese.

Application of HBM

HIV risk in Iranian females (Khani et al., 2010)

Aim: To investigate **perceptions** of HIV in Iranian females.

Method: A questionnaire was given to 180 female students from three high schools in Yazd, Iran.

Results: Students' beliefs about HIV and how it was spread were linked to their perception of their risk status. They perceived themselves as not at risk as they did not see themselves as 'typical' of a HIV at-risk group. This resulted in problems: students believed they were not at risk and so they actually engaged in risky behaviours (e.g. sex without condom use). Khani et al. (2010) show how people who believe they are at risk (e.g. prisoners who use drugs) decreased their HIV high-risk behaviours (e.g. used clean syringes) when they *believed* in the effectiveness of strategies.

Conclusion: Education strategies should target the belief system of sub-groups (e.g. female students; prisoners) and not offer one general message.

Model 2: Theory of Reasoned Action (TRA) and the Theory of Planned Behaviour (TPB)

Model sentence: Some of the problems of the HBM are addressed by the *Theory of Reasoned Action* (TRA) developed by Fishbein and Ajzen (1975).

The assumptions are:

- People's behaviour is not always in-line with their stated beliefs.
- **Attitudes:** People's *beliefs* based on ***interpretations*** of information influence how they make decisions. A simple presentation of facts is not enough.
- **Subjective norms:** People's friends' and family's *beliefs* also influence how they make decisions. These carry different ***weights***. For example, a work colleague asking you to exercise will carry less weight than a wife or husband.
- These lead to ***intention*** and this is the best **predictor** of behaviour.

In sum: A person's attitude, combined with the attitudes of others, forms their *behavioural intention.*

TRA was influenced by Self-Efficacy Theory (SET) put forward by Bandura (1977). *Self-efficacy* assumes one can successfully engage in a behaviour to produce desired outcomes (e.g. eat healthily and exercise regularly to lose weight). Bandura argued *motivation*, *performance*, and *feelings of frustration* will all affect how an individual approaches a problem.

Application of TRA/TPB

Obesity in Chinese Americans (Liou, 2007)

Aim: To examine the beliefs and attitudes related to obesity and its prevention in Chinese Americans using elements of HBM and TRA.

Method: Qualitative study with 40 Chinese Americans. Common themes were identified, **coded**, and compared using computer software.

Results: Traditional Chinese food was seen as more healthy but the participants had a positive attitude to America and wanted to **adopt** an American lifestyle. This meant they ate less traditional food. This was **coupled with** a traditional Chinese belief that a larger body is more attractive.

Conclusion: The attitudes of the participants (America is a place I want to be) and the subjective norms of their own culture (bigger body sizes are more attractive) influenced their unhealthy food choices.

Application: Health promotion strategies should consider attitudes and cultural norms of any group they are targeting.

> **Hints for success:** Use logical sub-headings to separate your answers. They will give a clear structure and focus – in this case *The Health Belief Model* and the *Theory of Reasoned Action*.

Synonyms

interpretations . understandings

weights........... influences/ powers

coded.............. labelled

adopt.............. take on

coupled with.... joined/ together with

Subject vocabulary

subjective norms the usual ways a person/group of people view something

qualitative study a study that produces qualitative data that is usually in the form of *words* taken from interviews showing thoughts, feelings, and experiences of the participants

Glossary

intention a plan/desire to do something

predictor shows what will happen in the future

Discuss the effectiveness of health promotion strategies

Opening sentence:

In this answer I will discuss the effectiveness of the *Measurement of Outcomes Approach* and the *Population Health Approach.*

Measurement of Outcomes Approach (MOA)

Model sentence: MOA is an approach to health promotion that aims to:

- **standardize** the measurement of health
- standardize the measurement of treatments
- use an evidence-based approach.

The aim is to discover if any change in health can be **related to** the **intervention**.

Why is it necessary?

Medical practitioners can use individual experiences with a treatment that are **subjective** and not based on evidence from large-scale realistic studies.

Therefore an MOA approach focuses on: efficacy and effectiveness.

Efficacy refers to improvement in health as the result of an intervention in a controlled trial. It is a more *scientific* way to approach the problem.

Effectiveness refers to improvement in health as the result of an intervention in a more everyday setting. It is a more *realistic* way to approach the problem.

An example of the effectiveness of the Measurement of Outcomes Approach (MOA)

Weisz and Gray (2008) wanted to know if the best treatments were being reviewed in medical literature and were being taught to new doctors. Using a Measurement of Outcomes Approach, they only focused on treatments that had clear evidence they worked in realistic settings.

Aim: To what extent are evidence-based treatments (EBTs) being used for children with emotional and behavioural problems?

Method: A meta-analysis of academic papers assessing treatment for children with behavioural and emotional problems with a focus on *evidence-based treatments (EBTs).*

Results: Treatments were mostly being tested in unrealistic settings (e.g. lab conditions to test drug therapies).

Research literature for treatments shows very few that work in real-world practice conditions.

Training programmes for doctors focus too much on general approaches to treatments.

Conclusion: The best treatments for children with behavioural and emotional problems were not making their way into training or everyday practice of **clinicians**.

Application: Doctors should use a Measurement of Outcomes Approach by focusing on treatments that have a successful record of treating children with behavioural and emotional problems.

Subject vocabulary

health promotion strategies that can be defined as: a way of helping people change their lifestyle to move toward a state of good health (Minkler, 1989)

meta-analysis a review of many studies into the same phenomena to see what broad conclusions can be made

Synonyms

promotion ..... encouragement/ support

related to .... linked to

medical practitioners doctors

Glossary

to standardize to make the same

intervention an action taken to create a change

subjective based on personal opinion

clinician a doctor who focuses on treating people instead of doing research themselves

Evaluation

Advantages:

It focuses on outcomes not outputs. Outcomes are an improvement in health in realistic and everyday settings. Outputs are things that make that happen. An example would be a health service that has to improve its treatment of children with emotional and behavioural problems. The output is the treatments they use; the outcome is happier and healthier children. An MOA approach would ask: *Are the children happier and healthier?* Not: *Are treatments being **implemented**?*

Disadvantages:

It requires a clearly defined population and a reasonable control of variables within it - this is often unrealistic.

Many non-measureable variables (such as culture and self-belief) affect health outcomes.

Population Health Approach (PHA)

A PHA is a mental **framework** for thinking about why some populations are healthier than others and then aims to improve the health of the unhealthier populations.

Why is this approach effective?

It is effective because it considers how different populations: have different attitudes to health; have different education levels; and have different ways of viewing messages and have different opinions of government messages.

Example: Government anti-drug campaigns (Advisory Council on the Misuse of Drugs, 1984)

The problem: The UK Advisory Council on the Misuse of Drugs (1984) argued government anti-drug campaigns were not effective after researching drug use among the target population of *young people*. The campaigns mainly used **scare tactics** aimed at shocking young people about how dangerous drugs were.

However, certain types of young people were more *likely* to try drugs because: governments specifically told them not to; the scare campaigns made the drugs look mysterious; and the anti-drug campaigns made drug users look **rebellious**.

The solution: Anti-drug campaigns became more **subtle**. Facts were presented **coldly** and **maturely**. Scary, dramatic tactics were **toned down**. Government symbols were removed (e.g. Department of Health).

Model sentence: **A *Population Health Approach* to drug research showed government anti-drug use campaigns were in some cases actually encouraging young people to try drugs. Therefore, using a Population Health Approach and focusing on the attitudes and needs of young people, anti-drug campaigns became more factual, less official, and more subtle to make drugs appear less mysterious and rebellious.**

Synonyms

- **implemented** ...... used/applied
- **framework** .... outline
- **scare** .... shock
- **tactics** .... approaches/methods
- **subtle** .... small/less obvious
- **toned down** .... softened/used less

Glossary

- **rebellious** deliberately not following rules
- **coldly** in an unfriendly way and without emotion
- **maturely** in an adult way

Hints for success: Clearly define what a health promotion strategy is. Then demarcate your answer with sub-headings (if the question is plural) for the two health promotion strategies.

GLO 1: To what extent do biological, cognitive, and sociocultural factors influence health-related behaviour?

Biological factors

Biological factor 1: *Genes and obesity*

The chances of a non-obese parent having an overweight child are only 7 per cent (Garn et al., 1981). The US Centers for Disease Control and Prevention (2010) states genes can directly cause obesity in **disorders** such as Prader-Willi syndrome. These disorders are rare but their existence shows a genetic link to obesity. The American Academy of Child and **Adolescent** Psychiatry (2008) states if one parent is obese, there is a 50 per cent chance children will also be obese; when both parents are obese, children will have an 80 per cent chance of being obese. However this may not be genetic: children will learn to be obese from parents who model unhealthy lifestyles.

Biological factor 2: *Alcoholism has a clear connection to biological factors*

- Alcoholism runs in families and is particularly common with males. This suggests a clear biological link. However, this may be due to environmental factors as well such as **modelling** from other people.
- Men are twice as likely as women to be **alcoholics** which may suggest a biological link.
- Genes can express themselves differently in different cultures. One gene has been identified that might be responsible for a **nervous** personality (COMT Met158Met). For example: Native American tribes who are stressed and have COMT Met158Met are less likely to become alcoholic. European white men who are stressed and have COMT Met158Met are more likely to become alcoholic (Cross, 2004).
- Alcoholics have fewer GABA receptors in the frontal lobes. GABA is a neurotransmitter (gamma-aminobutyric acid) that is involved in calming the body. PET scans were used to find this. Fewer GABA receptors might suggest a greater chance of feeling **anxiety** leading to an increased likelihood for alcoholism as alcohol can be used to **reduce** those feelings (Lingford-Hughes, 2005). However, it is not clear if the brain differences cause alcoholism or are a **consequence** of it.

Cognitive factors

Stress Inoculation Training (SIT)

Model sentence: The aim of SIT is to alter the way the person thinks about potential stressors. This is a cognitive approach to stress regulation and can influence health-related behaviour.

Subject vocabulary

biological related to biological processes (such as the effects of hormones, neurotransmitters, genes, and gender)

cognition/cognitive related to mental processes (such as perception, memory, problem-solving)

sociocultural (factors) related to social and cultural issues

genes molecular units which are the building blocks for characteristics

Prader-Willi syndrome a rare but wide-ranging condition with many characteristics. One characteristic is an increased need to eat which leads to obesity. It demonstrates there is a genetic link to obesity

frontal lobes the front part of the brain associated with planning and judgement

neurotransmitters chemicals in the brain that are involved with communication

Glossary

obesity being fat in an unhealthy way

alcoholism addiction to alcohol

to model/modelling to provide example behaviour or copy for someone or something

alcoholic a person who is addicted to alcohol

stressor a situation which usually causes stress

Synonyms

disorders	illnesses
adolescents	teenagers/young people
nervous	anxious/worried
anxiety	nervousness/fear
reduction	decrease/fall
consequence	result
alter	change
regulation	control

Conceptualization phase (how to view a problem): A good relationship is established between the client and the therapist. The client is educated about stress. Clients are encouraged to see stressful events as problems-to-be-solved.

Re-conceptualization then takes place (the problem is seen in a different way): During talks a new way of looking at the problem is agreed between client and therapist. It must be hopeful and helpful for the client.

Rehearsal phase: Skills for **coping with** the stress are rehearsed such as breathing techniques, relaxation training, social and communication skills training, attention diversion procedures (e.g. thinking about something else or going for a walk), and using family and friends.

Application phase: Clients imagine stressful events and apply the skills they have learned. This involves role playing/acting with the therapist.

Therefore, the aims of SIT are to: alter the way the client **perceives** potential stressors and then practise behavioural techniques for coping with stressors.

Sociocultural factors

Sociocultural factor 1: *Sociocultural factors and obesity*

Factors which influence whether or not the observer decides to **imitate** and learn are consistency, the level of rewards/punishment, and levels of **association**:

Consistency

- If a model behaves in a way that is consistent across situations - for example, always eating healthy food - then the observer will be more likely to imitate them. Tibbs et al. (2001) gave parents questionnaires to find out how often parents model dietary behaviours for their children. They found inconsistency for healthy snacks and eating fruit and vegetables which may lead to children not learning how to eat healthily.
- Parental modelling has been shown with smoking, seatbelt use, and physical activity, and suggests that observational learning is in part responsible for the **transmission** of health-**promoting** (eating healthily) or risky behaviour (eating unhealthily) in children (Tinsley, 2003).

Rewards/punishment

- Encouragement, helping with transport, payment of fees, and buying equipment (for example, football boots) can be seen as rewards for physical activity. There is a **correlation** between parents who do this and how active their children are (Sallis et al., 2007).
- Punishment can come in the form of price increases. Khan et al. (2012) looked at the correlations between fast-food consumption in kindergarten children and the price of the food. They found a 10 per cent increase in the price of fast food resulted in a 5.7 per cent reduction in children eating it. This suggests fat-taxes would work to a certain degree. Other studies show a high taxation rate but only a small effect on behaviour.
- For example: $0.45 tax per soft drink led to a 26 per cent **decline** in sales. So, a 20 per cent tax on sugary drinks in the USA would reduce obesity levels by 3.5 per cent - from 33.5 per cent to 30 per cent among adults (Mytton, 2012).

Synonyms

rehearsal .... practice
coping with .... dealing with
perceives .... views/understands
imitate .... copy
associate .... relate/connect
transmission ...... passing on
promoting .... encouraging/supporting
correlation .... link
decline .... decrease/fall

Subject vocabulary

cultural norms expected or usual ways to behave

independent variable (IV) the variable an experimenter controls or changes

to operationalize *how* the IV is manipulated and *how* the DV is measured

dependent variable (DV) the variable an experimenter measures

insulin a hormone that lowers the level of glucose (a type of sugar) in the blood

diabetes a condition whereby the body does not produce enough insulin (or cells stop responding to the insulin that is produced) which leads to glucose not being used properly

Glossary

addiction a strong desire to have/do something regularly

commercials TV advertisements

to hypothesize to suggest an explanation which has not yet been proven true

Synonyms

significant........... major/large

interpret............. understand

offspring............. young/babies

secretion............. production

impaired............. damaged

Association

People associate fast food with positive experiences. This is particularly true for children. For example:

- McDonald's operates more playgrounds designed specifically to attract children and their parents to its restaurants than any other private entity in the USA (Schlosser, 2006).
- Coca-Cola was the only corporate partner for *Harry Potter and the Sorcerer's Stone*. Pepsi bought the rights to Yoda, the *Star Wars* creature (McCarthy, 2005).
- A UK consumer advice group, Which? found 38 per cent of 8- to 11-year-olds preferred McDonald's as their favourite restaurant because of the toys/Happy Meals the company marketed to them.

Sociocultural factor 2: *Sociocultural factors and alcoholism*

- Cultural norms: Alcohol has been made for around 12 000 years. It is a widely accepted part of many cultures around the world. Pubs are a central part of many UK communities; bars are a central part of many US communities; cafes that sell alcohol are a central part of many European communities. These normalize alcohol use and make **addiction** more likely.
- **Commercials** by alcohol companies have a **significant** influence on young people. Young people who see more alcohol advertisements drink more on average (Snyder et al., 2006).
  - A survey in Ireland found young people identified alcohol advertisements as their favourites and believed the advertisements were targeted at them. This was because the advertisements showed scenes associated with young people - dancing, clubbing, and music (Dring and Hope, 2001).
- Teenagers can **interpret** alcohol advertisements as thinking alcohol is an effective way to achieve social and sexual success (Dring and Hope, 2001). This still happens even though the rules for alcohol advertising state that it should not be associated with sexual success.

GLO 2: Evaluate psychological research (that is, theories and/or studies) relevant to health psychology

Study 1: Fat father rats

Fang Ng et al. (2010) **hypothesized** poor diet of the father rat (and not the mother) over the life time of the individual would negatively impact on the **offspring**.

Method: The independent variable (IV) was poor diet and was operationalized by giving 40 per cent more calories than to the control rats making them fat. The dependent variable (DV) was the extent to which it would biologically affect the offspring and was operationalized by glucose intolerance and insulin **secretion**. Glucose intolerance means there is too much blood sugar and is considered a serious health condition.

Results: The rats became obese and began developing diabetes, including glucose intolerance and high resting levels of insulin. After the rats were mated, the researchers analysed the offspring. They noted the female offspring were more sensitive to the effects of their father's diet so the team focused on female pups (baby rats). By 6 weeks old, the young female rats were glucose intolerant. By 12 weeks of age, they had **impaired** insulin secretion.

Evaluation: Animals were used so caution should be used when generalizing the results to humans. However, this is a tightly controlled experiment with clear IVs and DVs and a cause-effect relationship can be established (methodological evaluations). The rats were bred for research purposes and were used **sparingly** (ethical evaluation).

Study 2: Correlating genes with obesity (Lombard et al., 2012)

Method: A longitudinal study using 990 black South Africans. Body Mass Index (BMI) was used to assess how obese the participants were. The participants had their genetic history mapped out.

Results: There was a significant association between four genes and obesity. Each risk gene was associated with an estimated average increase of 2.5 per cent in BMI.

Conclusion: There is a clear link between genes and obesity.

Evaluation: This is a very culturally specific study so caution should be used when generalizing to other cultures (cultural evaluation). Correlational evidence is not cause-effect evidence so caution should be used when assuming genes cause the effect of obesity. However, the only way to be sure of a cause-effect relationship is to carry out an experiment and this is not ethically possible while investigating genes and obesity in humans (methodological evaluation). Genes would have to be manipulated (the IV) and then the level of obesity measured (DV).

Hints for success: Always use previously learned material to support a GLO answer and use examples of research to support each point you are making.

Subject vocabulary

to generalize/generalization the extent to which we can apply results to other circumstances

cause-effect relationship where there is confidence that the effect on the dependent variable (DV) has been caused by the manipulation of the independent variable (IV)

longitudinal research that has taken place over a long period of time, usually years

Glossary

sparingly as few as possible

Distinguish between altruism and prosocial behaviour

Glossary

to distinguish (between) to identify the difference between two or more things

donation a gift of money usually given to a charity

to rescue to save from danger

stranger someone you do not know

Subject vocabulary

altruism/altruistic/altruistically a specific type of prosocial behaviour. Altruism is doing pro-social actions without expecting them to benefit oneself

egoistic focused on oneself

Opening sentence:

In this answer I will **distinguish** between altruism and prosocial behaviour.

Prosocial behaviour is behaviour that is intended to benefit others. For example, giving **donations**, **rescuing** someone in danger, sharing or carrying a bag for a **stranger**.

Altruism is a specific type of prosocial behaviour. Altruism is doing prosocial actions *without expecting them to benefit oneself*. If a person does something prosocial because they expect a benefit for themselves, it is not called altruistic behaviour; this is called egoistic behaviour.

Hints for success: You do not need to refer to research for this part of the question.

Contrast two theories explaining altruism in humans

Opening sentence:

In this answer I will contrast *kin selection* and the *empathy-altruism hypothesis*.

Model sentence: I will first give a brief description of the two theories.

Kin selection

Kin selection is an evolutionary theory. It **assumes** that human behaviour exists because it has an *adaptive function*; this means that it has helped human beings to survive.

People are **motivated** to help others who are genetically similar to themselves because we are motivated to make sure the genes survive. Therefore in an emergency, people are more likely to help someone who is in their family or when there is a degree of similarity because he or she is **perceived** to be in the *in-group*.

The empathy-altruism hypothesis

The empathy-altruism hypothesis is a cognitive theory.

According to this theory:

- A person must first recognize that there is a need.
- A person will act altruistically if he or she feels genuine empathy for another person in need. This focus on empathy to explain why a person will act altruistically is a limitation of the hypothesis because there may be other reasons for helping.
- The person must *perceive* a benefit for himself or herself before he or she is *motivated* to help. A benefit might be the removal of **distress** because when someone is in need, it causes discomfort. Helping to remove distress will reduce that feeling.

Differences

Model sentence: The two theories have different assumptions about human behaviour.

Assumptions

Kin selection is an evolutionary theory; this means that it is focused on biological reasons for altruistic behaviour. For example, behaviour can be inherited through genes. This means that kin selection sees altruism as an adaptive response that is natural in animals and humans.

Kin selection assumes that people put themselves in *danger* for other people. It focuses on extreme events.

Subject vocabulary

kin family member

empathy the ability to recognize emotions that are being experienced by someone else

altruism/altruistic/altruistically a specific type of prosocial behaviour. Altruism is doing prosocial actions *without expecting them to benefit oneself*

hypothesis the idea being tested by a study

evolutionary theory argues species compete for resources in a challenging environment. Those individuals which are better adapted have more chance of survival

in-group the group we are in or we want to be in

cognition/cognitive related to mental processes (such as perception, memory, problem-solving)

adaptive function/response an adaption that is the result of the processes of evolution that makes the organism better adapted to the environment and therefore more likely to survive

Synonyms

motivated........... keen that something will happen

perceived .... seen

distress .... extreme unhappiness

Glossary

to assume/assumption to think that something is true but without any evidence to prove it

Kin selection assumes that behaviour is only altruistic if there is a cost to the person who helps.

Kin selection theory fails to explain altruism when people help strangers who are not related to them.

The empathy-altruism hypothesis is cognitive in nature. For example, behaviour is guided by information processing (such as perception and motivation), and therefore empathy-altruism focuses on the psychological processes instead of assuming that behaviour is purely biological.

The empathy-altruism model can be applied to almost any helping situation and not just extreme events.

The empathy-altruism model assumes that if people feel empathy towards another person they will help them.

Empathy-altruism can explain altruism when people help strangers who are not related to them.

Empirical support

Model sentence: The two theories have different types of support.

Kin selection theory has been found cross-culturally and with animals.

Example 1: Vampire bats are more likely to share blood with close relatives (Wilkinson, 1984).

Example 2: Squirrels are more likely to **warn** relatives than non-relatives that there are **predators** nearby (Sherman, 1985).

Example 3:

Aim: To test kin selection theory in a laboratory setting in two countries (Madsen et al., 2007).

Method: The researchers asked student participants in the UK to do a painful physical exercise for as long as possible. They promised the students that one of their biological relatives would receive money according to how long he or she could stay in this position. They then compared the length of time students were able to stay in the painful position and correlated this with how genetically close the relative was, for example the researchers compared how long a student would stay in the position for a cousin or an aunt. In South Africa, they used the same position with students of **Zulu** origin. In order to make this test more culturally appropriate, food was offered as the reward instead of money.

Independent variable (IV): degree of biological relatedness.

Dependent variable (DV): time spent in a painful position.

Results: In both countries biological relatedness was correlated with the amount of money given. However, the Zulu males helped their cousins as much as their brothers. This is because in Zulu culture, cousins are considered to be family and part of the social in-group.

Conclusion: There is empirical support for kin selection. However, there are also sociocultural factors that influence behaviour.

Subject vocabulary

empirical data from standardized and properly conducted research studies

participant someone who takes part in a research study

correlated related

independent variable (IV) the variable an experimenter controls or changes

dependent variable (DV) the variable an experimenter measures

sociocultural (factors) relating to social and cultural issues

Glossary

to warn to indicate something dangerous might happen

predator an animal that eats or kills other animals

Zulu a tribe from southern Africa

The empathy-altruism model has supporting research *with humans* but not with animals.

Example:

Aim: To test if levels of empathy and cost had an impact on how much people would help another person (Toi and Batson, 1982).

Method: Female psychology students listened to a radio interview with a psychology student named Carol who had broken both her legs in a car accident. The researchers then gave participants the opportunity to help Carol with class notes.

Independent variable A: Empathy level

Condition 1: Participants were asked to imagine how Carol is feeling (high empathy condition).

Condition 2: Participants were asked to be objective and not concerned with how Carol felt (low empathy condition).

Independent variable B: High or low cost conditions

Condition 1: High cost. Carol would be in the class. It would be embarrassing to refuse to give her the lecture notes.

Condition 2: Low cost. Carol would not be in the class. It would not be as embarrassing to refuse to give her the lecture notes. **Results:** Groups who were told to focus on Carol's feelings were much more likely to offer to help her.

Results: The high empathy group were equally likely to help in either condition. The low empathy group was more likely to help Carol in the high cost condition.

Conclusion: The most important factors in people's decision to help is how much empathy they feel and the perceived cost to themselves for helping or not helping.

Concluding comments

The theories are not opposites, instead one **complements** the other. For example, it is highly likely that the cognitive processes described in the empathy-altruism model (empathy, perception, and motivation) are the result of evolutionary processes.

Hints for success: Use the studies to support your ideas: this means you should always be clear that you are comparing the theories, not the studies.

Glossary

to complement to make a good combination

Using one or more research studies, explain cross-cultural differences in prosocial behaviour

Opening sentence:

In this answer I will explain cross-cultural differences in prosocial behaviour with reference to two studies.

Model sentence: **Prosocial behaviour is behaviour that is intended to benefit others.**

Explanation 1: Economic development

Aim: To **compare** the rate of helping behaviour in different cities around the world (Levine et al., 2001).

Method: 23 countries were chosen around the world, and the researchers visited one major city in each of these countries. They recorded how often someone helped in the following conditions: a person pretending to be blind waiting to cross the road; a person walking along the street in a **leg brace** and dropping magazines; a person dropping a pen while walking along the street.

Results: Rio de Janeiro (Brazil) and San Jose (Costa Rica) were the cities considered to be most helpful in the three situations. They are both cities with low levels of economic development. Sofia (Bulgaria), Amsterdam (Holland), and Singapore (Singapore) were the cities considered to be the least helpful. Amsterdam and Singapore are considered to be cities with high levels of economic development.

Conclusion: Countries with low economic development tend to have stronger values about the importance of **ethical** behaviour in a **community**.

Glossary

to compare to look for similarities

leg brace a support which is placed around the leg to help the person move about

ethical relating to the idea of what is right or wrong

community an organization of people

Explanation 2: Levels of simpatia

Simpatia is a concern for the social well-being of others and is important in South American countries. In Levine et al.'s (2001) study the two highest scoring countries were South American where there is a culture of simpatia. It was also noted that many of the South American countries are mainly *Roman Catholic*. Therefore, belief in a religion may also influence levels of prosocial behaviour.

Subject vocabulary

simpatia concern for the social well-being of others

Explanation 3: Cultural differences in what is considered close kin

Aim: To test kin selection theory in a laboratory setting in two countries (Madsen et al., 2007).

Method: The researchers asked student participants in the UK to do a painful physical exercise for as long as possible. They promised the students that one of their biological relatives would receive money according to how long the student could stay in this position. They then compared the length of time students were able to stay in the painful position and correlated this with how genetically close the relative was, for example comparing how long a student would stay in the position for a cousin or an aunt. In South Africa, they used the same position with students of **Zulu** origin. In order to make this test more culturally appropriate, food was offered as a **reward** instead of money.

Independent variable (IV): degree of biological relatedness.

Dependent variable (DV): time spent in a painful position.

Results: In both countries biological relatedness was correlated with the amount of money given. However, the Zulu males helped their cousins as much as their brothers. This is because in Zulu culture, cousins are considered to be family and part of the social in-group.

Conclusion: **Perceptions** about who is considered to be close kin influence prosocial behaviour. In cultures where cousins are considered to be close, prosocial behaviour is higher.

Countries with low economic development tend to have stronger values about the importance of ethical behaviour in a community.

Simpatia is a concern for the social well-being of others and is important in South American countries.

In cultures where cousins are considered to be close, prosocial behaviour is higher.

Hints for success: This learning outcome cannot be asked alone: it will always be part of a bigger question. The most important thing is to make the reasons for the differences clear.

Subject vocabulary

kin family member

participant someone who takes part in a research study

to correlate/correlational to find a close connection between variables

independent variable (IV) the variable an experimenter controls or changes

dependent variable (DV) the variable an experimenter measures

in-group the group we are in or we want to be in

Glossary

Zulu a South African tribe

to perceive/perception to see or understand information

Synonyms

reward............... positive consequence

Examine factors influencing bystanderism

Glossary

bystander a person who watches something that is happening but does not take part

epileptic seizure brain seizure

seizure when the brain stops working properly

victim a person who suffers as the result of something bad happening to them

Subject vocabulary

diffusion of responsibility responsibility can be spread around so individuals feel less inclined to act

participant someone who takes part in a research study

independent variable (IV) the variable an experimenter controls or changes

dependent variable (DV) the variable an experimenter measures

in-group the group we are in or we want to be in

Synonyms

diffused .... spread out

Opening sentence:

When someone needs help in public and other people are around but not directly involved, they are called **bystanders**. Bystanderism is when bystanders do *not* help. I will examine factors influencing bystanderism.

Factor 1: Diffusion of responsibility

Model sentence: Diffusion of responsibility assumes that bystanders are influenced by the number of people around at the time of an event.

If there is only one observer (bystander), he or she will feel a lot of responsibility to act. The more observers there are, the smaller the possibility that they will help because the responsibility has been **diffused**.

Assumption: Someone else will act.

Supporting study

Aim: To test if the number of other people present influences a person's decision to help (Darley and Latané, 1968).

Method: 72 participants agreed to go into a room to be part of a recorded conversation about problems at university. Each person was in the room alone and heard the same recorded voices in the same order. The researchers told them that either there was one other participant or five other participants. However, there were no other participants, all of these others were just recorded voices. At some point one person seems to have an ***epileptic seizure*** and asks for help. The researchers measured how long it took for the real participant to come out of the room and try to help.

Independent variable (IV): Number of people the real participant thinks are also present to hear the call for help – 'alone with **victim**' or 'with four others and victim'.

Dependent variable (DV): Amount of time taken to try to help.

Results: Within the first 2 minutes, 85 per cent of the 'alone' participants tried to help, compared to 31 per cent of those who thought four other people could help. Within 6 minutes, 100 per cent of the alone group had tried to help, compared with 62 per cent of the other group.

Conclusions: The number of other people that bystanders think are also present is a very powerful influence on whether they help or not.

Factor 2: Similarity

Model sentence: Social Identity Theory (SIT) assumes we establish relationships with members of different groups and label them as in-groups and out-groups. The resulting social identity can influence our behaviour.

In an emergency we are more likely to help someone if there is a degree of similarity.

Assumption: People who look like us are in our in-group.

Supporting study

Aim: To test whether Manchester United football **fans** are more likely to help a fan of the same football team than a fan of a different team (Levine et al., 2005).

Method: Manchester United fans walked between two buildings at the university. A man ran past each participant, wearing either a Manchester United football shirt, a Liverpool football shirt, or a plain white shirt. After the man fell over and pretended to be hurt, observers recorded how much help the participants gave him.

Results: There was little difference in the help offered to the man when he wore a Liverpool shirt or a plain white shirt, but the participants were much more likely to help him if he was wearing a Manchester United shirt.

Conclusions: We are more likely to help someone if we believe they are in our in-group.

Factor 3: Culture

Model sentence: Research testing cultural differences in bystanderism assumes that behaviour is influenced by economic development and by cultural notions such as simpatia.

Assumption: Poorer people need to struggle to survive. Helping each other helps their own survival. Richer people do not need to be as **reliant** on other people for their own **well-being**.

Supporting study

Aim: To compare the rate of helping behaviour in different cities around the world (Levine et al., 2001).

Method: 23 countries were chosen around the world, and the researchers visited one major city in each of these countries. They recorded how often someone helped in the following conditions: a person pretending to be blind waiting to cross the road; a person walking along the street in a **leg brace** and dropping magazines; a person dropping a pen while walking along the street.

Results: Rio de Janeiro (Brazil) and San Jose (Costa Rica) were the cities considered to be most helpful in the three situations. They are both cities with low levels of economic development. Sofia (Bulgaria), Amsterdam (Holland), and Singapore (Singapore) were the cities considered to be the least helpful. Amsterdam and Singapore are considered to be cities with high levels of economic development.

Conclusion: Countries with low economic development tend to have stronger values about the importance of **ethical** behaviour in a community.

Hints for success: Make sure that you include information on the assumptions of the factors you use and you support them with research.

Synonyms

fans .... supporters

notions .... ideas

reliant .... dependent

Subject vocabulary

simpatia concern for the social well-being of others

Glossary

well-being the state of feeling healthy and happy

leg brace a support which is placed around the leg to help the person move about

ethical relating to the idea of what is right and wrong

Examine biological, psychological, and social origins of attraction

Opening sentence:

In this answer I will examine the biological, psychological, and social **origins** of attraction.

Attraction is when one person experiences interest in forming some kind of relationship with another person.

Biological origins of attraction

Assumption: Attraction has a survival purpose. It is known as having an ***adaptive function***.

This is shown by:

Males and females find different **characteristics** attractive. Males generally prefer younger women and they pay attention to physical details such as **breast** size and shape, teeth and lip colour, hair length and shine, hip size, and smooth skin. These represent **fertility** as female fertility is limited by age, so signs of youthfulness are **sought** out by men. Females generally prefer older men and they pay attention to **ambition**, wealth, intelligence, height, energy levels, and good health. These represent the ability to provide for any **offspring**. These general characteristics have cross-cultural support.

Biological origins assume attraction occurs between two people because the combination of their genes with the other person's genes would result in healthy offspring. The assumption is based on the idea that pheromones contained in **sweat** can provide information about a person's immune system. It is assumed that genetically *different* immune systems **complement** each other and the mixture of the two immune systems should produce a child with a good immune system.

Supporting study: Sweaty t-shirts

Aim: To test if a woman will judge a sweaty t-shirt as more attractive if it is from a man with different immune system genes (Wedekind et al., 1995).

Method: 49 female and 44 male students were tested to see what type of immune system genes they had. The males were asked to wear a plain white t-shirt for 2 days. The t-shirts were then put in closed boxes until the females were asked to smell them. They were asked to judge the shirts for **pleasantness** and sexiness.

Results: The women judged the t-shirts to be more pleasant and sexy if they came from a man with a different set of immune genes.

Conclusion: People are instinctively **motivated** to find a mate with different immune system genes so that the offspring will have stronger immune systems.

Synonyms

origins .... causes

characteristics..... traits/features

sought .... looked for

offspring............ young/babies

pleasantness .... niceness

Subject vocabulary

adaptive function/response an adaption that is the result of the processes of evolution that makes the organism better adapted to the environment and therefore more likely to survive

pheromones chemicals that make people smell

immune system the physiological system that protects us from sickness

instinctively naturally predetermined

Glossary

breasts the two round parts on a woman's chest which produce milk when she has a baby

fertility the ability to have babies

ambition a strong wish to be successful, powerful, and rich

sweat/sweaty salty liquid produced by the body

to complement to make a good combination

to motivate/motivation a reason to want to do something

Psychological origins of attraction

Psychological origins of attraction assume that psychological events (such as *fear*) interact with biological processes (such as *arousal*) and this can lead to attraction.

Supporting study: Love on a bridge

Aim: To test if physiological arousal can influence attraction (Dutton and Aron, 1974).

Method: The researchers selected two bridges in Canada. One bridge was higher and shook more than the other and was therefore more frightening. A female interviewer stopped men between 18 and 35 years old and asked them various questions. She then asked them to write a story connected with a picture she gave them. She gave them the telephone number of the psychology department and said they could call if they wanted to talk further. She told participants a different name depending on which bridge they were on.

Independent variable (IV): Levels of fear and arousal operationalized by type of bridge (one was higher and shook and the other was lower and did not shake).

Dependent variable (DV): Levels of attraction operationalized by number of phone calls (quantitative data) and levels of sexual content in stories (qualitative data).

Results: Only 2 of the 16 men from the regular bridge called the phone number, compared with 9 out of 18 from the frightening bridge. In addition, there was more sexual content in the stories from the frightening bridge.

Conclusions: Attraction is stronger when there is more physiological arousal from the danger of the bridge. The researchers suggest that attraction occurs when physiological arousal is *interpreted* as sexual excitement.

Social origins of attraction

Social origins of attraction assume that social factors such as proximity can lead to attraction.

Supporting study: Best friends on the same floor

Aim: To test if more friendships are found among people who live in proximity (Nahemow and Lawton, 1975).

Method: **Residents** in Manhattan, New York, were asked who their three best friends were in the housing area and gathered information about how far away these friends lived.

Results: 88 per cent of the people named a person living in the same building as their first best friend, and nearly half lived on the same floor.

Conclusion: We are attracted to others for friendship if they are physically close to us.

Subject vocabulary

arousal bodily and psychological alertness

physiological related to the body

independent variable (IV) the variable an experimenter controls or changes

to operationalize *how* the IV is changed and *how* the DV is measured

dependent variable (DV) the variable an experimenter measures

proximity how near something is

Glossary

residents people who live in a location

Hints for success: Make sure that when you use studies to answer this question, you identify which assumptions they are connected to.

Discuss the role of communication in maintaining relationships

Opening sentence:

In this answer I will discuss the role of communication in **maintaining** relationships.

Communication between people in an **intimate** relationship includes both *what* people say to each other and *how* they say it.

Communicating openness and assurance

Openness means talking about shared experiences and telling your partner things about yourself that they do not know. Giving **assurances** means offering comfort and showing an interest in his or her emotional **well-being**.

Study: How couples maintain marriages

Aim: This study **investigated** what kind of maintenance strategies married couples use and how satisfied they are with their marriage (Weigel-Ballard and Reisch, 1999).

Method: Married couples were asked to complete a questionnaire. The average age of participants was 39 and they had been married between 1 and 46 years.

Results: Traditional couples viewed themselves as more **dependent** on each other. They had high levels of assurance but low levels of openness. Independent couples communicated more and had higher levels of openness.

Conclusion: Traditional couples wanted to avoid **conflict** and so they were less open. Independent couples wanted to solve problems rather than avoid them.

Avoiding negative emotions

Key assumption: Communication can maintain relationships. One of the main causes of divorce is communicating too much negative emotion.

Aim: To test if older married couples and younger married couples have different ways of managing conflict, and to test if this is connected with unhappiness in the marriage (Gottman et al., 2003).

Method: 156 married couples went to a laboratory after not talking to each other for 8 hours. In the laboratory, they were observed discussing three topics, and **physiological** measurements such as heart rate were also taken. The couples discussed what happened that day, and agreed on a pleasant topic and another topic that they knew they would disagree about. The discussions were video recorded and different emotions were observed.

Results: Older couples with longer marriages communicated more **affection** to their partner during the discussions. Couples in unhappy marriages **expressed** more negative emotions. Couples in happy marriages **displayed** more positive emotions.

Conclusions: People learn to communicate with their partner in a way that avoids negative results. Communication styles change over time in order to maintain relationships.

Synonyms

- **maintaining** ...... keeping
- **intimate** .... close
- **dependent** .... reliant
- **conflict** .... disagreement/ a difference
- **expressed** .... described
- **displayed** .... showed

Glossary

- **assurance** a promise that something will happen or is true
- **well-being** the state of feeling healthy and happy
- **to investigate** to try to find the reasons for something
- **affection** showing feelings of love or care for another person

Subject vocabulary

- **key assumption** important underlying idea
- **physiological** related to the body

The role of listening

Arranged marriages are normal in several cultures. When a marriage is arranged, it means that the people who get married do not choose their partner alone. Normally the parents make the decision or, in some cases, find possible partners for their child and let them make the decision. In extreme cases, the person who gets married has no choice at all about the partner or the marriage.

Aim: To test if couples who believe in traditional roles in a marriage have less satisfaction (Ahmad and Reid, 2008).

Method: 114 married people of South Asian **descent** were asked to complete a questionnaire. Only one partner completed the questionnaire, and the researchers used a snowball method to contact participants: the first participants were given copies of the questionnaire to give to friends and family. The questionnaire contained questions about their attitudes towards marriage, their communication style in the marriage, and their satisfaction with the marriage.

Results: There was no direct relationship between beliefs about traditional roles and satisfaction. However, there was a connection between these beliefs and the listening style in the relationship. Those who have traditional beliefs and did not listen in order to understand their partner were less likely to be satisfied.

Conclusion: Arranged marriages with beliefs about traditional roles can be satisfying, but it is necessary for the partners to *practise listening* in order to understand how the other partner feels. This is important because it suggests that communication may have a stronger role in maintaining happy relationships than the cultural factors that cause people to marry.

Communicating openness and assurance, avoiding negative emotions, and listening (to improve communication) all help to maintain relationships.

Hints for success: The command term *discuss* means you should offer a balanced review in your answer. For this reason you should emphasize that communication can have positive and negative effects, and that listening is as important as speaking.

Glossary

descent where your family comes from

Subject vocabulary

snowball method/sampling the researcher asks existing participants in the study if they know other possible participants who are willing to take part and then these are recruited for the study

Explain the role that culture plays in the formation and maintenance of relationships

Opening sentence:

In this answer I will explain the role that culture plays in the **formation** and **maintenance** of relationships.

Culture can be defined as: 'A set of attitudes, behaviours and **symbols** shared by a large group of people and usually communicated from one generation to the next' (Shiraev and Levy, 2004).

Attitudes include beliefs (for example, political, religious, and moral beliefs), values, **superstitions**, and **stereotypes.**

Behaviours include norms, customs, traditions, and fashions.

Formation

Model sentence: Culture influences what we find attractive in other people, and therefore plays an important role in the formation of relationships. This is because there are cultural norms that guide who we can expect to have a relationship with and who we expect a good partner to be.

Attraction and culture

Aim: To test if close relationships are best explained by evolutionary theory or by social norms (Pines, 2001).

Method: A structured interview was used with 93 young Americans and 89 young Israelis. The interviews asked them about their current and past **romantic** relationships and what attracted them to their partner. Answers were *coded* so that the researcher could take into consideration whether variables such as physical attraction and **status** were the reasons for attraction.

Results: Men from both cultures were more likely to mention physical appearance than women as a reason for their attraction to their partner. Eight per cent of the Americans mentioned the status of their partner, while none of the Israelis mentioned status.

Conclusions: Culture has an influence on whether status is seen as attractive in close relationships. There are also cross-cultural similarities (such as men valuing physical appearance) which affect attraction.

Maintenance

Culture and traditional roles

Traditional marriage refers to a model where the man focuses on providing economically for the family (the **breadwinner**) and the woman focuses on taking care of the home and being the main carer for the children (Parker, 2002). It does not mean that the woman cannot work outside of the home; it means her focus is also on making the home a comfortable place to be.

Glossary

formation creation

maintenance keeping things the same

symbol a picture, shape or person that has a particular meaning for a group of people

superstition a belief that certain objects or actions are lucky or unlucky

stereotype a belief about what a particular person or group of people is like

status position of someone within society

breadwinner the member of the family who provides the money to support the others

Subject vocabulary

norms expected or usual ways to behave

customs norms within a culture

evolutionary theory argues species compete for resources in a challenging environment. Those individuals which are better adapted have more chances of survival

to code to label a theme or idea generated by research

Synonyms

romantic............ loving

Norwegian culture has high levels of gender **equality**. However, divorce rates for couples who did equal amounts of **housework** was approximately 50 per cent higher than that of more traditional couples where the woman did all the housework (Hansen, 2012). Women *willingly* did the housework - they were not being forced to do it. Traditional roles mean there are clear rules for each person. Traditional roles may also be the result of **innate** differences as a result of evolutionary processes - men are predisposed to provide resources from outside the home; women are predisposed to care and **nurture** inside the home.

Arranged marriages

Arranged marriages are normal in several cultures. When a marriage is arranged, it means that the people who get married do not choose their partner alone. Normally the parents make the decision or, in some cases, they find possible partners for their child and let them make the decision. In extreme cases, the person who gets married has no choice at all about the partner or the marriage.

Study 1

Epstein (2012) interviewed 70 couples and also performed a meta-analysis of studies of arranged marriages. He concluded that arranged marriages last longer and are happier because: feelings of love in arranged marriages tend to increase gradually over time; arranged marriages usually happen based on the *recommendation* that it will be a good match from a third party (e.g. parents); feelings (which are very changeable) are not the only factor involved, there is also an intellectual element; 'love marriages', where attraction is based on **passionate** emotions, are less stable as passion decreases over time (e.g. as much as 50 per cent after only 18 to 24 months of marriage).

Study 2

Aim: To test if couples who believe in traditional roles in a marriage have less satisfaction (Ahmad and Reid, 2008).

Method: 114 married people of South Asian **descent** were asked to complete a questionnaire. Only one partner completed the questionnaire, and the researchers used a snowball method to contact participants: the first participants were given copies of the questionnaire to give to friends and family. The questionnaire contained questions about their attitudes towards marriage, their communication style in the marriage, and their satisfaction with the marriage.

Results: There was no direct relationship between beliefs about traditional roles and satisfaction. However, there was a connection between these beliefs and the listening style in the relationship. Those who have traditional beliefs and did not listen in order to understand their partner were less likely to be satisfied.

Conclusion: Arranged marriages with beliefs about traditional roles can be satisfying, but it is necessary for the partners to *practise listening* in order to understand how the other partner feels. This is important because it suggests that communication may have a stronger role in maintaining happy relationships than the cultural factors that cause people to marry.

Glossary

equality having the same status

innate a quality or ability you are born with

to nurture/nurturing to take care of a child in terms of education, and the physical and mental attention paid to the person

descent where your family comes from

Synonyms

housework.......... jobs around the home

passionate .... intense

Subject vocabulary

evolutionary processes processes which allow a species to adapt over time to the challenges in its environment

predisposed to be more likely to act or think in a particular way

meta-analysis a review of many studies into the same phenomena to see what broad conclusions can be made

snowball method/sampling the researcher asks existing participants in the study if they know other possible participants who are willing to take part and then these are recruited for the study

Hints for success: This question will only be asked together with another question. There is no need to evaluate the research in this part of the question: the focus should only be on why relationships change and end.

Analyse why relationships may change or end

Opening sentence:

In this answer I will analyse why relationships may change or end.

Reason 1: Communication changes

Study 1

Knapp and Vangelisti (1996) **proposed** a model to describe the stages that people go through from the beginning to the end of a relationship. For example: at the start, people become closer by using 'we' instead of 'I' when talking to other people in order to emphasize their status as a partner. In the later stages, there is less communication and 'I' is used more often. This is a sign that the relationship might end.

Study 2

Key assumption: Communication can maintain relationships. One of the main causes of **divorce** is communicating too much negative emotion.

Aim: To test if older married couples and younger married couples have different ways of managing **conflict**, and to test if this is connected with unhappiness in the marriage (Gottman et al., 2003).

Method: 156 married couples went to a laboratory after not talking to each other for 8 hours. In the laboratory, they were observed discussing three topics, and **physiological** measurements such as heart rate were also taken. The couples discussed what happened that day, and agreed on a pleasant topic and another topic that they knew they would disagree about. The discussions were video recorded and different emotions were observed.

Results: Older couples with longer marriages communicated more **affection** to their partner during the discussions. Couples in unhappy marriages expressed more negative emotions. Couples in happy marriages **displayed** more positive emotions.

Conclusions: People learn to communicate with their partner in a way that avoids negative results. Communication styles change over time in order to maintain relationships.

Reason 2: Cultural changes

- Divorce became easier in some cultures and so became more common. For example: **no-fault divorce** became possible in some US states in the 1950s. Couples no longer needed to prove that one person was responsible for the failure of the marriage. They could simply say that the marriage had broken down. By 1970, almost all states had laws allowing no-fault divorces. From 1940 to 1965, the divorce rate remained near to ten divorces for every 1000 married women. By 1979, the rate was 20 for every 1000 married women.
- Religion has declined in Western societies and is no longer a major influence on people's decisions.

Synonyms

proposed .... suggested

conflict .... disagreements/ a difference

displayed .... showed

Glossary

divorce legal ending of a marriage

affection showing feelings of love or care for another person

no-fault divorce legal ending of a marriage where there is no need to show who is responsible for its failure

Subject vocabulary

physiological relating to the body

- Women have become less dependent on their husbands for economic stability.
- The ***welfare state*** in the UK means women do not need to have a job when they leave their husbands and set up home after a divorce.

Reason 3: Communication problems

Model sentence: Couples who do not talk about their problems are more likely to break up.

- If partners cannot talk to one another then they are less likely to solve problems. Work hours (and travel time) can prevent partners from being able to talk to one another if they are home at different times or they are too tired to start talking about their problems (Duck, 1982).
- The most common causes of conflict in marital relationships include communication, money, children, sex, housework, and **jealousy** (Gottman, 1979; Mead et al., 1990).
- Communication problems may hide deeper problems and these are not solved as there is less communication overall. They may be problems with power and **intimacy** (e.g. disagreements about how much time to spend together; the sharing of house jobs).

1. *Communication styles change over time.*
2. *Successful relationships communicate more affection and show less negative emotion.*
3. *Divorce became easier in some cultures and so became more common. For example: no-fault divorce became possible in some US states in the 1950s. Couples no longer needed to prove that one person was responsible for the failure of the marriage.*
4. *Religion has declined in Western societies and is no longer a major influence on people's decisions.*

Hints for success: This question will only be asked together with another question. There is no need to evaluate the research in this part of the question: the focus should only be on why relationships change or end.

Glossary

welfare state a system where the government helps people with money when they do not have a job

to break up to end a relationship

Synonyms

jealousy .... envy

intimacy .... closeness

Evaluate sociocultural explanations of the origins of violence

Synonyms

origin................. cause

imitation............ copying

Glossary

honour the respect you feel and get from other people

aggression/aggressive behaving in an angry or threatening way

Subject vocabulary

experiment a method where the independent variable is changed to measure the effect on the dependent variable while controlling for other variables

independent variable (IV) the variable an experimenter controls or changes

dependent variable (DV) the variable an experimenter measures

Opening sentence:

In this answer I will explain and evaluate sociocultural explanations of the **origins** of violence.

I will explain and evaluate *Social Learning Theory* and the *Culture of* ***Honour*** theory.

Explanation 1: Social Learning Theory

Model sentence: Social Learning Theory can explain how we learn aggression from people around us.

Supporting study: Bobo doll experiment

Aim(s): To show that learning can occur through observation alone of a model and that **imitation** can occur when the model is not present.

Method: Children were shown either an aggressive model playing with a Bobo doll or a non-aggressive model who played with the same doll in a non-aggressive way (independent variable – IV). All children then went into a room which contained both aggressive toys (e.g. a 3-foot-high Bobo doll, a mallet, dartguns, and a tether ball) and non-aggressive toys (e.g. a tea set, dolls, and colouring paper), and levels of aggressive behaviour (dependent variable – DV) were observed.

Results: Children in the aggressive model condition copied the model's physical and verbal aggression and the model's non-aggressive verbal responses significantly more than children who saw the non-aggressive model. Children in the non-aggressive model condition showed very little aggression. Boys would imitate male models significantly more than girls for physical and verbal aggression. Boys imitated male models more than female models. Girls imitated female models more than boys. Children exposed to the aggressive model were also more likely to act in *verbally* aggressive way than those who were not exposed to the aggressive model.

Conclusion: Aggression can be learnt from role models. The gender of the role model is important.

How does the theory explain the origins of violence?

The theory is based on a well-conducted study. The study separated key variables (types of aggression; types of model; levels of imitation) while controlling for irrelevant variables (e.g. location, toys, age). It clearly shows that violence can be learnt through imitation. Bandura states that people can learn from observing what happens to others. The models were not punished and this may have encouraged the children to imitate the aggression. SLT is able to explain how watching movies, playing violent video games, or being in a home with a violent role model can lead to violent behaviour.

However: it does not consider biological factors (other than gender). For example, it does not explain why boys are more likely to commit violent acts than girls – particularly when they have been exposed to the same role model.

Explanation 2: Culture of Honour

A culture of honour is a norm. It can be described as follows: when a man has been even slightly **offended** by another person, he must respond with physical violence in order to protect his honour.

Cohen et al. (1996) state that in the southern states of the USA a culture of honour is common.

Supporting study: Aggression in a university corridor

Aim: To test if people from a culture of honour will react more violently to a mild **insult**. The participants were students at a university in the northern part of the USA. Half of them were originally from the south of the USA and half were originally born in the North (Cohen et al., 1996).

Method: 42 Northerners and 41 Southerners were asked to fill out a questionnaire and take it to the end of a long, narrow corridor. A confederate who was working in the corridor **bumped into** the participant and called him an '**asshole**'. He did not bump into or insult members of the control group. Observers recorded emotional reactions such as anger and **amusement**.

Results: Northerners were more likely than Southerners to be amused when the confederate insulted them.

Conclusion: The differences between those students from the North and the South must be cultural. People from an area with social norms that **approve** of violence are more likely to react negatively to insults and are more likely to consider violence an **appropriate** response.

How does the theory explain the origins of violence?

It shows that behaviour can be learnt not only from direct observation of family violence, but also from norms about violence in the culture. This shows how someone who did not grow up in a violent family might become violent.

One limitation of the theory is that it does not focus on individual differences in aggression. For example, not all people from the southern states in the USA are violent. In addition, many people who do not come from a culture of honour are violent; **domestic violence** occurs in most cultures around the world even if there is no culture of honour.

Aggression can be learnt from role models and influenced by culture.

Hints for success: You need to explain at least two theories to answer this question, and you must be sure that when you are evaluating, you evaluate the theory, not just the studies you use. In addition, remember to include a conclusion.

Subject vocabulary

norms expected or usual ways to behave

confederate fake participants who are pretending to not know about the experiment

Glossary

to offend to make someone upset by doing or saying something which is unkind or rude

to insult to say something rude or unkind that upsets another person

to bump into to knock against someone or something

asshole an example of a mild insult

amusement the feeling that something is funny

to approve of to think something is suitable

domestic violence behaviour intended to physically hurt members of the family in the home

Synonyms

appropriate .... suitable

Discuss the relative effectiveness of two strategies for reducing violence

Opening sentence:

In this answer I will discuss the relative **effectiveness** of two strategies for **reducing** **violence**.

Effectiveness can be judged in two main ways: firstly, do violent individuals become less violent because of the strategy; and, secondly, is there less violence in society because of the strategy?

Strategy 1: Group treatment

Group treatment is when several different people who have carried out acts of **domestic violence** visit a **therapist** or **counsellor**. It includes anger-management training, which helps people identify what makes them angry and how to manage their anger without violence.

Example: The Broward County experiment in Florida

Aim: To test the effectiveness of group treatment compared with no treatment for men who had been **convicted of** domestic violence (Feder and Dugan, 2002).

Method: 404 males aged between 19 and 71 who had been convicted of domestic violence were put into either the experimental group, which received 26 weeks of group treatment, or the control group, which received no treatment. The researchers looked at **police** and **probation records** and interviews with the men to judge the effectiveness of the **programme** after 6 and 12 months.

Results: There was no **significant difference** between the control group and the experimental group in terms of their attitudes towards women or in the amount of violence they carried out after treatment. However, those who attended more sessions **committed** less crime afterwards. Those who were older and who had jobs for a longer time also committed less violence.

Conclusions: Group treatment is not enough: attention needs to be paid to the other factors that influence **motivation** such as employment.

Strengths:

- Group treatment is relatively cheap compared with individual treatment.
- When new **perpetrators** join a group that includes older, more **reformed** members who have already learnt not to be violent, the older members can be role models for the new members.

Limitations:

- It cannot change the social and cultural causes of violence, such as a culture's attitudes towards women and violence.
- **Participants** can learn more about violence and possibly learn new ways to express power at home and avoid being arrested.
- Participants have usually not chosen to participate. This is not a problem of the treatment, but it can help explain why it is not perfectly effective: participants may be very **resistant** to **compulsory** treatment.

Glossary

effectiveness how successful something is

to reduce/reduction to make something smaller in size

domestic violence behaviour intended to physically hurt members of the family in the home

therapist a person who is trained to give particular types of medical treatment

counsellor a person who provides help for people with problems

to be convicted of to be guilty of a crime

police records information about a person's criminal behaviour

probation records information about the behaviour of criminal who is not sent to prison for a crime that they have done. Instead, they can remain in society but they must behave well

programme a course of education

to commit to do

to motivate/motivation a reason to want to do something

perpetrator a person who does something wrong or illegal

to reform to change something for the better

be resistant to not want to do

compulsory something that you have to do

Subject vocabulary

violence behaviour that is intended to hurt someone physically

experiment a method where the independent variable is changed to measure the effect on the dependent variable while controlling for other variables

significant difference a difference that has been identified by using mathematical tests and that can be considered large enough for social scientists to look for causes

participant someone who takes part in a research study

Strategy 2: Primary prevention

Primary **prevention** means stopping something from happening as early as possible. In the case of domestic violence, this means trying to educate young people so that when they are older they are not violent.

The main aims are to make young people think about causes and effects of violence and **alternative** solutions, and to give them training in better social skills in order to prevent **conflict**.

It is very difficult to judge how effective this approach is because we do not know which young people might become violent in the future. The only way to consider effectiveness is to look at **rates** of domestic violence in society.

Example: The Safe Dates programme (Foshee et al., 2004)

Aim: To test the effectiveness of the Safe Dates programme in schools after 4 years.

Method: In 1994, several schools in North Carolina in the United States ran a Safe Dates programme. This programme intended to raise awareness about the differences between healthy, supportive relationships and **abusive** relationships between young people in the early stages of a close relationship. Participants were also taught effective ways to deal with conflict in relationships. Four years later, this study investigated the rates of violence carried out by participants and carried out on participants to see if there was a long-term effect.

Results: Those who had taken part in the Safe Dates programme reported much less violence, either as **victims** or perpetrators, than the control group.

Conclusion: The Safe Dates programme had significant, positive long-term benefits for participants and therefore seems to be a good strategy for reducing violence.

Strengths:

- It tries to solve many **underlying** causes of violence, such as social norms, and therefore it is able to stop violence before it happens, not just react to it.
- It does not only focus on perpetrators. For example, the Safe Dates programme also focuses on helping people avoid becoming victims. Therefore it may be effective for everyone who takes part in the programme.

Limitations:

- Longitudinal studies have not measured the effects for long enough: the Safe Dates study measured effects up to 4 years, which is a long time for a study like this, but 4 years is still a short time in a person's life.
- This is a problem because there may be important differences at the beginning between participants who complete the programme and those who do *not* complete the programme.

Hints for success: The question asks you to discuss. Therefore, you do not need to make a conclusion about which strategy is better. 'Discuss' requires balance so make sure you include the strengths and limitations of both strategies.

Glossary

prevention programme a course of education to stop something from happening

rate the speed at which something happens, like a heart beating

date a romantic meeting

to abuse/abusive to be physically and/or verbally violent

victim a person who suffers as the result of something bad happening to them

Synonyms

alternative .... other

conflict .... disagreement/ a difference

underlying .... basic/root

Subject vocabulary

social norms expected or usual ways to behave

longitudinal study research that has taken place over a long period of time, usually years

Discuss the effects of short-term and long-term exposure to violence

Opening sentence:

In this answer I will discuss the effects of short-term and long-term **exposure** to violence.

Exposure to violence means seeing **aggression** or being the **victim** of aggression.

Short-term exposure means exposure for a short time, for example one **incident** of violence. Long-term exposure means months or years of exposure to violence.

Short-term exposure to violence

Supporting study: Bobo doll experiment

Aim(s): To show that learning can occur through observation alone of a model and that **imitation** can occur when the model is not present.

Method: Children were shown either an aggressive model playing with a Bobo doll or a non-aggressive model who played with the same doll in a non-aggressive way (independent variable – IV). All children then went into a room which contained both aggressive toys (e.g. a 3-foot-high Bobo doll, a mallet, dartguns, and a tether ball) and non-aggressive toys (e.g. a tea set, dolls, and colouring paper), and levels of aggressive behaviour (dependent variable – DV) were observed.

Results: Children in the aggressive model condition copied the model's physical and verbal aggression and the model's non-aggressive verbal responses significantly more than children who saw the non-aggressive model. Children in the non-aggressive model condition showed very little aggression. Boys would imitate male models significantly more than girls for physical and verbal aggression. Boys imitated male models more than female models. Girls imitated female models more than boys. Children exposed to the aggressive model were also more likely to act in *verbally* aggressive way than those who were not exposed to the aggressive model.

Conclusion: Aggression can be learnt from role models. The gender of the role model is important.

The study separated key variables (types of aggression; types of model; levels of imitation) while controlling for irrelevant variables (e.g. location, toys, age). It clearly shows that violence can be learnt through imitation. Bandura states that people can learn from observing what happens to others. The models were not **punished** and this may have encouraged the children to imitate the aggression. SLT (Social Learning Theory) is able to explain how watching movies, playing violent video games, or being in a home with a violent role model can lead to violent behaviour. The children reacted immediately (within minutes) and were directly imitating the same behaviour (including verbal statements) as the models.

Glossary

exposure having contact with/ experience of

aggression/aggressive behaving in an angry or threatening way

victim a person who suffers as the result of something bad happening to them

incident an event or situation where something happens

to punish to make a person suffer for something they have done which is wrong

Synonyms

imitation............ copying

Subject vocabulary

experiment a method where the independent variable is changed to measure the effect on the dependent variable while controlling for other variables

independent variable (IV) the variable an experimenter controls or changes

dependent variable (DV) the variable an experimenter measures

Social Learning Theory (SLT) a theory that states behaviour (in particular aggression) can be learnt from the environment

Long-term exposure to violence

Example 1: Physical and mental health of men

Aim: To test what mental health problems are present in men who are victims or **perpetrators** of domestic violence (Rhodes et al., 2002).

Method: Men who visited a public hospital for **non-urgent** physical treatment were asked to complete a 20-minute health assessment questionnaire on a computer. Over 1000 men completed the questionnaire, which asked about their exposure to violence and their own mental health. The researchers compared the **symptoms** of mental health problems in men who were victims and/or perpetrators of violence, and those who reported no violence.

Results: The least mental health problems were found in men who reported no violence at home. The worst mental health problems were found in men who were both victims and perpetrators of violence at home. For example, **suicidal thoughts** were reported by 0.7 per cent who were not exposed to violence, 3.5 per cent who were victims of violence, 2.5 per cent who were perpetrators of violence, and 23.4 per cent who were both a victim and a perpetrator of violence. Depression rates were similar.

Conclusion: Long-term exposure causes symptoms of psychological disorders in men, both those who are the victim and the perpetrator of violence.

Model sentence: Men who commit violence may also suffer long-term psychological health problems such as depression and suicidal thoughts.

Example 2: Battered woman syndrome

The main **assumption** of this condition is that when a woman has been exposed to violence for a long period of time, she begins to **empathize** with her partner (usually the husband) and **blame** herself for the violence.

Aim: To investigate differences between women who are victims of domestic violence and women who are not victims (Anson and Sagy, 1995).

Method: Women who gave birth in one particular hospital were invited to take part in an interview. Over 150 completed the interview. Women who reported at least one incident of violence in the last year were **classified** as 'in a violent relationship' and their responses were compared with those who did not report at least one incident of violence in the last year.

Results: 18 per cent of the women were classified as being in a violent relationship. These women were more likely to consider **marital violence** normal or *to blame themselves for the violence.* They were more likely to judge their *partner* as being unhappy.

Conclusions: There is some evidence that women in violent relationships try to empathize with their partner.

Model sentence: The long-term effects on women who are exposed to violence may mean they start to empathize with their perpetrators of the violence.

Hints for success: Because the learning outcome is 'discuss', you do not need to have a conclusion, but you may write one if you want. Make sure that you include the research and evaluate what you are writing so that you are not just describing the effects of violence.

Glossary

perpetrator a person who does something wrong or illegal

symptoms signs of an illness

suicidal thoughts thinking about killing oneself

to batter to hit

to assume/assumption to think that something is true but without any evidence to prove it

to empathize to be able to understand the feelings of others

to blame to say that someone is responsible for something bad

to classify to put into a group

marital violence behaviour between people who are married which intends to physically hurt the other person

Synonyms

non-urgent .... not serious

Subject vocabulary

psychological disorders abnormal behaviour which needs treatment

syndrome a collection of symptoms that form together to make a clearly recognizable illness

domestic violence violence that takes place inside the home

GLO 1: To what extent do biological, cognitive, and sociocultural factors influence human relationships?

Biological factors

Model sentence: Biological factors can be used to explain attraction in humans.

Assumption: Attraction has a survival purpose. It is known as having an *adaptive function*.

This is shown by:

Males and females find different **characteristics** attractive. Males generally prefer younger women and they pay attention to physical details such as **breast** size and shape, teeth and lip colour, hair length and shine, hip size and smooth skin. These represent **fertility** as female fertility is limited by age, so signs of youthfulness are sought out by men. Females generally prefer older men and they pay attention to **ambition**, wealth, intelligence, height, energy levels, and good health. These represent the ability to provide for any **offspring**. These general characteristics have cross-cultural support.

Biological origins assume attraction occurs between two people because the combination of their genes with the other person's genes would result in healthy offspring. The assumption is based on the idea that pheromones contained in **sweat** can provide information about a person's immune system. It is assumed that genetically *different* immune systems **complement** each other and the mixture of the two immune systems should produce a child with a good immune system.

Supporting study: Sweaty t-shirts

Aim: To test if a woman will judge a sweaty t-shirt as more attractive if it is from a man with different immune system genes (Wedekind et al., 1995).

Method: 49 female and 44 male students were tested to see what type of immune system genes they had. The males were asked to wear a plain white t-shirt for two days. The t-shirts were then put in closed boxes until the females were asked to smell them. They were asked to judge the shirts for pleasantness and sexiness.

Results: The women judged the t-shirts to be more pleasant and sexy if they came from a man with a different set of immune genes.

Conclusion: People are instinctively **motivated** to find a mate with different immune system genes so that the offspring will have stronger immune systems.

Cognitive factors

Attraction

Psychological origins of attraction assume that psychological events (such as *fear*) interact with biological processes (such as *arousal*) *and this* can lead to attraction. Dutton and Aron (1974) suggest that attraction occurs when physiological arousal is *interpreted* as sexual excitement.

Subject vocabulary

biological related to biological processes (such as the effects of hormones, neurotransmitters, genes, and gender)

cognition/cognitive related to mental processes (such as perception, memory, problem-solving)

sociocultural (factors) related to social and cultural issues

attraction when a person experiences interest in forming some kind of relationship with another person

adaptive function/response an adaption that is the result of the processes of evolution that makes the organism better adapted to the environment and therefore more likely to survive

attractive beautiful, good looking

origins causes

pheromones chemicals that make people smell

immune system the physiological system that protects us from sickness

arousal bodily and psychological alertness

physiological related to the body

Synonyms

characteristics..... traits/features

offspring............ young/babies

Glossary

to assume/assumption to think that something is true but without any evidence to prove it

breasts the two round parts on a woman's chest which produce milk when she has a baby

fertility the ability to have babies

ambition a strong wish to be successful, powerful, and rich

sweat/sweaty salty liquid produced by the body

to complement to make a good combination

to motivate/motivation a reason to want to do something

Supporting study: Love on a bridge

Aim: To test if physiological arousal can influence attraction (Dutton and Aron, 1974).

Method: The researchers selected two bridges in Canada. One bridge was higher and shook more than the other and was therefore more frightening. A female interviewer stopped men between 18 and 35 years old and asked them various questions. She then asked them to write a story connected with a picture she gave them. She gave them the telephone number of the psychology department and said they could call if they wanted to talk further. She told participants a different name depending on which bridge they were on.

Independent variable (IV): Levels of fear and arousal operationalized by type of bridge (one was higher and shook more and the other was lower and did not shake).

Dependent variable (DV): Levels of attraction operationalized by number of phone calls (quantitative data) and levels of sexual content in stories (qualitative data).

Results: Only two of the 16 men from the regular bridge called the phone number, compared with nine out of 18 from the frightening bridge. In addition, there was more sexual content in the stories from the frightening bridge.

Conclusions: Attraction is stronger when there is more physiological arousal from the danger of the bridge. The researchers suggest that attraction occurs when physiological arousal is *interpreted* as sexual excitement.

Sociocultural factors

Model sentence: Research testing cultural differences in bystanderism assumes that behaviour is influenced by economic development and by cultural notions such as simpatia.

For example, one idea is that helping behaviour is more common in less economically developed cultures and in those cultures that have the notion of simpatia.

Supporting study

Aim: To compare the **rate** of helping behaviour in different cities around the world (Levine et al., 2001).

Method: 23 countries were chosen around the world, and the researchers visited one major city in each of these countries. They recorded how often someone helped in the following conditions: a person pretending to be blind waiting to cross the road; a person walking along the street in a **leg brace** and dropping magazines; a person dropping a pen while walking along the street.

Results: Rio de Janeiro (Brazil) and San Jose (Costa Rica) were the cities considered to be most helpful in the three situations. They are both cities with low levels of economic development. Sofia (Bulgaria), Amsterdam (Holland), and Singapore (Singapore) were the cities considered to be the least helpful. Amsterdam and Singapore are considered to be cities with high levels of economic development.

Conclusion: Countries with low economic development tend to have stronger values about the importance of **ethical** behaviour in a community.

Subject vocabulary

participant someone who takes part in a research study

independent variable (IV) the variable an experimenter controls or changes

to operationalize *how* the IV is changed and *how* the DV is measured

dependent variable (DV) the variable an experimenter measures

simpatia concern for the social well-being of others

Glossary

bystander a person who watches something that is happening but does not take part

leg brace a support which is placed around the leg to help the person move about

ethical relating to the idea of what is right and wrong

Synonyms

notions .... ideas

rate .... level/ amount

GLO 2: Evaluate psychological research (that is, theories and/or studies) relevant to the study of human relationships

Model sentence: Social Learning Theory can explain how we learn aggression from the social environment around us. It can be evaluated by:

Positives

- The Bolso doll study separated key variables (types of aggression; types of model; levels of **imitation**) while controlling irrelevant variables (e.g. location, toys, age) and clearly showed that behaviour can be learnt through imitation.
- Gender was taken into consideration in terms of the models and the children.

Negatives

- In the 1960s, gender was probably a clearer concept than it is today. Care should be taken when applying the results to a modern situation as they relate to 'gender'.
- Very strange adult behaviour (hitting the doll together with unusual aggressive words such as '**sock him on the nose**') is not usual for children to see.
- The non-aggressive model was *also* very strange with an adult playing with a doll (non-aggressively) for 10 minutes.
- The doll is designed to be hit which could be seen as encouraging the children's aggressive behaviour.
- Aggression was taught to children although the behaviour was well within the normal behavioural norms of this age group.
- Care should be taken when generalizing the findings to a modern environment as the study is very culturally specific both in terms of when (1960s) and where (USA) it took place.
- The **artificial** nature of the experiment means that care should be taken when generalizing the results to real life situations such as domestic violence.

Model sentence: Social Identity Theory (SIT) assumes we establish relationships with members of different groups and label them as in-groups and out-groups. The resulting social identity can influence our behaviour.

In an emergency we are more likely to help someone if there is a degree of similarity.

Supporting study

Aim: To test whether Manchester United football fans are more likely to help a fan of the same football team than a fan of a different team (Levine et al., 2005).

Method: Manchester United fans walked between two buildings at the university. A male confederate ran past each participant, wearing either a Manchester United football shirt, a Liverpool football shirt, or a plain white shirt. After the man fell over and pretended to be hurt, observers recorded how much help the participants gave him.

Subject vocabulary

Social Learning Theory (SLT) a theory that states behaviour (in particular aggression) can be learnt from the environment

to generalize/generalization the extent to which we can apply results to other circumstances

violence behaviour that is intended to hurt someone physically

in-group the group we are in or we want to be in

confederate fake participants who are pretending that they do not know about the experiment

Glossary

aggression/aggressive behaving in an angry or threatening way

sock him on the nose hit him on the nose

Synonyms

imitation .... copying

artificial .... not real/unnatural

Evaluation:

Positives

- This was a very **robust** study as there was a clear IV (type of t-shirt) and clear DV (how much help they gave the man who fell over). This means that there is a cause-effect relationship. The control group was also very clear (plain white t-shirt).
- Ethically this was a good study because only a low level of deception was used.
- It has ecological validity (it is common to see people wearing football t-shirts).

Negatives

- The extent to which the study can be generalized to women is limited because it was a male confederate who needed help. If it had been a female confederate than the level of help may have increased.

Hints for success: Always use previously learnt material to support a GLO answer and use examples of research to support each point that you make.

Synonyms

robust................. strong

Subject vocabulary

cause-effect relationship where there is confidence that the effect on the dependent variable (DV) has been caused by the manipulation of the independent variable (IV)

control group the group in an experiment that does not experience the manipulation of the variable

to deceive/deception to make someone believe something that is not true

ecological validity having realism and being able to generalize to real-life situations

Evaluate theories of motivation in sport

Subject vocabulary

motivation wanting or a desire to do something

self-efficacy feelings of confidence in one's ability to do something

expectation what you think or hope will happen

arousal bodily and psychological alertness

feedback a response that gives information

face validity a theory of method that appears to work or make sense. This is especially useful for non-experts

self-report method a type of data collection method (e.g. survey, questionnaire) where participants read the question and select a response by themselves without researcher interference

participant someone who takes part in a research study

correlation a relationship between variables

Synonyms

desire .... want

efficacy........... effectiveness

persuasion...... encouragement

coach.............. trainer

appropriate .... suitable

Glossary

performance how well a person does something

peer a person who is the same age as you or has the same position in society

to investigate to try to find the reasons for something

aerobics a type of exercise

Opening sentence:

In this answer I will evaluate two theories of motivation in sport. Motivation can be defined as the **desire** to do something. In sports psychology, theories of motivation try to explain the desire to play or compete in sports.

Model sentence: I will evaluate Self-Efficacy Theory and Achievement Goal Theory with reference to studies.

Theory 1: Self-Efficacy Theory

Self-Efficacy Theory is a social-cognitive theory that focuses on the role of a person's *expectations*. Bandura (1997) wrote about outcome expectations and **efficacy** expectations.

- Outcome expectations are our expectations about what behaviour will lead to a particular result.
- Efficacy expectations are our expectations about our ability to actually do this.

Bandura suggests that we learn our expectations through successful **performance**, indirect experience, verbal **persuasion** (such as a **coach**'s voice and a person's own voice) and emotional arousal. These are all obtained through training. Feedback is obtained from our **peers**, coaches, and teachers, but also from our own bodies.

Model sentence: According to self-efficacy theory, our motivation will be highest when we have appropriate knowledge and skills and high efficacy expectations for a particular task. We are motivated to do things that we believe we can do.

Strengths

It has very good *face validity*: sportspeople and coaches around the world can easily understand the idea as it *seems* to make sense.

It is *useful* because it gives some clear suggestions for psychologists and coaches about how they can improve motivation and performance through self-efficacy.

Limitations

It is very difficult to measure self-efficacy. Most studies use self-report measures, and even if participants try to tell the truth, they may not feel comfortable saying that they are very confident about their abilities.

Most of the research into self-efficacy is correlational. This means that we cannot be sure if self-efficacy is a cause or an effect of motivation and performance. People who are very motivated may also become more confident in their abilities. However, those with high levels of talent may become more confident.

Supporting study: Self-efficacy and aerobics

Aim: To **investigate** reasons for participation in **aerobics** for exercise (McAuley, Wraith, and Duncan, 1991). Many people begin exercise for external reasons such as health or appearance, but continuing to exercise may be related to more internal factors such as self-efficacy.

Method: 265 participants who were doing university aerobic dance classes, including only 11 males, completed questionnaires in the ninth week of their class. The questionnaires measured motivation, self-efficacy for aerobics, and **perceptions** of success.

Results: Participants with high levels of self-efficacy were more motivated than others, whether they were beginners or more advanced.

Conclusion: Self-efficacy is an important factor that influences how motivated people are to continue with exercise programmes.

Synonyms

perceptions .... opinions/understanding

Theory 2: Achievement Goal Theory

People involved in sports can have two different goal orientations (a goal orientation is a way to interpret the meaning of success in sport):

1. Task orientation - people who are more task oriented focus on improving skill or knowledge.
2. Ego orientation - people who are more ego oriented focus on being better than others.

Task orientation and goal orientation are separate from each other. A person can be high on one or both orientations.

Subject vocabulary

ego orientation a focus on the self

Strengths

It can clearly explain the differences between many people who do sport.

It is quite simple to measure using self-report questionnaires because this kind of motivation is very conscious: people usually know if they are task oriented or goal oriented.

It is very useful because it allows coaches to identify each individual's motivation and to try and deal with them appropriately. For example, not everyone in a team will be motivated to be better than other people. As a result training should include opportunities both for internal team competition and for individual skill development in order to keep team members interested.

Limitation

It does not explain differences in skill level and the effect these have on motivation.

Supporting study: Males versus females, individuals versus teams

Aim: To investigate differences in goal orientation among male and females in individual and team sports (Hanrahan and Cerin, 2009). Individual sports are those where the individual performs alone (e.g. swimming or golf). In team sports the whole team performs at the same time (e.g. football).

Method: Questionnaires were given to 272 Australian athletes who spent on average 9 months a year doing team and individual sports. The questionnaire contained items about their goal orientation.

Results: There were no differences between males and females in how much ego orientation they had, but females had a stronger *task orientation* at all levels of sport than males. Those who played individual sports had a higher ego orientation.

Conclusion: People who have a high ego orientation are more attracted to individual sports because these sports give clear feedback about who is best.

Hints for success: You might be asked to evaluate one or two theories. If you are asked to evaluate two, it is not necessary to compare them.

Using one or more research studies, explain the role of goal-setting in the motivation of individuals

Opening sentence:

In this answer I will explain the role of goal-setting in the **motivation** of individuals with reference to research.

Motivation and goal-setting

Motivation can be defined as the **desire** to do something. In sports psychology, theories of motivation try to explain the desire to play or compete in sports.

Some psychologists suggest that all behaviour is goal-directed and therefore it is important to understand our motivation in sport according to how we set goals. A goal is the expected result that we want to achieve.

According to goal-setting theory, we are most motivated to **perform** well if our goal is clear and it is something that we can achieve. Coaches and sports psychologists can be very helpful in setting **achievable** goals for sportspeople so that they are motivated.

Model sentence: There are four requirements for goals to be motivating (Locke et al., 1981):

1. Goals must be clear and specific (e.g. not just to win, because that is too **vague**).
2. Goals should be difficult to achieve.
3. Goals must be accepted by the person who has to achieve them.
4. Feedback must be **provided**, **preferably** about progress towards the goal.

Research study: Goal-setting and behaviour change (Schofield et al., 2005)

Model sentence: The effectiveness of goal-setting is shown in this experiment that clearly shows that appropriate goals cause an increase in motivation.

Aim: To test if goal-setting really can cause increased motivation to **participate** in exercise (Schofield et al., 2005).

Method: 85 teenage girls who were identified as 'low-active' from different schools were divided into three different groups. One group received a pedometer, a small **device** that can be attached to a person's belt to count the number of steps they take. This device was used to set a goal of a certain number of steps per day, and feedback about progress was constantly available. A second group was given time-based goals; they were asked to walk for a set period of time each day. The control group received nothing. The participants were asked about their physical activity before the study, then after 6 and 12 weeks. For the pedometer group, the device provided them with a quantitative measure of their exercise level.

Subject vocabulary

goal a target, something a person wants to achieve

to set goals to decide what you want to do and how you are going to achieve it

feedback a response that gives information

participant someone who takes part in a research study

quantitative measure data that usually involves numbers

Glossary

to motivate/motivation a reason to want to do something

to perform/performance to do

achievable something that you can succeed in doing

effectiveness how successful something is

to participate to take part in something

Synonyms

desire .... want

requirements ...... needs

vague .... unclear

provided .... made available

preferably .... the best option

device .... machine

Results: After 6 weeks, the group using the pedometer increased their physical activity the most. After 12 weeks, the group with time-based goals was showing the same increase in physical activity as the pedometer group. Both were much higher than the control group.

Conclusion: Motivation can be increased quickly by using appropriate goal-setting that meets the four requirements above (for example, the pedometers were very clear and gave immediate feedback. However, it is still effective to use goals that do not meet these requirements.

Motivation can be defined as the desire to do something. In sports psychology, theories of motivation try to explain the desire to play or compete in sports.

According to goal-setting theory, we are most motivated to perform well if our goal is clear and it is something that we can achieve. Coaches and sports psychologists can be very helpful in setting achievable goals for sportspeople so that they are motivated.

Hints for success: This question can only be asked together with another question because the learning outcome is 'explain'. You do not need to evaluate goal-setting theory, but you need to link the study to the theory by mentioning the four requirements for goals to be motivating.

Discuss theories relating arousal and anxiety to performance

Subject vocabulary

arousal bodily and psychological alertness

anxiety a state of fear and uncertainty

physiological relating to the body

hormone a chemical messenger that transports a signal from one cell to another. Hormones differ from neurotransmitters as they travel through the blood stream while neurotransmitters travel across synapses (the gaps) between neurons

response time the amount of time a sportsperson responds to a stimulus

inverted U a U shape upside down

hypothesis the idea being tested by the study

face validity a theory or method that appears to work or make sense. This is especially useful for non-experts

phenomenon a fact or situation that is observed to exist or happen

ethical relating to the idea of right or wrong behaviour

cognition/cognitive related to mental processes (such as perception, memory, problem-solving)

Glossary

to perform/performance to do

to activate/activated to make something work or switch something on

talent skill

to define to describe correctly

Opening sentence:

In this answer I will discuss two theories linking arousal and anxiety to **performance**.

Arousal and anxiety

Arousal is a physiological state that prepares the body for action. Through the release of hormones and the **activation** of various parts of the brain, a person's alertness increases and their response times decrease.

Arousal can be helpful but also sometimes brings anxiety, which includes uncomfortable physical feelings and worrying thoughts, and these are sometimes responsible for problems in performance.

Theory 1: Inverted-U hypothesis

This theory tries to explain why people who experience high anxiety sometimes begin to perform very badly. For example, many football players make terrible mistakes in very important games, for example, missing a penalty kick in the final game of a competition. However, some arousal is also helpful for performance. Many players find their **talent** seems to change when they are under stress; some give their best performance, others give their worst.

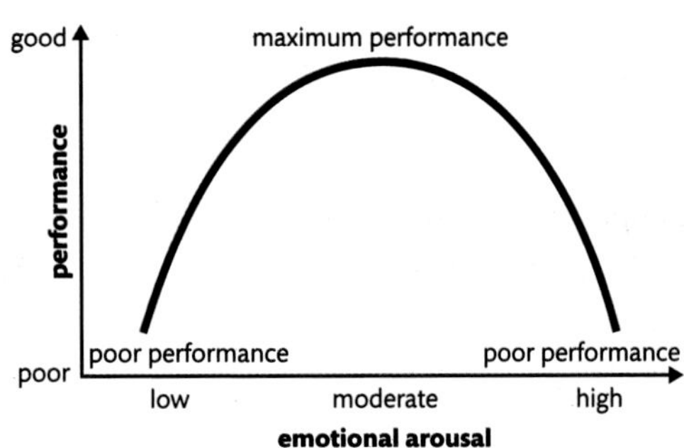

Inverted U-hypothesis graph of performance against arousal.

The name of the theory describes the shape of a graph in which performance is measured against arousal. At first, performance increases with arousal, but after a certain point, it begins to drop. The highest performance is associated with moderate arousal, and the worst performance is associated with very low or very high arousal.

Strength: It has face validity: it describes and explains a phenomenon that has been experienced by many sportspeople and coaches.

Limitation: The theory makes it very difficult to conduct true experiments because it is not ethical to cause high levels of anxiety. This means we cannot be sure about the effect of anxiety on performance. This is a general problem with theories about anxiety in sport.

A general problem with theories about anxiety and arousal in sport is that these terms have not been clearly **defined**. For example, anxiety is not usually divided into physical and cognitive types, and these can have very different effects. In addition, it is not always clear that there is a direct relationship between arousal and anxiety. It is difficult to know at what point arousal changes into anxiety.

Supporting study: Yips

Yips are something that happens to some golfers when they are under pressure. They suddenly lose their ability to swing the golf club correctly, either hitting the ball too hard or too softly.

Aim: To investigate the relationship between physiological arousal and performance in golf (Smith et al., 2000).

Method: Golfers who reported (by questionnaire) that they had the yips took part in an experiment which tested muscle **tension** in their arm, **grip** strength, and heart **rate** in various different situations on the golf course.

Results: The participants who had the yips had worse performance and a higher average heart rate than the others. They also gripped their clubs more tightly than golfers who did not have the yips.

Conclusions: Anxiety levels are associated with the yips. Performance decreases in golfers who experience high levels of arousal.

Theory 2: Individual Zone of **Optimal** Functioning (IZOF) theory

IZOF is similar to the inverted-U hypothesis because it also states that the relationship between anxiety, arousal, and performance is not simple. Some arousal is necessary for good performance, but it suggests that each person has a *zone of optimal arousal:* a person will perform well as long as he or she is aroused at approximately the right level for that person.

Strength: It tries to explain *individual differences* in performance in different sports. It is useful: it is quite simple to study an individual **athlete**'s performance, to identify their IZOF, and to help them work out strategies to increase or decrease their arousal.

Limitation: It does not clearly **distinguish between** anxiety and arousal. Most researchers who use the theory test for anxiety; they do not measure arousal. While there is usually a relationship between arousal and anxiety in people, individuals can be high on only one of these. For example, a person could be physiologically aroused but not be very anxious.

Supporting study: **Finnish** athletes

Aim: To test if IZOF theory explains differences in performance in a group of Finnish athletes (Salminen et al., 1995).

Method: Athletes (runners, gymnasts, and ice skaters) were asked to remember how they felt before a successful competition and completed a questionnaire about their anxiety levels. This was done to calculate each person's zone of optimal functioning. Next, they completed a questionnaire before an actual competition to test if their pre-competition anxiety was in their own zone of optimal functioning or not. After the competition, they were asked to rate their level of **satisfaction** with their performance from 0 to 10.

Results: For the most important competitions, being in the zone *did* predict performance satisfaction. However, for less important competitions, this was less true.

Conclusion: IZOF theory appears to accurately explain satisfaction with performance for more important competitions. This means that those people who stay within their optimal zone of arousal before an important competition are more likely to be successful.

Glossary

tension tightness or stiffness

to grip to hold something tightly in the hand

rate the speed at which something happens, like a heart beating

athlete a sportsperson

to distinguish between to recognize the difference between two or more things

Finnish a person from Finland

Synonyms

optimal .... the highest point/best/ideal

satisfaction .... happiness

Subject vocabulary

yips difficulties controlling movement because of anxiety

individual differences differences between people

Hints for success: When you are asked to discuss, you must remember to include research and to include some negative and some positive comments about the theories.

Evaluate techniques for skill development used in sport

Subject vocabulary

mental imagery imagining something in a visual way

technique way of doing something

frontal lobes the front part of the brain associated with planning and judgement

neurons nerves

longitudinal research research that has taken place over a long period of time, usually years

Synonyms

skill .... ability

outcome .... result

injured .... hurt

regain .... get back

Glossary

to activate/activated to make something work or switch something on

to perform/performance to do

ritual something that is always done in the same way in the same situation

water polo a ball game played in a swimming pool with two teams

to take a penalty a chance to have a kick/hit the ball into the goal because the other team has broken a rule

to personalize to make something that is suitable for one particular person

Opening sentence:

In this answer I will evaluate *mental imagery* and *self-talk*.

Model sentence: Skill development can be defined as improving the skills that are important in a sport. Coaches and psychologists try to help sportspeople develop their skills by using various techniques.

Technique 1: Mental imagery

Mental imagery is a technique in which sportspeople use their imagination to see good **outcomes** – for example, kicking a ball into the correct place in goal.

It can be used to learn new skills, to improve existing skills, or to reduce anxiety. It is also useful for sportspeople who are **injured** and need to **regain** skill or confidence.

Strengths

- There are biological explanations for how the theory may work: various parts of the frontal lobes are **activated** when people imagine doing something, and these are also activated during physical **performance**. Therefore, *from the brain's point of view*, using mental imagery may be as good as physical practice for the brain.
- Mental imagery causes mirror neurons to be activated. Mirror neurons are neurons that are active when we observe *other people's* behaviour (Rizzolatti, 2004).

Model sentence: When a sportsperson watches others and then imagines himself or herself doing the same action this is a form of practice for the brain.

Limitation

It is difficult to know whether the participants are really using imagery in the way that they were taught. It is also difficult to know whether a control group is *not* using mental imagery.

It is not clear whether using mental imagery is a cause or an effect of skill development. Longitudinal research could help by showing changes over time. It is possible that poor sportspeople are also bad at imagining successful performance, and therefore mental imagery may not work for everyone.

Supporting study: Pre-performance rituals in water polo

Aim: To test if using mental imagery can improve water polo players' skill in **taking penalties** (Marlow et al., 1998).

Method: Three experienced water polo players who had never used mental imagery before were interviewed and then given **personalized** pre-performance rituals by a sports psychologist. The rituals included relaxation breathing, concentration focus (staring at the ball to concentrate), and then imagining the perfect shot. Before they started and then several times over a period of weeks, the researchers measured skill development by asking the players to take five penalties and rating them between 1 and 10 according to how similar they were to the perfect shot.

Results: The three players all improved, by 21 per cent, 25 per cent, and 28 per cent compared to their baseline performance.

Conclusion: Mental imagery is a technique that can improve skill development.

Technique 2: Self-talk

Self-talk is statements which a person says to himself or herself. Self-talk can be either instructional or motivational. Instructional self-talk is when athletes remind themselves how to complete a task. For example, a tennis player might remind herself 'Get your feet planted'. Motivational self-talk is when a sportsperson tries to encourage himself or herself, for example 'Come on, you can do it'.

Strengths

It is quite simple to train people to use self-talk as it requires no special equipment, and most people already talk to themselves.

Limitation

It is very difficult to know what kind of things athletes say to themselves. They may or may not be able to tell the researcher what they heard in their own heads.

The cause-effect relationship is unclear. The most successful athletes are also the ones that use self-talk well. Therefore does self-talk improve skill, or does skill improve self-talk?

Supporting study: Self-talk in tennis

Aim: To test the **effectiveness** of self-talk in improving skill in tennis (Hatzigeordiadis et al., 2009).

Method: 72 Greek tennis players were divided into two groups. The first group was the experimental group and they were taught self-talk, for example they should say 'shoulder' to focus their attention on how they moved their shoulder. The other group was a control group who were not taught self-talk. The players then had to perform a difficult shot. The researchers **rated** each shot according to how close it was to the **baseline** on the other side of the court.

Results: The experimental group showed more improvement in the task and a larger increase in **self-confidence**.

Conclusion: Self-talk is an effective way to increase performance.

Mental imagery is a technique in which sportspeople use their imagination to see good outcomes – for example, kicking a ball into the correct place in goal.

Self-talk is statements which a person says to himself or herself. Self-talk can be either instructional or motivational.

Subject vocabulary

baseline original score before an intervention

motivation wanting or a desire to do something

cause-effect relationship where there is confidence that the effect on the dependent variable (DV) has been caused by the manipulation of the independent variable (IV)

Synonyms

effectiveness....... success

Glossary

to rate to judge the level or quality of something

baseline (tennis) the line at the back of a tennis court

self-confidence a person's belief that they can do things effectively

Hints for success:
Remember that 'evaluate' means you need to include both strengths and limitations. Use the supporting studies as examples of the strengths of the theories.

To what extent does the role of coaches affect individual or team behaviour in sport?

Synonyms

coach .... trainer

affects .... influences

climate .... atmosphere

perception .... opinion/ understanding

Glossary

mentor an experienced person who helps and advises a less experienced person

athlete a sportsperson

to motivate/motivation a reason to want to do something

to perform/performance to do

handball a team sport where players score points by throwing a ball into a goal

competence the ability to do something

to drop out to stop attending

Subject vocabulary

self-fulfilling prophecy a situation which you expect will happen and you act in such a way that it does happen

goal orientation being focused on goals

correlation a relationship between variables

Opening sentence:

In this answer I will discuss the extent to which the role of **coaches affects** individual or team behaviour.

The role of the coach can mean five different things: teacher, organizer, competitor, learner, friend/**mentor** (Short and Short, 2005).

People who have the role of coach can influence individual and team behaviour in positive and negative ways.

There is also research that shows that the role of the coach is not as important as other factors.

The main problem in trying to understand the role of coaches is that there are so many factors that influence behaviour. An example of this is the research which found that coaches can often predict who will be successful. However, they also usually spend more time with those **athletes** they think will be successful. This creates a **self-fulfilling prophecy**.

Effect 1: Coaches can create a **motivational climate**

There are two types of motivational climate:

- a *mastery climate* – in which there is a focus on improvement and achieving goals
- a ***performance*** *climate* – where there is a focus on competitive success.

Mastery climates are associated with more motivation, enjoyment and better performance, especially among younger athletes.

Supporting study: Motivational climate in handball

Aim: To investigate the effects of a motivational climate (a mastery climate) on teams of female handball players (Balaguer et al., 2002).

Method: 181 female handball players completed questionnaires which had items about motivational climate, **perceptions** of improvement, **goal orientations**, satisfaction, the coach, and performance. The researchers **correlated** various variables with motivational climate to see what effects this climate has.

Results: Players who reported that the team had a motivational climate also reported feelings of **competence** and a sense of improvement. They did not report more team improvement.

Conclusions: The motivational climate has very positive effects on individual improvement but it did not necessarily have very positive effects on team improvement.

Effect 2: **Dropout** rates

Model sentence: A coach can convince young players to continue with their sport when they are thinking about giving up.

Supporting study: Teenage swimmers and dropout

Aim: To investigate the reasons for dropping out of swimming (Fraser-Thomas et al., 2008).

Method: Semi-structured interviews were conducted with 20 teenage swimmers, ten who had dropped out of the sport, and ten swimmers who had not dropped out. The researchers carried out a *thematic content analysis*. This means that they looked for the same **themes** among one of the groups of teenagers and then they put these together.

Results: There were three main differences relating to the coach: dropouts were less likely to have more than one coach; dropouts were less likely to have a **democratic** relationship with their coach; and dropouts talked more about coaches who ignored weaker swimmers and showed **favouritism** to better swimmers.

Conclusions: The relationship between a coach and an athlete is extremely important as even **subtle** factors in the relationship can cause the athlete to lose motivation.

Effect 3: Coaches can have a democratic coaching style

Model sentence: A democratic coaching style allows team members to make decisions about choosing goals and training routines.

Supporting study: Goal-setting and team cohesion

Team cohesion can be **defined** as 'the tendency for a group to stick together and remain united' as it tries to achieve its objectives and/or as it satisfies its team members' emotional needs (Carron et al., 1998).

Aim: To test if a democratic approach to goal-setting would increase team cohesion (Senecal et al., 2008).

Method: A longitudinal experiment was conducted with 86 female high school basketball players. Half of the teams used a democratic goal-setting **strategy** (independent variable - IV) for the whole **season**, and the other four teams were used as controls, with no intervention. The experimental group chose their goals and decided on their own **targets**. At the beginning and at the end of the study, the researchers measured team cohesion using a questionnaire, and they measured performance (dependent variable - DV) according to the percentage of games won at the end of the season.

Results: The basketball teams had similar **ratings** of team cohesion at the beginning of the season (which were quite high) but the experimental teams who did democratic goal-setting gave significantly higher ratings of team cohesion than the control groups at the end of the season. This was not because their team cohesion increased, but because cohesion among the other groups went down.

Conclusion: Democratic goal-setting is useful as a way to prevent teams becoming less cohesive.

Hints for success: When 'to what extent' is asked, you must remember to provide an answer to the question, and you can do this in the introduction and in the conclusion or summary at the end.

Subject vocabulary

semi-structured interview an interview guide is prepared which lists the topics that should be explored during the interview. The interviewers try to make sure that the same topics are explored with all the participants in the study

thematic content analysis a method of analysis where themes are identified in the participants' responses

to set goals to decide what you want to do and how you are going to achieve it

team cohesion the extent to which a team can stick together while pursuing its objectives

longitudinal something that takes place over a long period of time, usually years

experiment a method where the independent variable is changed to measure the effect on the dependent variable while controlling for other variables

control group the group in an experiment that does not experience the manipulation of the variable

significant difference a difference that has been identified by using mathematical tests and can be considered large enough for social scientists to look for causes

Glossary

theme the main subject or idea

democratic when decisions are made by everyone together

favouritism when you treat one person better than others

routine the usual order in which you do something

strategy a plan of action

season the period when there are sports competitions, e.g. football

target something you are trying to achieve

rating a measurement of how good or interesting something is

Synonyms

subtle .... small/less obvious

defined .... described fully and correctly

Explain relationships between team cohesion and performance

Subject vocabulary

cohesion/cohesive sticking together

task cohesion sticking together to complete a task

social cohesion sticking together socially

team norms expected behaviour in a group

micro-culture norms and behaviours within a small group such as a team or group of friends

Synonyms

train .... practise

commitment....... loyalty/faithfulness

Glossary

to perform/performance to do

off-season the period when there are no competitions in a sport, e.g. football

attachment feelings of loyalty/being faithful to someone or something

to sacrifice to give up something important

to socialize to spend time with friends or people you know

Opening sentence:

In this answer I will explain relationships between team cohesion and **performance**.

Team cohesion can be defined as 'the tendency for a group to stick together and remain united' as it tries to achieve its objectives and/or as it satisfies its team members' emotional needs (Carron et al., 1998).

There are two types of cohesion:

- Task cohesion is how much a team works together to achieve the goals that the members have in common.
- Social cohesion is how much the members of a team enjoy each other's company and like the other members of the team.

Model sentence: There are two reasons why there is a relationship between team cohesion and performance.

Reason 1: Successful teams become more cohesive: in other words, cohesion does not cause better performance, but better performance causes the team to enjoy working together more.

Reason 2: *Team norms* develop over time and are important in the relationship between cohesion and performance. Each team is a micro-culture with its own unwritten rules of behaviour, and each team member will feel pressure to follow these rules. For example, it is more common among some teams to **train** in the **off-season**. It is possible that lazy players will leave these teams, but more active players will fit in and therefore feel more **attachment** to their team. Other norms include **sacrificing** behaviour, such as giving up personal social life. Many high level sportspeople **socialize** with members of their team because their **commitment** to the team means it is difficult to socialize regularly with people who are outside the team. This will lead to high social cohesion because sportspeople who do not want to make sacrifices will probably leave teams which have sacrificing norms.

Model sentence: There is a relationship between team cohesion and performance but it is not necessarily a cause-effect relationship. It cannot be assumed team cohesion leads to better performance because better performance will also lead to greater team cohesion.

Supporting study: Team pressure to work hard

Aim: To examine the importance of team norms in the relationship between team cohesion and performance (Patterson et al., 2005).

Method: 298 adult **athletes** from various team sports took part in the study. They used both interdependent team sports such as football, and co-active team sports such as wrestling and swimming. These participants completed a questionnaire about team norms for **practice**, competition, and social situations.

Results: The greatest effort was shown by teams which had strong norms for **social interaction** and high team social cohesion.

Conclusions: Norms play an important role in the relationship between cohesion and performance but more research is needed to understand it.

Team cohesion can be defined as 'the tendency for a group to stick together and remain united' as it tries to achieve its objectives and/or as it satisfies its team members' emotional needs (Carron et al., 1998).

Successful teams become more cohesive.

Team norms develop over time and are important in the relationship between cohesion and performance.

Each team is a micro-culture with its own unwritten rules of behaviour, and each team member will feel pressure to follow these rules.

Hints for success: Remember that the question asks you to explain *the relationship* between cohesion and performance, not just to explain cohesion or performance.

Synonyms

athletes.............. sportspeople

social interaction socializing

Glossary

to practise/practice to do an activity or using a skill regularly in order to get better at it

Subject vocabulary

cause-effect relationship where there is confidence that the effect on the dependent variable (DV) has been caused by the manipulation of the independent variable (IV)

interdependent sport individual members' performance is dependent on the team (for example, a football team)

co-active sport individual members' performance is independent of the team (for example, a golfing team)

participant someone who takes part in a research study

Describe aids and barriers to team cohesion

Subject vocabulary

aid something that is helpful

barrier something that is unhelpful

goal a target, something a person wants to achieve

to set goals to decide what you want to do and how you are going to achieve it

longitudinal something that takes place over a long period of time, usually years

experiment a method where the independent variable is changed to measure the effect on the dependent variable while controlling for other variables

independent variable (IV) the variable an experimenter controls or changes

control group the group in an experiment that does not experience the manipulation of the variable

dependent variable (DV) the variable an experimenter measures

Glossary

cohesion sticking together

coach a trainer

democratic when decisions are made by everyone together

routine the usual order in which you do something

season the period when there are sports competitions, e.g. football

target something you are trying to achieve

to perform/performance to do

rating a measurement of how good or interesting something is

Opening sentence:

In this answer I describe aids and barriers to team **cohesion**.

Team cohesion can be defined as 'the tendency for a group to stick together and remain united' as it tries to achieve its objectives and/or as it satisfies its team members' emotional needs (Carron et al., 1998).

There are two types of cohesion:

- Task cohesion is how much a team works together to achieve the goals that the members have in common.
- Social cohesion is how much the members of a team enjoy each other's company and like the other members of the team.

Aid 1: **Coaches** can have a **democratic** coaching style

Model sentence: A democratic coaching style allows team members to make decisions about choosing goals and training routines and prevents teams from becoming less cohesive.

Supporting study: Goal-setting and team cohesion

Aim: To test if a democratic approach to goal-setting would increase team cohesion (Senecal et al., 2008).

Method: A longitudinal experiment was conducted with 86 female high school basketball players. Half of the teams used a democratic goal-setting strategy (independent variable – IV) for the whole **season**, and the other four teams were used as controls, with no intervention. The experimental group chose their goals and decided on their own **targets**. At the beginning and at the end of the study, the researchers measured team cohesion using a questionnaire, and they measured **performance** (dependent variable – DV) according to the percentage of games won at the end of the season.

Results: The basketball teams had similar **ratings** of team cohesion at the beginning of the season (which were quite high) but the experimental teams who did democratic goal-setting gave significantly higher ratings of team cohesion than the control groups at the end of the season. This was not because their team cohesion increased, but because cohesion among the other groups went down.

Conclusion: Democratic goal-setting is useful as a way to prevent teams becoming less cohesive.

Aid 2: Strong norms for social interaction

Model sentence: If teams socialize together they will increase their cohesion.

Supporting study: Team pressure to work hard

Aim: To examine the importance of team norms in the relationship between team cohesion and performance (Patterson et al., 2005).

Method: 298 adult athletes from various team sports took part in the study. They used both interdependent team sports such as football, and co-active team sports such as wrestling and swimming. These participants completed a questionnaire about team norms for practice, competition, and social situations.

Results: The greatest effort was shown by teams which had strong norms for social interaction and high team social cohesion.

Conclusions: Norms play an important role in the relationship between cohesion and performance but more research is needed to understand it.

Barriers to team cohesion

Model sentence: There are also several barriers to cohesion (Weinberg and Gould, 2003).

1. Difficult relationships between team members: This can be because of a **clash of personalities** in the team or because of communication problems between members, or because of **confusion** about roles in the team.
2. Power structure problems: One or more members want to have power.
3. Frequent change of members: This means that people leave the team and are replaced quite often.
4. Team members do not agree with the group goals: This can happen if the goal-setting process was not democratic or if some members are not allowed to express their opinions.

Team cohesion can be defined as 'the tendency for a group to stick together and remain united' as it tries to achieve its objectives and/or as it satisfies its team members' emotional needs (Carron et al., 1998).

Aid is something that is helpful.

Barrier is something that is unhelpful.

Hints for success: This question cannot be asked by itself: it will always be asked together with a longer question that asks you to discuss or examine, for example. You do not need to evaluate the information for this learning outcome but you may want to include it in other relevant questions.

Subject vocabulary

norms expected or usual ways to behave

interdependent sport individual members' performance is dependent on the team (for example, a football team)

co-active sport individual members' performance is independent of the team (for example, a golfing team)

participant someone who takes part in a research study

Glossary

clash of personalities a situation where people are not friendly because they are different

confusion not understanding something because it is not clear

Discuss athlete response to stress and chronic injury

Synonyms

athlete .... sportsperson

stress .... anxiety

injury .... being hurt

depression .... sadness

mature .... sensible and reasonable

overall .... including everything

Glossary

response a reaction

frustration a feeling of being annoyed or upset because you cannot do something

butterflies a feeling you get in your stomach when you are nervous

to grieve/grief to feel extremely sad (usually after a death)

reaction what you do or feel because of something that has happened

setback a problem that makes a situation worse than it was before

patient a person who is getting medical treatment

clinic a place where people can get medical treatment

session time spent on a particular activity

trend a general direction in which something is going

Subject vocabulary

cognition/cognitive related to mental processes (such as perception, memory, problem-solving)

rehabilitation the process of getting better after injury

face validity a theory of method that appears to work or make sense. This is especially useful for non-experts

physiotherapist someone who treats physical injuries

Opening sentence:

In this answer I will discuss **athlete response** to **stress** and chronic **injury**.

Stress in sport can mean cognitive anxiety or worry, thoughts about failure, pressure or **frustration**, and physical sensations such as '**butterflies**' in the stomach.

Chronic injury can be defined as an injury that happens over a longer period of time because of weakening or overuse.

Model 1: **Grief-reaction**-response model

This model was originally intended to outline the stages a person goes through when they know they are going to die, but it has been used to understand how athletes respond to serious injuries.

Harris (2003) describes the stages a person goes through when their injury first happens:

- Denial - for example, when an athlete continues to play or returns to the sport early.
- Anger - when the athlete realizes that the injury may mean the loss of an entire career.
- Bargaining - this involves trying to find a solution to the situation.
- **Depression** - this occurs when rehabilitation takes longer than expected or when there are **setbacks**.
- Acceptance and reorganization - this occurs if the athlete is **mature** enough and has strong social support.

Supporting study: Emotional experiences of injured athletes

Aim: To investigate the emotions of athletes after injury (Dawes and Roach, 1997).

Method: The researchers gave questionnaires to 52 **patients** who were attending **clinics** for sports injuries. The questionnaires included items about emotions, social support, and the injury itself. The patients completed the questionnaire each time they arrived at the clinic so that the researchers could note changes in emotions over five **sessions**.

Results: There were generally very negative emotions, including frustration, before the first treatment. However, this seemed to disappear after treatment started, although there was a brief increase again between the second and third treatment. Feelings of both anger and excitement were common.

Conclusion: There were no **overall trends**. The grief-reaction-response model has face validity. However, this study shows that athletes with chronic injuries have many different reactions after they begin therapy. Therefore, it is important for physiotherapists to pay attention to each individual's emotions.

Model 2: Cognitive Appraisal Theory (Weinberg and Gould, 2003)

The theory assumes that differences in the ways athletes react to injury and stress are because of the way that individuals **process** the information about events.

Udry et al. (1997) use five steps to describe how Cognitive **Appraisal** Theory works in sports:

- An injury occurs.
- Cognitive appraisal occurs. This involves the athlete's perceptions of how serious the injury is.
- The emotional response occurs. It may be the grief response or less significant.
- Coping response occurs. In general, this involves changing the cause of the stress or changing the appraisal.
- Following the behavioural response. This means following the treatment and rehabilitation programme. In this way, the positive appraisal of the situation is **maintained**.

Supporting study: Recovery from a rugby injury

Aim: To investigate appraisal while recovering from a sports injury (Vergeer, 2006).

Method: The researcher had several interviews with a 28-year-old man who had recently injured his shoulder. It was so serious that there was a 70 per cent chance he would never play again. She asked him questions over 20 weeks about how he was dealing emotionally with the injury and interviewed him again 3 years later. The results of these interviews were presented as a case study.

Results: There were two main sources of input that he needed to process. These were his contact with medical personnel, and his own body, particularly in terms of pain. For the first 5 or 6 weeks of rehabilitation, he was learning about how bad the injury was and thinking about his future. His emotions were linked to progress. When he was making progress, he was happy, and when he was afraid for his future, he was unhappy. She notes that his self-efficacy was an important factor in his recovery: he *believed* that he would be able to do the right things to get better.

Conclusion: It is appropriate to understand response to injury in terms of cognitive appraisal. For example, mental toughness is a personality characteristic that allows people to ***perceive*** threats as challenges, and to select an appropriate way to meet the challenge. Therefore, the results are linked to the way they are appraised (whether they are challenges to be overcome or not).

Hints for success: Show that the models can present *general trends* for athletes but there are also many individual differences for how athletes respond.

Subject vocabulary

cognitive appraisal an information processing system that judges threats and abilities

coping response how athletes cope with an injury

self-efficacy feelings of confidence in one's own ability to do something

Synonyms

maintained .... continued in the same way

recovery .... getting better

perceive .... see

Glossary

to process to carry out a series of steps in order to achieve a particular result

to appraise to judge

Examine reasons for using drugs in sport

Opening sentence:

In this answer I will examine two reasons for using drugs in sport.

Drugs

Drugs are sometimes used in sport to improve the performance of **athletes** although they are forbidden in most sports. Using them is called *doping*.

An example of a drug used in sport is an *anabolic steroid.*

Anabolic steroids have similar effects to testosterone in the body. They increase protein within cells, especially in muscles. They develop masculine **characteristics** such as muscle mass (physical) and **aggression** (psychological). They can cause heart damage, liver damage, hair loss, and a **retraction** of the testes in men, and in women, they cause masculine characteristics to develop such as a deep voice and broad shoulders.

Assumption 1: Drugs improve self-esteem

Model sentence: **Self-esteem is a measurement of how we feel about ourselves. High self-esteem means we feel good about ourselves.**

Example study: French teenagers and doping

Aim: To investigate the reasons given by high school athletes for using drugs in sport, and their **attitudes** towards doping (Laure et al., 2004).

Method: 2500 high school students who were members of a school sports association were asked to complete a questionnaire at their school on a particular day. The questionnaire asked about their use of drugs in sport and outside sport, their beliefs about doping, and their opinions about their own health.

Results: Only 4 per cent of the sample said they had used drugs for sport, more often boys. When asked if they thought doping was effective in improving performance, 68 per cent said it improved performance; 6 per cent stated that doping is not cheating. The key finding was that those students who had tried doping were more likely to have bad relations with parents, to be unhappy, and to have no girlfriend/boyfriend. This suggests that they have low esteem.

Conclusions: There is a group of athletes who is more likely to use drugs. Young people who are having problems socially and use sport as a way to gain self-esteem are the ones most likely to try doping and then to continue doing it when it has some positive results such as an increase in physical size.

Model sentence: **It can be assumed from this research that athletes use drugs to improve their self-esteem.**

Subject vocabulary

performance how well you do something

testosterone a hormone found in large amounts in males. It is responsible for male physical characteristics (such as broad shoulders) and is thought to play a significant role in male behaviour traits

protein molecules which (among other roles) help build muscle in the body

testes/testicles male sex organs

assumption an underlying idea that a theory is built on

Synonyms

athletes.............. sportspeople

characteristics..... traits/features

attitudes............ opinions

Glossary

aggression/aggressive behaving in an angry or threatening way

retraction moving inward

Assumption 2: The doping **dilemma** – 'other people use them'

The doping dilemma is the problem that athletes have when they are not sure if other athletes are using drugs or not.

Haugen (2004) summarizes the assumptions like this:

> Two equal athletes compete in the same sports event and have the choice to use drugs or not to use drugs. Both assume the drug is effective in increasing performance. This means that if one athlete takes the drug and the other does not, the drug taker will win. If both athletes take the drug, then they are equal again. Therefore the **logical** decision for the athlete is to take the drug because the worst possibility is being equal with the other drug-taking athletes.

This approach assumes that these factors increase the chances of athletes using drugs:

- **uncertainty** about how many others are using drugs
- uncertainty about the chances of being found out
- uncertainty about possible health risks compared to certainty about benefits.

Glossary

dilemma a situation when it is very difficult to make a decision

uncertainty when you are not sure about something

Synonyms

logical................ reasonable/ sensible

Supporting study: Doping in Turkey

Aim: To investigate the amount of doping among Turkish athletes and the reasons for drug use (Özdemir et al., 2005).

Method: The researchers gave a questionnaire to 433 licensed athletes and 450 non-athletes living in Turkey.

Results: 14.5 per cent of the athletes reported doping or using drugs which improved their performance. Most used steroids. Of these people, 79 per cent said they believed that their main opponents were using doping, compared with 54.5 per cent of the non-users.

Conclusions: The number of athletes who use drugs is low. The number of those who *believe* other athletes use drugs is very high. It is likely that their belief that others are doping is a key factor in the decision of athletes to break the rules and use drugs.

Model sentence: It can be assumed from this research that athletes use drugs because they believe others are also using drugs and they want to compete equally with them. The results also suggest that they have *faulty thinking* as the number of athletes who use drugs is quite low.

Hints for success: Remember that the instruction 'examine' means that you must include details of the reasons for the assumptions.

Discuss effects of drug use in sport

Subject vocabulary

performance how well you do something

testosterone a hormone found in large amounts in males. It is responsible for male physical characteristics (such as broad shoulders) and is thought to play a significant role in male behaviour traits

protein molecules which (among other roles) help build muscle in the body

testes/testicles male sex organs

libido sex drive

personality disturbance a negative effect on an individual's personality, such as increased amounts of anger

Glossary

retraction moving inward

weightlifter a person who tries to lift up heavy pieces of metal which weigh a particular amount

to investigate to try to find the reasons for something

seminar a meeting to discuss an educational topic

mood how a person feels

side effect an expected or unwanted effect of taking a drug

irritability getting annoyed quickly

insomnia an inability to sleep

acne red spots/pimples usually on the face and neck

frustration a feeling of being annoyed or upset because you cannot do something

Synonyms

athletes............... sportspeople

characteristics..... traits/features

aggression .... anger/violence

Opening sentence:

In this answer I will discuss three effects of drug use in sport.

Drugs

Drugs are sometimes used in sport to improve the performance of **athletes** although they are forbidden in most sports. Using them is called *doping*.

An example of a drug used in sport is an *anabolic steroid*.

Anabolic steroids have similar effects to testosterone in the body. They increase protein within cells, especially in muscles. They develop masculine **characteristics** such as muscle mass (physical) and **aggression** (psychological). They can cause heart damage, liver damage, hair loss, and a **retraction** of the testes in men, and in women, they develop masculine characteristics such as a deep voice and broad shoulders.

Negative effect 1: Physical and psychological change

Supporting study 1: Effects of steroid use in weightlifters

Aim: To **investigate** what psychological and physical states are associated with steroid use in weightlifters (Bahrke, Wright, Strauss, and Catlin, 1992).

Method: 50 male weightlifters who attended a **seminar** about steroid use were invited to take part in the study. In exchange, they were promised free health checks and that the information they provided would not be shown to anyone. They filled in a questionnaire about **mood** and physical **side effects**.

Results: Current users of steroids were heavier. Increased aggression was reported by 91 per cent of current users and 73 per cent of previous users. A similar increase in **irritability** was found. A feeling of well-being or enthusiasm was reported by 45 per cent of current users and 73 per cent of previous users. Apart from these differences, the only differences between drug users and non-users were behavioural and physical, such as increases in libido, **insomnia**, and **acne**.

Supporting study 2: Nice guys finish last

Aim: To investigate the long-term effects of steroid use in weightlifters (Perry, Andersen, and Yates, 1990).

Method: The researchers placed advertisements in local newspapers and fitness centres and found 20 steroid-using athletes who agreed to take part in the study. A control group of 20 weightlifters who said they did not use steroids was also found. They completed questionnaires and attended an interview that asked for specific details about drug use and personality and psychological problems, and any changes they had noticed since they started to use drugs.

Results: 95 per cent of the steroid users reported that their testicles had shrunk, and 60 per cent that they had lost hair. The steroid users had more personality disturbances overall. Their reasons for steroid use were typical: to improve performance and/or appearance, because they believed other athletes were using them, or out of **frustration** that if you don't use drugs you can't win. This was described as a 'nice guys finish last' attitude.

General conclusion: The weightlifters' wish to increase muscle strength and body size are met when they take steroids, but there are also some side effects, such as increased aggression.

Negative effect 2: **Drug dependence**

Drugs can make an athlete become bigger, stronger, and more successful (Kashkin and Kleber, 1989). This means that young males in particular can become depressed when they do not use the drug.

Supporting study: Do young people become dependent on drugs in sport?

Aim: To investigate whether drug users become dependent on steroids used in sports (Copeland, Peters, and Dillon, 1999).

Method: The researchers sent questionnaires to or carried out interviews with 100 participants in Australia, using snowball sampling from known steroid users. All participants had used steroids within the previous 12 months.

Results: 73 per cent of participants reported at least one symptom of dependence or **abuse**, for example, most of the steroid users reported withdrawal symptoms when they were not using the drug. In total, 23 per cent of the steroid users could be considered to be dependent on steroids, and another 25 per cent could be considered to abuse steroids. The drug users who showed signs of dependence were more likely to have aggression problems.

Conclusions: Steroid use *does* appear to be addictive as there is clear evidence of the symptoms of dependence in this study.

Positive effect: Drugs improve self-esteem

Model sentence: Self-esteem is a measurement of how we feel about ourselves. High self-esteem means we feel good about ourselves.

Example study: French teenagers and doping

Aim: To investigate the reasons given by high school athletes for using drugs in sport, and their attitudes towards doping (Laure et al., 2004).

Method: 2500 high school students who were members of a school sports association were asked to complete a questionnaire at their school on a particular day. The questionnaire asked about their use of drugs in sport and outside sport, their beliefs about doping, and their opinions about their own health.

Results: Only 4 per cent of the sample said they had used drugs for sport, more often boys. When asked if they thought doping was effective in improving performance, 68 per cent said it improved performance; 6 per cent stated that doping is not cheating. The key finding was that those students who had tried doping were more likely to have bad relations with parents, to be unhappy, or to have no girlfriend/boyfriend. This suggests that they have low esteem.

Conclusions: There is a group of athletes who is more likely to use drugs. Young people who are having problems socially and use sport as a way to gain self-esteem are the most likely to try doping and then to continue doing it when it has some positive results such as an increase in physical size.

Glossary

drug dependence/dependent when a person is addicted to a drug

to abuse (drugs) to take too many drugs

Subject vocabulary

participant someone who takes part in a research study

snowball method/sampling the researcher asks existing participants in the study if they know other possible participants who are willing to take part and then these are recruited for the study

symptoms signs of an illness

withdrawal symptoms the symptoms that occur when an addict stops experiencing the cause of their addiction, usually a drug

addictive describes a substance (usually a drug) or activity that the user is unable to function without

Hints for success:
Remember that the instruction 'discuss' requires you to be balanced. Mention positive and negative effects.

Compare models of causes and prevention of burnout

Opening sentence:

In this answer I will compare the *Cognitive-Affective Stress Model* and *the Commitment Model* of causes and prevention of burnout.

What is burnout?

Burnout is what happens when a person loses energy, motivation, and interest, and their **performance** declines.

The focus is placed on what an **athlete** *feels* is happening (rather than what *is* actually happening).

Many athletes respond to burnout by giving up their sport.

Model 1: The Cognitive-Affective Stress Model

Burnout is the result of cognitive processes which are used in response to situational and environmental demands.

When an athlete is facing demands, they do a primary appraisal of how big the demands are. They then do a secondary appraisal of whether they are able to deal with those demands.

If the demands are **perceived** as too big, or if the person does not believe that they can cope, then they may reach burnout.

The athlete carries out a cost-benefit analysis to work out if they should leave the sport or not.

Supporting study: Burnout in Swedish athletes

Aim: To test if the cognitive-affective model is an **appropriate** way to understand burnout (Gustafsson et al., 2008).

Method: Athletes were interviewed about their feelings towards their sport. The interview questions focused on the feelings and experiences of the athletes during the time when they had experienced burnout. *Thematic content analysis* was carried out to identify factors that led to burnout.

Results: Common themes were a **perceived lack** of **accomplishment**, feeling **exhausted**, not feeling that the sport was important any more, feeling that there was not enough social support, feeling that other people expected too much.

Conclusions: The cognitive-affective model appears to be a useful way of understanding factors that lead to burnout, because these athletes report many perceptions of problems that can be understood as primary or secondary appraisals. For example, the perceived lack of accomplishment could be a primary appraisal. For some people this could be a *motivating challenge*, while for others it is a *demotivating threat*.

Subject vocabulary

cognition/cognitive related to mental processes (such as perception, memory, problem-solving)

affective related to emotions

model a representation of behaviour or an idea. They allow predictions to be made about behaviour

commitment how motivated an individual is to complete a task or be part of a team

motivation wanting or a desire to do something

situational demands demands created by the specific situation

environmental demands demands created by an environment

primary appraisal a judgement about how much of a threat something is

secondary appraisal a judgement about one's ability to deal with a threat

cost-benefit analysis a decision-making process considering what the cost will be and what the benefits will be. A decision is then made

thematic content analysis a method of analysis where themes are identified in the participants' responses

motivating challenge a positive factor that will motivate people

demotivating threat a negative factor that will demotivate people

Glossary

performance how well a person does something

to perceive/perception to see or understand information

a lack (of) not enough

accomplishment something that is achieved through a lot of effort and hard work

exhausted feeling extremely tired

Synonyms

athlete .... sportsperson

appropriate .... suitable

perceived .... seen

Model 2: The Commitment Model

Commitment has three components:

- the attractiveness of the activity
- the attractiveness of other activities
- **restrictions** that mean the athlete cannot leave the sport.

When an athlete feels that he or she 'must be' rather than 'wants to be' in the sport, then he or she is at risk of burnout. Players whose commitment is because of personal **desire** and interest are less likely to experience burnout.

This means that in order to prevent burnout, **coaches** and psychologists need to make sure that athletes are aware of the personal benefits they get from the sport and try to prevent the athlete feeling **trapped** in the sport.

Comparing the two models

- They both consider cognitive factors to be important. The Cognitive-Affective Stress Model involves *appraisal theory* and a *cost-benefit analysis*; the Commitment Model involves the relationship between different types of commitment, which is also a cost-benefit analysis.
- In both theories, when costs are greater than benefits, the athlete starts to experience burnout.
- The two models can be tested in similar ways. It is impossible to do experiments for either theory, because it would be **unethical** to cause burnout, and very difficult to **manipulate** emotions. This means that researchers must use questionnaires and interviews.
- Both models are useful. Coaches can use similar **strategies** based on these theories to prevent burnout, even when they do not know what the true cause of burnout is. For example, they can teach players relaxation techniques to help them to deal with problems better. This makes their sport seem more **attractive** and beneficial. They can offer social support and create a positive social team environment. This can be a clear benefit that makes the sport more attractive and also prevents players from feeling alone when they have a problem.

Evidence for both models is shown by Cresswell and Eklund (2005)

Aim: To investigate changes in burnout and motivation over a 12-week period (Cresswell and Eklund, 2005).

Method: 102 rugby players completed questionnaires about sports motivation and athlete burnout three times: before a 12-week competition, in the middle of the competition, and at the end of the competition.

Results: The most important influence seems to be the athlete's motivation earlier in the season. Those athletes who had more intrinsic motivation (rather than extrinsic motivation such as *earning money*) were less likely to experience burnout at the end of the season. Older, more experienced, and more injured players were all more likely to experience burnout.

Conclusion: There is evidence for the Commitment Model: when players believe that their involvement in the sport is externally controlled or managed (for example, because they are receiving financial rewards), they may lose interest in the sport itself and feel exhausted.

Glossary

restriction something that controls or limits what you can do

trapped a feeling of being in a difficult situation that you are unable to change

to manipulate/manipulation to control something or someone to your advantage

attractiveness the qualities a person has which draw you in

Synonyms

desire .... want

coach .... trainer

unethical .... morally unacceptable

strategies .... techniques

Subject vocabulary

experiment a method where the independent variable is changed to measure the effect on the dependent variable while controlling for other variables

intrinsic motivation motivation from inside the individual – for example, a desire to get thin

extrinsic motivation motivation from outside the individual – for example, earning money

Hints for success: The word 'compare' asks only for similarities which are outlined above. However, the command term may change to 'compare and contrast' (similarities and differences) in which case you should not attempt this question.

General Learning Outcomes

GLO 1: To what extent do biological, cognitive, and sociocultural factors influence behaviour in sport?

Biological factors

Model sentence: Arousal and anxiety show how biological factors influence behaviour in sport.

Arousal is a physiological state that prepares the body for action. Through the release of hormones and the **activation** of various parts of the brain, a person's alertness increases and their response times decrease.

Arousal can be helpful but also sometimes brings anxiety, which includes uncomfortable physical feelings and worrying thoughts, and these are sometimes responsible for problems in **performance**.

Supporting study: Yips

Yips are something that happens to some golfers when they are under stress. They suddenly lose their ability to swing the golf club correctly, either hitting the ball too hard or too softly.

Aim: To investigate the relationship between physiological arousal and performance in golf (Smith et al., 2000).

Method: Golfers who reported (by questionnaire) that they had the yips took part in an experiment which tested muscle **tension** in their arm, **grip** strength, and heart rate in various different situations on the golf course.

Results: The participants who had the yips had worse performance and a higher average heart rate than the others. They also gripped their clubs more tightly than golfers who did not have the yips.

Conclusions: Anxiety levels are associated with the yips. Performance decreases in golfers who experience high levels of arousal.

Cognitive factors

Model sentence: Self-Efficacy Theory shows how cognitive factors influence behaviour in sport.

Self-Efficacy Theory is a social-cognitive theory that focuses on the role of a person's *expectations*. Bandura (1997) wrote about outcome expectations and efficacy expectations.

- Outcome expectations are our expectations about what behaviour will lead to a particular result.
- Efficacy expectations are our expectations about our ability to actually do this.

Bandura suggests that we learn our expectations through successful performance, indirect experience, verbal **persuasion** (such as a **coach**'s voice and a person's own voice), and emotional arousal. These are all obtained through training. Feedback is obtained from our **peers**, coaches, and teachers, but also from our own bodies.

Subject vocabulary

biological related to biological processes (such as the effects of hormones, neurotransmitters, genes, and gender)

cognition/cognitive related to mental processes (such as perception, memory, problem-solving)

sociocultural related to social and cultural issues

arousal bodily and psychological alertness

physiological relating to the body

hormone a chemical messenger that transports a signal from one cell to another. Hormones differ from neurotransmitters as they travel through the blood stream while neurotransmitters travel across synapses (the gaps) between neurons

anxiety a state of fear and uncertainty

yips difficulties controlling movement because of anxiety

experiment a method where the independent variable is changed to measure the effect on the dependent variable while controlling for other variables

participant someone who takes part in a research study

expectation what you think or hope will happen

feedback a response that gives information

Glossary

to activate/activated to make something work or switch something on

performance how well a person does something

tension tightness or stiffness

to grip to hold something tightly in the hand

peer a person who is the same age as you or has the same position in society

Synonyms

persuasion...... encouragement

coach.............. trainer

Model sentence: According to Self-Efficacy Theory, our motivation will be highest when we have appropriate knowledge and skills and high efficacy expectations for a particular task. We are motivated to do things that we believe we can do.

Supporting study: Self-efficacy and aerobics

Aim: To investigate reasons for participation in aerobics for exercise (McAuley, Wraith, and Duncan, 1991). Many people begin exercise for external reasons such as health or appearance, but continuing to exercise may be related to more internal factors such as self-efficacy.

Method: 265 participants who were doing university aerobic dance classes, including only 11 males, completed questionnaires in the ninth week of their class. The questionnaires measured motivation, self-efficacy for aerobics, and perceptions of success.

Results: Participants with high levels of self-efficacy were more motivated than others, whether they were beginners or more advanced.

Conclusion: Self-efficacy is an important factor that influences how motivated people are to continue with exercise programmes.

Sociocultural factors

Model sentence: Coaches who create a motivational culture or climate show how sociocultural factors influence behaviour in sport.

There are two types of motivational **climate**:

- a *mastery climate* – in which there is a focus on improvement and achieving goals
- a *performance climate* – where there is a focus on competitive success.

Mastery climates are associated with more motivation, enjoyment, and better performance, especially among younger **athletes**.

Supporting study: Motivational climate in handball

Aim: To investigate the effects of a motivational climate on teams of female handball players (Balaguer et al., 2002).

Method: 181 female handball players completed questionnaires which had items about motivational climate, perceptions of improvement, goal orientations, satisfaction, the coach, and performance. The researchers correlated various variables with motivational climate to see what effects this climate has.

Results: Players who reported that the team had a motivational climate also reported feelings of **competence** and a sense of improvement. They did not report more team improvement.

Conclusions: The motivational climate has very positive effects on individual improvement but it did not necessarily have very positive effects on team improvement.

Glossary

to motivate/motivation a reason to want to do something

aerobics a type of exercise

handball a team sport where players score points by throwing a ball into a goal

competence the ability to do something

Synonyms

appropriate ...... suitable

skill .... ability

climate .... atmosphere

athlete .... sportsperson

Subject vocabulary

goal a target, something a person wants to achieve

goal orientation being focused on goals

correlation a relationship between variables

GLO 2: Evaluate psychological research (that is, theories and/or studies) relevant to the study of sport psychology

The theory of using mental imagery in sport

Mental imagery is a technique in which sportspeople use their imagination to see good outcomes - for example, kicking a ball into the correct place in goal.

It can be used to learn new skills, to improve existing skills, or to reduce anxiety. It is also useful for sportspeople who are **injured** and need to **regain** skill or confidence.

Strengths

- There are biological explanations for how the theory may work: various parts of the frontal cortex are activated when people imagine doing something, and these are also activated during physical performance. Therefore, *from the brain's point of view*, using mental imagery may be as good as physical practice for the brain.
- Mental imagery causes mirror neurons to be activated. Mirror neurons are neurons that are active when we observe *other people's* behaviour (Rizzolatti, 2004).

Model sentence: When a sportsperson watches others and then imagines himself or herself doing the same action this is a form of practice for the brain.

Limitations

It is difficult to know whether the participants are really using imagery in the way that they were taught. It is also difficult to know whether a control group is *not* using mental imagery.

It is not clear whether using mental imagery is a cause or an effect of skill development. Longitudinal research could help by showing changes over time. It is possible that poor sportspeople are also bad at imagining successful performance, and therefore mental imagery may not work for everyone.

Supporting study: Pre-performance rituals in water polo

Aim: To test if using mental imagery can improve water polo players' skill in **taking penalties** (Marlow et al., 1998).

Method: Three experienced water polo players who had never used mental imagery before were interviewed and then given **personalized** pre-performance rituals by a sports psychologist. The rituals included relaxation breathing, concentration focus (staring at the ball to concentrate), and then imagining the perfect shot. Before they started and then several times over a period of weeks, the researchers measured skill development by asking the players to take five penalties and **rating** them between 1 and 10 according to how similar they were to the perfect shot.

Results: The three players all improved, by 21 per cent, 25 per cent, and 28 per cent compared to their baseline performance.

Conclusion: Mental imagery is a technique that can improve skill development.

Evaluation: Clear independent variable (IV) (imagining the perfect shot) and a quantifiable dependent variable (DV) (success of making a perfect shot) means there is a good cause-effect relationship. It has some generalizability to other sports but caution should be used when generalizing beyond water polo.

Subject vocabulary

mental imagery imagining something in a visual way

technique way of doing something

frontal cortex the front part of the brain associated with planning and judgement

neurons nerves

longitudinal research a study that takes place over a long period of time, usually years

baseline original score before an intervention

independent variable (IV) the variable an experimenter controls or changes

dependent variable (DV) the variable an experimenter measures

cause-effect relationship where there is confidence that the effect on the dependent variable (DV) has been caused by the manipulation of the independent variable (IV)

generalizability the extent to which we can apply results to other circumstances

Synonyms

injured.............hurt

regain...............get back

Glossary

ritual something that is always done in the same way in the same situation

water polo a ball game played in a swimming pool with two teams

to take a penalty a chance to kick/hit the ball into the goal because the other team has broken a rule

to personalize to make something that is suitable for one particular person

to rate to judge the level or quality of something

Supporting study: Self-talk in tennis

Aim: To test the effectiveness of self-talk in improving skill in tennis (Hatzigeordiadis et al., 2009).

Method: 72 Greek tennis players were divided into two groups. The first group was the experimental group and they were taught self-talk, for example they should say 'shoulder' to focus their attention on how they moved their shoulder. The other group was a control group who were not taught self-talk. The players then had to perform a difficult shot. The researchers rated each shot according to how close it was to the **baseline** on the other side of the court.

Results: The experimental group showed more improvement in the task and a larger increase in **self-confidence**.

Conclusion: Self-talk is an effective way to increase performance.

Evaluation: There is always a problem with measuring how much the technique contributed to the improvement as these are internal psychological processes.

Hints for success: Always use previously learnt material to support a GLO answer and use examples of research to support each point that you are making.

Glossary

baseline (tennis) the line at the back of a tennis court

self-confidence a person's belief that they can do things effectively

Distinguish between qualitative and quantitative data

Researchers disagree over the correct definitions of qualitative and quantitative data and whether there is any clear difference at all. However, quantitative data is usually in the form of *numbers*. Numbers are easier to summarize and subject to statistical analysis. Qualitative data is usually in the form of *words* taken from interviews, thoughts, feelings, and experiences of the participants as well as observations, interpretations, and an attempt to report on experiences. A qualitative approach usually **acknowledges** that the researcher is part of the research process - this will take the form of the researcher giving their own thoughts, feelings, and **biases** and explaining how these influenced the research process.

Qualitative data is usually described as being 'rich' - detailed descriptions of thoughts, feelings, and experiences. Qualitative data will often report on *how* data was produced. When human beings speak or write down their thoughts, the results are less straightforward than numbered data as they can be complex and **contradictory**. Qualitative data attempts to report on this by focusing not just on the words or text but on the wider experience of *being human*. For example, a qualitative approach will report on how study participants use humour, **sarcasm**, pauses, how they change their **tone of voice** to make a point or make a joke, how they use eye contact to suggest different meanings, or handle objects (for example, a participant may play with their glasses while being interviewed - a researcher may interpret this as *nervousness*). A qualitative researcher will usually build a relationship with the participants to get to know their **mannerisms** and personalities.

In summary, quantitative data usually uses numbers to produce focused conclusions. Qualitative data involves an overall attempt to capture the richness and complexity of the human experience. This usually involves using words that report on the thoughts, feelings, and experiences of the participants. The conclusions from qualitative research often depend on how the researcher and then the reader interpret them.

It should be noted: Social science studies will often use both approaches.

Quantitative data is usually in the form of numbers. *Numbers are easier to summarize and subject to statistical analysis.*

Qualitative data is usually in the form of words *taken from interviews, thoughts, feelings, and experiences of the participants as well as observations, interpretations, and an attempt to report on experiences.*

Subject vocabulary

participant someone who takes part in a research study

Glossary

to acknowledge to accept

bias/biased unfairly preferring one person or group over another

sarcasm a style of humour where a person says one thing but means the opposite

tone of voice how someone speaks, such as in a happy way

mannerism a way of speaking or moving that is typical of a person

Synonyms

contradictory ...... conflicting/opposing

Explain strengths and limitations of a qualitative approach to research

Strengths:

- The thoughts and feelings of the researched and the researcher are acknowledged and built into the research process. Therefore, the biases of the researcher and how they influenced data collection and conclusions can be seen by the reader.
- Produces *rich* data in the form of observations, interpretations, and an overall attempt to capture human *experiences*.
- Particularly helpful for investigating complex and personal issues (usually by reporting on thoughts, feelings, and experiences) which cannot be reduced to 'numbered data'. Examples include: individuals who are involved in **abusive** relationships; the thoughts and feelings of people in a particular workplace; human sexuality.
- Can be seen as having greater *validity* – a researcher spends more time with the participants in order to record as much about their experiences as possible.
- Useful in exploring the experiences of individuals which are rare or unusual and cannot be quantified or recreated in an artificial setting.

Limitations:

- The **in-depth** approach usually means that *fewer* participants take part in any study – there is more depth but less **breadth**.
- Large amounts of data are produced. The data have to be edited and interpreted – *how* and *why* a researcher edits and interprets data is often complex and personal to the researcher and a reader may not always know how or why choices were made. Another researcher will edit and interpret the same data in different ways – therefore qualitative data is often seen as not being as *reliable* as numbered data.
- Qualitative data are broad and varied ideas – there is no agreement on one definition or approach (some may also see this as a strength). Therefore, studies that use qualitative data collection methods can vary hugely in quality as there are not many **consistent** rules or methods that researchers agree on.

Synonyms

in-depth .... thorough/ complete/ detailed

consistent .... the same

Glossary

to abuse/abusive to be physically and/or verbally violent

breadth how wide something is

Subject vocabulary

validity how accurate or correct a result is

reliable how much the same results can be repeated with other studies

To what extent can findings be generalized from qualitative studies?

Generalizing findings from a study means that the results can be applied to situations outside of the study itself. Qualitative research is a very broad term and how much can be generalized will usually depend on how the study was carried out. However, two general conclusions can be made:

Qualitative research usually has smaller sample sizes. Therefore, it can be said to have limited *representational generalization*, which means that findings from qualitative research studies are less relevant to populations which are not part of the study.

Qualitative research usually emphasizes the thoughts, feelings, and experiences of the researched and the researcher. This usually results in a lot of ideas and new directions. Therefore, it can be said to have a high amount of *theoretical generalization*, which means findings often lead to new ideas, research directions, and theories.

Subject vocabulary

findings the results of a study

to generalize/generalization the extent to which we can apply results to other circumstances

population the group of people participants are taken from and then the results can be generalized (e.g. nurses at a hospital)

Personal **conduct** with participants

The nature of qualitative research means that there should always be extra focus on how relationships are built and developed with the participants. It can be normal to have close personal contact over a long period of time and a researcher has to consider how close they become to their participants. This is especially true with **frail** or **vulnerable** groups such as the elderly or victims of abuse. A further consideration is *how* and *when* the relationship will end. A close personal relationship is helpful for data collecting; however, unless this builds into a true friendship, the relationship will have to end and this may have psychological **consequences** for the participant.

Informed consent and privacy

Participants need to be informed about how their responses will be used. If a researcher guarantees privacy then consideration has to be given to the participants' responses which may identify the participants. For example, if a researcher is interviewing lots of people from a large organization (such as a corporation or a hospital) then the participants may feel that their privacy is guaranteed because of the size of the study and because their names will not be used in the final report. However, they should be told *how* and *to what extent* their responses will be published. Participants may think they are talking **in confidence** but then it will be possible to identify them in the final report through their voice patterns, jokes, or information about where they work which they give in interview ('Well, here in the cardiology department we have a real problem with funding because of the problems with management...'). In summary, in qualitative research just changing the names of participants does not guarantee privacy. Participants may not be aware of that because it is not easy to hide a person's identity in a small qualitative research study.

The presentation of data back to the participants

Qualitative research involves exploring the thoughts, feelings, and experiences of people. Once data has been collated, edited, interpreted, and presented, some researchers have felt that for ethical reasons they need to present the data back to the participants for further thoughts and to check for accuracy. However, participants may not like how their views are being presented, or they may not like the **overall tone** of the report, or they may have forgotten what they said. They may **object to** having their personal views included when they see them in writing.

Participants' views can change with time, mood, and situation. For example, if they are interviewed in the staff cafeteria, or a bar, then they may feel that they can provide more personal information. However, they may then object when they see their words in writing a few months later when they are reading it in a more formal situation such as their workplace. For these reasons, many qualitative researchers do not present the data back to the participants. There is no correct ethical way to approach this problem but it should be taken into consideration by all qualitative researchers and they should choose a way that suits them and their research.

Synonyms

ethical .... moral

conduct .... behaviour

frail .... physically weak

vulnerable .... easily hurt

in confidence ...... secretly

Glossary

consequences something that happens as the result of an action

informed having a lot of information about something

overall tone general attitudes and feelings expressed

to object to to say you do not agree with something

Discuss sampling techniques appropriate to qualitative research (for example, purposive sampling, snowball sampling)

Samples in qualitative research are usually smaller because data sets tend to be larger and more in-depth. Qualitative researchers usually want to 'sort' through the data and large sample sizes make this difficult.

Purposive sampling

Purposive sampling **targets** a particular group of people that the researcher assumes would make good study participants because of their **characteristics**. 'Appropriate' characteristics would depend on the aim of the study. For example, if a researcher was interested in the experiences of foreign-born nurses in a hospital, then they would have to target nurses who were foreign born but also be *willing and able* to talk **at length** about their experiences. The researcher should also try to get a **diverse** sample, in terms of age and gender. An advantage is the researcher can choose who they want in the study. A disadvantage is that the researcher can be accused of bias - deliberately finding people who will agree with the research aims and express views the researcher would like expressed in the study.

Snowball sampling

The researcher asks existing participants in the study if they know other possible participants who are willing to take part. This is very useful for studies that focus on sensitive topics which participants may not want to take part in - for example, research into football **hooligan** gangs. The researcher can build trust with a small number of participants and become accepted and then use them to find more participants.

The advantage of snowball sampling is that it can be used to find *hidden populations* - people who the researcher would not be able to find but who would talk to another **likeminded** person. For example, a gang member may only talk to a researcher if another gang member has said that it is fine. The major limitation is that it is very difficult to avoid bias in the sample as likeminded people tend to group together and recommend other possible participants because they will confirm what has already been said. There are also **confidentiality** concerns, because the participants know the identity of other participants.

Subject vocabulary

sampling the methods used to create a group of participants for studying

data sets groups of data (e.g. groups of themes generated from interview; responses to questions on specific topics)

to sort through data to work through the data to identify themes

Glossary

to target to choose a particular person or group to do something to

hooligan/hooliganism a noisy, violent person who often wants to start fights

likeminded having the same interests or opinions

confidentiality keeping information a secret

Synonyms

characteristics..... traits/features

at length............. for a long time

diverse................ varied

Explain effects of participant expectations and researcher bias in qualitative research

Humans do not passively take part in research. They adapt as the interview and research process develops.

Participant expectations

This is where the fact that a participant is taking part in a study affects how he or she behaves. This is particularly common in qualitative research as human factors such as an informal relationship between the researcher and participant can mean that the participant tries to guess what kinds of responses are required and then provide those to the researcher. Participants may try and understand the aims of the research or give socially desirable answers to the researcher by saying what they think presents them in the most positive light. Researchers may find it difficult to hide what the study is about from the participant. Interviews can often become conversations which can lead to even more **informality**.

Researcher bias

This is when a researcher's own beliefs start to **dominate** the research process rather than the beliefs of the participants. The huge amounts of data produced through qualitative research allow a researcher to ignore data that do not match their aims. Their real aims, however, should be to allow the participants and the data to be the main focus. Researcher bias is often dealt with by using a ***reflexive tone*** throughout the report. This is where the researcher explains why he or she made certain choices about the literature and the data and specifically deals with researcher bias.

Subject vocabulary

expectations the researcher and participants will have expectations about how the research will proceed. This affects how they act and respond

reflexive tone refers to the careful attention the researcher pays to their own role in the research

Glossary

informality being relaxed and friendly

to dominate/dominant to have power or influence over other people

Explain the importance of credibility in qualitative research

Credibility refers to *trustworthiness*. Trustworthiness is established when the conclusions of the study accurately reflect the meanings as they were described by the participants. It is difficult for outside observers to establish this without carrying out a thorough investigation of the data. It is the researcher who reports the descriptions of the participants – they can be edited, **altered**, and invented to suit the research aims of the **hypothesis**.

In order to establish credibility, the researcher should leave a ***decision trail*** in the final report to explain how decisions were made about editing, interpreting, and presenting data. Other researchers will also carry out similar studies to test the accuracy of the original claims.

Subject vocabulary

credibility whether the methods used or the entire study is believable, and whether it can be trusted and therefore accepted as accurate

hypothesis the idea being tested by the study

decision trail an explanation to the reader about how the researcher arrived at decisions

Glossary

to alter to change

Explain the effect of triangulation on the credibility/trustworthiness of qualitative research

Triangulation is the use of **multiple** procedures or sources to collect data from different angles or perspectives.

Examples include:

- **Researcher triangulation**

  This involves using many observers, interviewers, or researchers to compare and check data collection and interpretation.

- **Method triangulation**

  This involves using different methods to collect data (for example, questionnaires, interviews, observations). This could also involve qualitative and quantitative methods. It can also be more **subtle** – for example, using different methods to carry out interviews.

Qualitative researchers rarely look for one *truth*. They may look for one *interpretation* of the data. Triangulation helps support that interpretation by showing it is supported from different perspectives and by different methods. The interpretation becomes more credible if it can be confirmed from different perspectives.

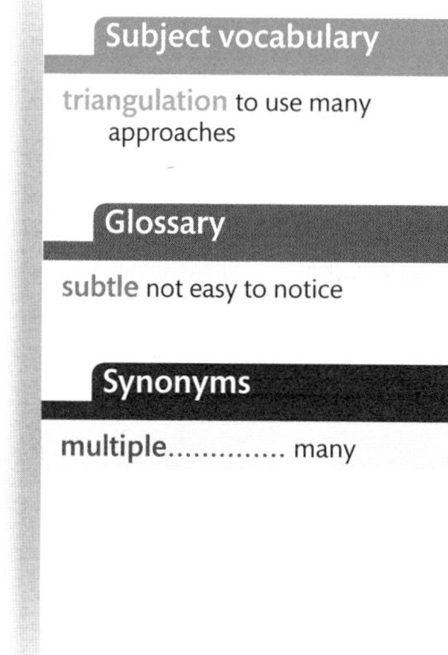

Subject vocabulary

triangulation to use many approaches

Glossary

subtle not easy to notice

Synonyms

multiple............. many

Explain reflexivity in qualitative research

Reflexivity in qualitative research refers to the careful attention the researcher pays to their own role in the research.

Reflexive questions for the researcher include:

- How did I come to the conclusions I came to?
- How did my beliefs affect how I edited and interpreted the data?
- Why did I decide to investigate this topic?
- If I approached the data from another perspective, how would that affect the results?
- If I used different data collection methods, would I arrive at the same conclusions?
- What has been **muted**, **repressed**, or unheard?

The questions show the reader how and why the researcher was able to arrive at his or her conclusions. Qualitative research involves summarizing large data sets by using editing and interpreting to arrive at conclusions – it is vital the reader knows which factors influenced those processes.

Synonyms

muted................ made quiet

repressed........... held back

Evaluate semi-structured, focus group, and narrative interviews

Semi-structured interviews

This is where an interview guide is prepared which lists the topics that should be explored during the interview. The interviewers try to make sure that the same topics are explored with all the participants in the study. The key **characteristic** of a semi-structured interview is the level of flexibility: wording, order, and level of detail of the questions can be changed as the interview is being carried out.

Advantages

Semi-structured interviews make it possible for researchers to carry out similar interviews. They also allow many interviews to be carried out by different interviewers.

They allow the researcher to be flexible while they still follow a **pre-designed** structure.

Disadvantages

The pre-designed structure may not be followed as closely by different researchers which may result in them carrying out completely different interviews.

The **artificial** nature of the interview may affect an interviewee and he or she may be less willing to discuss personal issues.

Focus group interviews

The researcher acts as a **facilitator** and participants answer questions in groups (typically of about five to 15 people). Participants discuss a topic and respond to what other participants say.

Advantages

This type of less formal discussion produces *rich data* for the researcher. This is because participants are encouraged to talk naturally (they can make **jokes**, use **sarcasm** and **slang**) and this puts them at their ease.

Focus group interviews produce large amounts of data from a wide range of participants in a short time period.

Disadvantages

Groupthink occurs. This is where participants behave differently when they are part of a group than when they are interviewed alone. For example, they may agree more with each other in order to cooperate with the other group members. Or they may disagree more in order to attract the attention of the researcher.

Strong personalities can often **dominate** group discussions and the researcher has to be well trained to allow participants to be able to speak freely.

They are not always suitable for investigating **sensitive** issues.

Glossary

semi-structured something that is only partly planned or organized

pre-designed planned or decided in advance

artificial not genuine or natural

facilitator a person who helps a group of people discuss something

joke something that you say which makes people laugh

sarcasm a style of humour where a person says one thing but means the opposite

slang very informal language

to dominate/dominant to have power or influence over other people

sensitive something that has to be dealt with very carefully

Subject vocabulary

participant someone who takes part in a research study

groupthink a decision made by a group that the individuals would not arrive at on their own

Synonyms

characteristic ...... trait/feature

Narrative interviews

Participants are encouraged to tell stories about their lives and experiences. It is seen as a **universal** human characteristic that people tell stories (narratives) about past events. The stories do not have to be true or entirely accurate – the aim is to see how the participants describe their experiences and then interpret them. For example, teachers might be encouraged to talk about their working lives by using stories about students they have taught or fellow teachers they have worked with. Different teachers will focus on different aspects of their working lives (some will tell stories about how the students behaved; some will focus on their grades; some will focus on student personalities or sporting achievements) and this can be seen in the stories they tell.

Advantages

Narrative interviews produce rich data that is highly personal.

They can be used to investigate very personal and sensitive issues.

Disadvantages

Stories are an interpretation of personal experiences that participants tell a researcher. The researcher then interprets this interpretation. Conclusions are very personal (for both the researcher and the participant) and therefore they can be seen as being difficult to **generalize** to other people and events.

It is difficult for the situation and the researcher to be **consistent** (and it may not be desirable). Therefore, the narrative interview technique should not be used to look for **themes** in a large sample with many different researchers.

Subject vocabulary

to generalize/generalization the extent to which we can apply results to other circumstances

Glossary

universal the same everywhere

to be consistent/consistency to remain or always behave in the same way

Synonyms

theme................. main subject/topic

Discuss considerations involved before, during, and after an interview (for example, sampling method, data recording, traditional versus postmodern transcription, debriefing)

Before

Sampling method

Interviews often involve sensitive or specialist topics. In order to find participants who can produce rich data it is acceptable to use a deliberate approach instead of using **random** sampling. Samples are usually smaller than those used in quantitative research as the data produced is richer.

Recording equipment

Researchers should ask themselves what type of recording equipment to use. It should not break down and be able to hold large amounts of data. For example, if a tape-recorder is used - how long will the tape and batteries last? Equipment should always be tested and checked beforehand in order to ensure that it is working.

During

Member checking

The researcher's theories and ideas which are emerging during the interviews need to be checked. This is done by repeating questions in different ways. Participants are encouraged to approach the same topics from different **perspectives**.

Thematic diaries

These are a record of the researcher's thought processes and can be written during the interview.

Data recording

The interview will usually be electronically recorded in some way. However, richer data are often produced when the recording equipment is turned off because the participants feel more at ease. The researcher should be aware of this possibility and be ready to take detailed notes.

After

Traditional versus postmodern transcription

Traditional transcriptions focus only on speech therefore other features of the social interaction are not included. Communication does not only involve words and more advanced transcription techniques are now being used more. This involves making either notes or a video so that non-verbal aspects of the interview (such as laughter, disgusted facial expressions, non-facial body language such as sitting back or leaning forward) can be recorded. The researcher explains how they chose which non-verbal aspects to record in the presentation of the final research.

Debriefing

Participants need to be debriefed for **ethical** reasons. This should happen in all research. A full debriefing after an interview includes how the recorded information will be used, who will have access to it, and when and how the participant will receive feedback about the researcher's findings from the interviews.

Glossary

transcript/transcription a written record of everything that is said

random chosen without a definite plan

ethical moral

Subject vocabulary

sampling the methods used to create a group of participants for studying

to debrief to give out information after an event (e.g. experiment)

to emerge to become clear from the data

Synonyms

perspective .... point of view

Explain how researchers use inductive content analysis (thematic analysis) on interview transcripts

Inductive content analysis involves allowing themes to emerge from data.

1. Reading and rereading the transcripts of each participant in order to become familiar with each participant's responses.
2. The researcher identifies general themes from each interview transcript. Themes are usually found in simple statements that participants have made. For example, in a piece of research investigating working experiences, a participant may say 'I enjoy working at home' – the theme would then be: *Working from home is a positive experience.*
3. Each theme is written separately (on a computer or a small card) and should show which participant is the source of that theme.
4. Statements from the participants are listed under each theme. For example, another participant might say: 'I like my boss but I prefer working at home.' This may be filed under the *Working from home is a positive experience* theme as well as a *Positive experience with boss* theme.
5. Under each theme, similar statements are grouped together. This process of grouping a participant's statements relies on the researcher understanding the meaning of these statements. Different themes will have different levels of support. Themes with weak support will be ignored or joined together with other more popular themes. Eventually, dominant or popular themes will emerge.
6. The researcher records how the process of coding and grouping was done.
7. It is useful for the researcher to talk to research peers in order to discuss the way they have grouped themes and to find out if they agree about how data should be grouped.
8. Researchers analyse the data until they feel they have reached a point where they can find no new information. This is called *data saturation.*

Subject vocabulary

thematic analysis the process where themes are identified in the data

research peers other researchers at the same standard of research usually working on the same area

Glossary

transcript/transcription a written record of everything that is said

Evaluate participant, non-participant, naturalistic, overt, and covert observations

Subject vocabulary

participant someone who takes part in a research study

ethical issues discussions about the correct or morally decent way to conduct research

patient an individual who is sick and is receiving treatment

Synonyms

criminal .... illegal

perspective .... point of view

create .... make

Glossary

hooligan/hooliganism a noisy, violent person who often wants to start fights

bias/biased unfairly preferring one person or group over another

sensitive something that has to be dealt with very carefully

Participant observations

This is where the researcher becomes part of the group they are observing. The aim is to develop a close relationship with the group in their environment in order to understand them better. It usually involves taking part in the behaviour that is being studied even if it is **criminal** (e.g. football **hooliganism**). This is because the researcher would no longer be a participant in the group if he or she did *not* take part.

Advantages

They produce rich, personal, and in-depth knowledge.

They avoid *researcher* ***bias*** because the researchers try to understand from the **perspective** of an *insider*.

Disadvantages

It is difficult to record data quickly when and where it takes place.

An extra participant (in the form of a researcher) influences group behaviour.

There are ethical issues concerning how much the researcher will ***create*** behaviour they are interested in studying.

Non-participant observations

The researcher is not part of the group being studied. The researcher observes participants from a distance, sometimes without their knowledge. The researcher does not take a part in the behaviour of the group.

Advantages

Participants with **sensitive** issues can be observed without knowing they are being observed. This avoids distress from knowing they are being observed.

Disadvantages

There are ethical issues with observing participants who are not aware they are being observed. Careful consideration needs to be given to how informed consent should be reached. In the example of people who are mentally sick, should the hospital give informed consent or the patient's family as well?

Naturalistic observations

Naturalistic observations are very similar to non-participant observations but the researcher tries hard to focus the research on the participants' *natural* environment and to avoid influencing the behaviour they are observing.

Advantages

Participants are observed in their natural environments. Participants with sensitive issues can be observed, e.g. the mentally sick.

Disadvantages

Participants react to being observed and may not behave naturally (the Hawthorne effect).

The researcher may not have a full understanding of the natural environment and may place more importance on events that they do not fully understand. For example: observing mentally sick patients in a hospital setting. Psychiatric hospitals are complex places and a researcher who spends a small amount of time there may not fully understand the details they can see (such as patient distress; relationships between doctors and patients).

Overt and covert observations can be seen as *approaches* to naturalistic and non-participant observations.

Subject vocabulary

psychiatric hospital a hospital that treats abnormal behaviours

approach ways of viewing

Overt observations

Participants know they are being observed but they might not know the exact reasons. For example, a researcher may say they are simply writing a book when they are really collecting research data.

Advantages

Participants are usually observed in their natural environments. Participants with sensitive issues can be observed, e.g. the mentally sick.

Disadvantages

Participants react to being observed and may not behave naturally (the Hawthorne effect).

Covert observations

Participants are not aware of being studied and so they have not agreed to it. The researcher has to make up a story to explain why they are present. The method is used in sensitive situations or when it is important that the presence of a researcher does not affect the behaviour of the participants.

Advantages

Participants are not aware of being studied and so their behaviour can be seen as more natural.

Disadvantages

There are ethical issues with observing participants who are not aware they are being observed. Careful consideration needs to be given to how informed consent should be reached. In the example of people who are mentally sick, should the hospital give informed consent or the patient's family as well?

Discuss considerations involved in setting up and carrying out an observation

Personal **conduct** with participants

The nature of observational research means that there should always be extra focus on how relationships are built and developed with the participants. It can be normal to have close personal contact over a long period of time and a researcher has to consider how close he or she becomes to their participants. A researcher may want to design an observation that means he or she does not have close personal contact with the participants. Avoiding contact may be a good thing in cases of violent or ill people. However, building a close relationship may be a good thing with **frail** or **vulnerable** groups such as the elderly or victims of abuse. A further consideration with participant observations is *how* and *when* the relationship will end – a close personal relationship is helpful for collecting data; however, the relationship will have to end and this may have psychological consequences for the participants.

Glossary

to abuse/abusive to be physically and/or verbally violent

consequences something that happens as the result of an action

prisoner someone who is kept in a jail

Synonyms

conduct .... behaviour

frail .... physically weak

vulnerable .... easily hurt

aggressive .... angry/threatening

schedule .... timetable

The Hawthorne effect

This refers to how participants change their behaviour when they know they are being observed. This will depend on the group. For example, prisoners may become more **aggressive**; patients may act more sick; teachers will teach better. A researcher should consider how to keep this to a minimum – for example, not saying that he or she is a researcher; not saying what the observation **schedule** is in advance; pretending to observe another group (e.g. students) while he or she is really observing the teacher.

Discuss how researchers analyse data obtained in observational research

Observational data is usually large and in-depth. The aim of analysis is to reduce these data to more a manageable size and then use the reduced version of the data to find meaning in the behaviour and environment observed. There are several ways to approach the data:

1. There is a problem with having to deal with large amounts of data. The data has to be edited and interpreted – *how* and *why* a researcher edits and interprets data is often complex and personal to the researcher and a reader may not always know how or why choices were made. A researcher should keep a notebook explaining how they made decisions with data.
2. The researcher looks for **themes** in the data and codes the observations based on these themes.
3. The researcher keeps notes to explain how the coding of the themes was done. In order for readers to feel that the research is **credible**/**trustworthy**, a complete description of the coding process must be provided.
4. The themes and codes are used to **reconstruct** the 'story' of the observation. This should be a descriptive account of what was observed and should include the themes identified, the codes used, the researcher's notes made during observation, and the researcher's interpretation of these.
5. The thoughts and feelings of the researched and the researcher should be acknowledged and built into the research process. Therefore, the biases of the

Synonyms

theme .... main topic/subject

credible .... believable

trustworthy .... reliable

reconstruct .... rebuild

Subject vocabulary

to code to label a theme or idea generated by research

researcher and how they influenced data collection and conclusions can be seen by the reader. This is a key advantage of qualitative research processes.

Reflexivity

Reflexivity in qualitative research refers to the careful attention the researcher pays to their own role in the research. When conducting observations, researchers should always ask reflexive questions such as:

- How did I come to the conclusions I came to?
- How did my beliefs affect how I edited and interpreted the data?
- Why did I decide to investigate this topic?
- If I approached the data from another perspective, how would that affect the results?
- If I used different data collection methods, would I arrive at the same conclusions?
- What has been **muted**, **repressed**, or unheard?

The questions show the reader how and why the researcher was able to arrive at his or her conclusions after conducting observations.

Synonyms

muted .... made quiet

repressed .... held back

Evaluate the use of case studies in research

Subject vocabulary

to generalize/generalization the extent to which we can apply results to other circumstances

data sets groups of data (e.g. groups of themes generated from interview; responses to questions on specific topics)

reflexive approach where the researcher thinks carefully about his or her own motivations and how this may affect the data

findings the results of a study

Synonyms

rare .... uncommon

perspectives........ points of view

unique................ one of a kind

Glossary

to contradict to disagree with/ to say the opposite is correct

established existing for a long time

emotional influenced by what you feel about something

A case study is an in-depth research approach to an *individual unit*. The individual unit can be an individual person, a family, a hotel chain, a prison, a hospital, a football team, etc. A case study will use multiple methods and is not considered to be one method alone; it is a research *strategy*. For example, it may use interviews, questionnaires, and observations to carry out the aims of the research.

Advantages

A case study can be used to study **rare** events that would be difficult to recreate - for example, a rare brain injury.

It is in-depth and produces data from different **perspectives** and methods.

It places the research unit in *context* - the research unit is researched in their natural environment - for example, the family home.

It can be used to **contradict established** theories because established theories are often generalized from large data sets and they may ignore individual details. Case studies focus on individual details to create rich data.

It leads to new research by presenting in-depth data that generate new ideas from multiple perspectives.

Disadvantages

They take time and cost a lot of money to do well.

A researcher can become **emotionally** involved as they have such close, in-depth contact with the participants. However, if the researcher uses a reflexive approach and good research skills this should not cause problems.

The fact that each case study is **unique** makes it difficult to generalize the findings to other situations.

Explain how a case study could be used to investigate a problem in an organization or group

Glossary

absenteeism staying away from work without a good reason

employee a person who is paid to work for someone

employer a person who pays someone for the work they do

interviewee a person who is interviewed by someone

Subject vocabulary

anonymous the name of the person is not known by other people

Absenteeism in a company

Absenteeism is a common problem in organizations. That is where **employees** are not at work when they are supposed to be there. A case study in this situation could start with the analysis of interview data collected from various members of staff in management and non-management positions. A *focus group* where the causes of absence could be discussed would be a particularly good way to collect data. However, employees may find it uncomfortable to admit to bad behaviour and it would be important to have arranged with the **employer** in advance that the **interviewees** would be completely anonymous. Diaries would also provide good data for this study: employees could make a note every time they were not where they should be and why they were not there. Anonymous questionnaires could also be used. In-depth interviews could be conducted with a small number of employees.

After data from these sources have been analysed, it may be possible to identify **common factors** that lead to absenteeism. The company can then make changes that deal with the problem. Such changes might involve **flexitime** systems that allow employees to work at times more convenient for them, changing employer attitudes about how many hours employees should work, offering an on-site medical service, introducing **fines** for lateness, or making the workplace a nicer environment (e.g. free coffee, more staff areas for socializing). As part of the case study approach, a **follow-up study** could be carried out to find out how successful the changes had been.

Synonyms

common factors.. similar reasons

Glossary

flexitime a system which allows people to start work early and finish early, or start late and finish late

fine money you have to pay as a punishment

Subject vocabulary

follow-up study a study that happens later to check the details of the first study and to find out if things have changed

Discuss the extent to which findings can be generalized from a single case study

A case study will probably use a small sample that has been specially selected - therefore there are problems in generalizing to a larger group. Small samples may not be **representative** of the larger **population** they claim to represent. Case studies may involve the investigation of a group or organization because they are unique or special in some way. Their uniqueness makes it difficult to generalize the findings. If case studies cannot be used to produce generalizations they can at least be used to explore them.

The question can be asked: What can we learn from studying only *one* of anything? The answer: All we can. Each case study is unique, but not so unique that we cannot learn from it and apply the lessons we learn.

Subject vocabulary

representative the sample is similar in terms of the important characteristics to the population it claims to represent

population the group of people participants are taken from and then the results can be generalized (e.g. nurses at a hospital)

Introduction to the Internal Assessment (Standard Level)

The Internal Assessment (IA) should be a simple experiment. An experiment is a method where a variable (an independent variable – IV) is changed to measure the effect on another identified variable (the dependent variable – DV) while controlling for other variables. Therefore, an independent variable (IV) is the variable an experimenter *manipulates*. The dependent variable (DV) is the variable an experimenter *measures*. **Manipulate** *one* IV and measure its effect on *one* DV. Students should note: The IA is *not* an opportunity for you to show you can **conduct** independent research – you are being measured on your ability to follow clear guidelines about how to write up a simple experiment. A good experiment has a clear IV and a clear DV. Students are very strongly advised to conduct a very simple, safe experiment such as those found in the Psychology course guide or the following.

Examples of research include:

1. **Aim:** To measure the effect of leading verbs on speed **perception**.
   Source study/idea: Loftus and Palmer.
   IV: The **intensity** of a leading verb.
   DV: Speed perception as measured by estimation of speed.
   Design: Independent measures.

2. **Aim:** To measure the effect of **context** on **recall**.
   Source study/idea: Godden and Baddeley.
   IV: The context of recall.
   DV: Amount of recall.
   Design: Independent measures.

3. **Aim:** To measure the effect of interference on cognition.
   Source study/idea: The Stroop effect.
   IV: Word lists are congruent or incongruent.
   DV: Interference as measured by the time taken to complete the task.
   Design: Repeated measures.

4. **Aim:** To measure the effect of physiological **arousal** on perception of attractiveness.
   Source study/idea: Dutton and Aron.
   IV: Presence or absence of physiological arousal on perception of attractiveness.
   DV: Perception of attractiveness as measured by attractiveness **rating**.
   Design: Independent measures.

Abstract

Suggested word count: 200

The abstract is a clearly written summary of the experimental study, including the results. State the relevant aspects of the procedure and the main findings.

What was the experiment's aim?

What was the experiment's **scope**; what did it do, and to whom?

What were the results?

What is the experiment's conclusion?

Subject vocabulary

to control for experimenters control variables and the experimental settings so they can be sure they are manipulating and measuring what they *assume* they are manipulating and measuring

to manipulate to change

independent measures different participants are used in the different conditions of the research process

interference disruption

cognition/cognitive related to mental processes (such as perception, memory, problem-solving)

congruent similar

incongruent dissimilar

repeated measures the same participants are used in every condition of the research process

physiological related to the body

Synonyms

manipulate .... change

conduct .... carry out

recall .... remember

Glossary

to perceive/perception to see or understand information

intensity how strongly you feel about something

context situation in which something happens

arousal bodily and psychological alertness

rating a measurement of how good or interesting something is

scope the extent/range that a subject deals with

Introduction

Suggested word count: 300

The introduction should contain the academic background to the study. It should *clearly* show where the main ideas came from and how the aim is based on previous research.

The study replicated is clearly identified and relevant details of the study are explained.

You must explain the aim, method, results, and conclusions of the study you are replicating. Aim can be defined as the overall research goal (usually the research question). It does not need to be copied from the original study; you can use your own words. Method can be defined as what happened in the study. Results can be defined as exactly what was found in terms of their data. Conclusions can be defined as the broader meaning that comes from the results.

Example paragraph:

> Loftus and Palmer (1974) aimed to show that **eyewitnesses** do not accurately 'replay' what they saw. Instead they reconstruct events based on their schemas or simplified mental representations. Loftus and Palmer aimed to show that participants' perceptions of a car's speed could be manipulated by **leading questions**. An independent measures laboratory experiment was conducted, with 45 undergraduate students being presented with seven **film clips** of traffic accidents. The experiment's IV was a key verb that took five conditions in the question: 'About how fast were the cars going when they smashed into each other?' 'Smashed' was substituted with 'collided', 'bumped', 'contacted', and 'hit'. The mean speed associated with 'smashed' was 40.8 mph while the mean for 'hit' was 31.8 mph. Loftus and Palmer (1974) concluded that eyewitness **testimony** can be manipulated by using different words in a leading question.

You do not need to replicate every detail of the study. You will probably have to simplify it in some way. For example, with Loftus and Palmer you may need to use fewer participants and show fewer films.

The aim of the study is clearly stated.

The aims are statements of what the research tries to show. Do not use the word 'investigate' when stating the aim because the IA is an investigation. You should state the aim precisely, so use words such as measure, discover, explain, evaluate, and **explicate**. You can also use the aim of the IA in the title.

Example sentence:

> **Aim:** To measure the effect of leading verbs (IV) on speed perceptions (DV).

Synonyms

replicated .... copied

explicate .... explain

Glossary

(eye)witness a person who sees something, usually a crime

leading question a question that encourages the desired answer

film clip short extract from a movie

testimony a (formal) statement of what is true

Subject vocabulary

schema a frame for understanding the world

participant someone who takes part in a research study

condition the experimental situation the experimenters have created to test something

mean a form of central tendency usually referred to as the 'average'

Method

Suggested word count: 400

The Method section contains information on how and why the experiment was designed, how it was carried out, and who it was carried out with (the participants). The word 'method' should appear at the top of the new section in the middle of the page and then each sub-section should have clearly labelled sub-headings of *design*, *participants*, and *procedure*.

Design

The independent variable and dependent variable are accurately identified and operationalized.

State the IV and DV and then describe how they will be operationalized. Operationalizing an IV means showing how it will be **manipulated**. Operationalizing a DV means showing how it will be measured.

Example sentence:

The IV is leading verbs. It will be manipulated by changing the verb. Participants will be **exposed** to the verb 'smashed' or 'hit' in a question about a traffic accident. The DV is **perception**. It will be operationalized by asking participants to **estimate** a car's speed in miles per hour (mph).

You can use a table to make them clearer.

	IV	DV
Identified...	The IV is the verb in the question, i.e. ...	The DV is the car's estimated speed
Operationalized...	IV1 = hit IV2 = smashed	Measured in miles per hour (mph)

The experimental design is appropriate to the aim and its use is appropriately justified.

Experimental designs are usually either:

Repeated measures (the same participants experience the IV's two conditions) or

Independent measures (different participants experience the IV's two conditions)

'Justified' means to give reasons for using a particular design. Repeated measures are used because they require fewer participants and variables such as participants' intelligence can be controlled in each condition. Independent measures avoid demand characteristics such as participants guessing what the experiment is trying to find out and then not responding naturally.

Example paragraph:

Independent measures were used to control for demand characteristics. Participants would probably guess the nature of the study if they were exposed to both verbs and so their responses would be unnatural.

Subject vocabulary

participant someone who takes part in a research study

condition the experimental situation the experimenters have created to test something

demand characteristics participants form an interpretation of the experiment's purpose and then change their behaviour to fit that interpretation. It is why deception is sometimes necessary

to control (for) experimenters control variables and the experimental settings so they can be sure they are manipulating and measuring what they *assume* they are manipulating and measuring

Glossary

to manipulate/manipulation to control something or someone to your advantage

to expose/exposure to see/to be shown

to perceive/perception to see or understand information

Synonyms

estimate............. guess

appropriate .... suitable

There is clear indication and documentation of how ethical guidelines were followed.

The IBO publishes ethical guidelines. If your IA breaks these guidelines you could receive zero marks.

You must include clear evidence that your experiment is ethical.

In practice, the term ethical guidelines refers to how participants **consented** to be involved, whether the experiment was safe, whether the participants were **deceived**, and how participants were **debriefed**. Mild deception is often necessary but must be reasonable. A simple guide is to ask yourself how you would feel if you were the participant?

Example sentence:

Mild deception was necessary so the participants did not guess the nature of the experiment. The deception did not cause **discomfort** or **humiliation** and so was considered by the researcher and his supervisor to be reasonable, and was clearly addressed in the debriefing session.

You should put **blank** consent and debrief **forms** in the Appendix.

Example sentence:

Participants were asked to read and sign an **Informed** Consent form (Appendix I). Participants were debriefed after the experiment (Appendix II).

Sample informed consent form (to be included in the IA's Appendix)

To whom it may concern,

As part of my IB Diploma Psychology course I am **conducting** an experiment that investigates the **cognitive** process of perception and I would like to invite you to participate.

The experiment will involve you watching a brief video of a traffic accident. There are no disturbing images of injuries in the video.

You will then be asked to complete a brief questionnaire.

The experiment is being supervised by the school's Psychology teacher and he has approved the study as being safe for participants. No personal information will be kept.

If you agree to participate, please sign below.

____

Do not tell the participants what the experiment is about on the consent forms. Put a blank consent form in the Appendix.

Subject vocabulary

ethical relating to the idea of right or wrong behaviour

to debrief to give out information after an event (e.g. experiment)

cognition/cognitive related to mental processes (such as perception, memory, problem-solving)

Glossary

to consent to agree to something

to deceive/deception to cause someone to believe something that is not true

discomfort a feeling of not being at ease

humiliation making a person feel stupid or ashamed

blank nothing written on it

informed having a lot of information about something

Synonyms

forms .... official documents

conducting .... carrying out

Example debrief form

Dear Participant,

Thank you for participating in the experiment. Its aim was to measure the effect of leading verbs on participants' perceptions of speed. As participants, you were asked to watch a traffic accident and then estimate a car's speed. I averaged these estimates to make a concluding statement about the effect of the leading verb on speed perception.

The experiment's conclusion is that the **intensity** of the verb used in the question (hit or smashed) **affects** participants' perception of the car's speed. In general, participants who were asked how fast the car was travelling before it smashed into the other car estimated a higher speed than those who were asked how fast the car was travelling before it hit the other car.

The experiment's results will only be used in my internal assessment. Participants were assigned a number and so cannot be identified in the report. No personal information was collected about participants.

If you have any questions or **concerns** about your involvement in the experiment, please contact me or my supervisor, in the school's Psychology Department.

Glossary

intensity how strongly you feel about something

to affect to influence

criterion a standard by which you measure something

Synonyms

concerns .... worries

characteristics ..... traits/features

urban .... towns/cities

Participants

Relevant characteristics of the participants are identified.

You must identify relevant characteristics to describe the group of participants who took part in the experiment. Relevant characteristics of participants in Loftus and Palmer (1974) include driving experience, exposure to **urban** traffic situations, experience with/in traffic accidents, exposure to speed-related interests such as go-kart racing, playing WRC on the PlayStation, studying Physics. Before including a characteristic, you should think about whether it is relevant.

It is important that you think about this assessment **criterion** before you set up your experiment. How will you collect this information about the participants?

Example sentence:

Twenty participants were included in the experiment: 12 girls and eight boys, aged between 16 and 17, all students at the International School of [. . .]. The speed limit around the school is 40 mph and so all the participants are regularly exposed to traffic speeds in the range of the car shown in the experiment's video. Eleven of the participants were Hungarian, but nine were Chagos Islanders. There are no cars on the Chagos Islands and so these participants had very little exposure/experience of estimating speeds. Eight participants drive themselves to school and so they have a high level of experience of estimating traffic speed. Four have been involved in traffic accidents and seven more have witnessed traffic accidents recently. Twelve have been participants in other psychology experiments and six of the participants have studied psychology.

The sample is selected using an appropriate method and the use of this method is explained.

Sampling means choosing participants from the wider population and this section requires you to describe how and why you chose the participants.

Purposive sampling: Purposive sampling targets a particular group of people who would make good study participants because of their characteristics. 'Appropriate' characteristics would depend on the aim of the study.

Example sentence:

> We chose purposive sampling because the experiment required a good command of English. We deliberately approached good English speakers who we knew because having some participants with native English skills and others who have English as a second or third language would make the results less reliable.

Opportunity sampling: This is where members of a target population are asked to take part just because they are available. In this situation, you ask possible participants that you see in the corridor or in lessons. This is sometimes called convenience sampling.

Example sentence:

> We chose an opportunity sampling method because it is quick and convenient and because we needed the full agreement of a teacher in advance to use their classes for our experiment. We approached a supportive teacher and agreed in advance to use their lesson time for our experiment. We used 22 participants because this was the class size.

Random sampling: Each member of a target population has the same chance of being sampled. In this situation, you write each name on a separate piece of paper and put them into a container and then pull out the required number of participants. Do not use the phrase 'random selection' as it is not a suitable way to describe this process.

Example sentence:

> We chose a random sampling method to achieve an unbiased sample. We placed every name from our grade level onto a piece of paper and then put them in a hat and pulled out 20.

Subject vocabulary

target population the group a researcher is interested in and the group about which the researcher wishes to draw conclusions

unbiased free from personal influence or opinion

Subject vocabulary

procedural referring to the method used to carry out an experiment

raw data information that has not been processed

Synonyms

replicable .... repeatable

materials .... equipment

Procedure

The procedural information is relevant and clearly described, so that the study is easily replicable.

You should include a step-by-step guide of how the experiment was conducted. Include details of when and where the experiment was carried out. Make sure that you only describe the experiment's procedure, not the whole IA.

Details of how the ethical guidelines were applied are included.

You should state when you handed out the informed consent forms. You should also explain how and when you debriefed your participants.

Example sentence:

Participants were given consent forms and then asked to read and sign them. These were then collected by the researchers and filed for later reference. After the experiment was over participants were each given a debriefing form and asked to read it. Consent and debriefing forms can be found in the appendices (I and II).

Necessary materials have been included and referenced in the appendices.

Necessary materials can be written as a list. After each one, add the appendix Roman numeral reference in brackets. Necessary materials include: questionnaires, consent and debrief forms, pens, scrap paper, recording equipment, video references, raw data forms (which can include print outs from websites and/or Excel worksheets).

Example sentence:

Example of questionnaire (Appendix IV)

Raw data forms (Appendix V)

Results section

Suggested word count: 200

Results are clearly stated and accurate and reflect the aim of the research.

The results section must show whether the IV caused a change in the DV.

Appropriate descriptive statistics (one measure of central tendency and one measure of dispersion) are applied to the data and their use is explained.

A common mistake is to calculate more than one measure of central tendency (mean, median, mode) and one measure of dispersion averages (range, standard deviation, variance, inter-quartile range). Use one of each.

A measure of central tendency shows the most likely, the most probable, the typical piece, or the average piece of data. Choose from the mean, median, or mode.

Use the mean to describe the typical, most likely, piece of data. If there are extreme outliers (unusually high or low pieces of data), the mean will be distorted. As a result, it does not describe the typical data. If there are outliers, use the median.

If the data is not continuous, use the mode. If a group includes five girls and 15 boys, the most likely gender is male. It would not make sense to say that the typical gender is 0.75 male.

A measure of dispersion shows how **varied** the group of data is or how dispersed the data is from the normal or central data. The actual measure used depends on the data set you have collected. The range is a good measure to use unless there are extreme outliers.

Use the standard deviation if the data is continuous and the data set is normally distributed and use the inter-quartile range if the data is skewed.

Make sure that you include information on *what* the statistics are describing. For example, the mean speed is not 35.5, it is 35.5 miles per hour.

Example sentence (if the score is low):

> The low value indicates the data tends to be very close to the mean suggesting there is a great deal of similarity in the data set.

Example sentence (if the score is high):

> The high standard deviation indicates the data is spread out over a large range of values suggesting there is less similarity in the data set.

Synonyms

reflect................ show

Subject vocabulary

results data that has been processed – for example, turned into a mean

descriptive statistics statistics which summarize the data

dispersion measures how spread out a data set is

mean a form of central tendency usually referred to as the 'average'

median the middle value separating the higher half of a data set from the lower half

mode the value that appears most often in a data set

standard deviation shows how much variation, spread, or dispersion exists from the average or expected value

variance the average of the squared differences from the mean

inter-quartile range an accepted measure of dispersion

outliers results/responses that are very different form the other results/responses

distorted changed

continuous data data that can be measured on a scale and compared with other data

data sets groups of data (e.g. groups of themes generated from interview; responses to questions on specific topics)

normal distribution refers to a type of data that is symmetrical around the mean

skewed a lack of symmetry in the data set

Glossary

varied including different types (of things or people)

Subject vocabulary

axis the vertical and horizontal lines on a graph

raw data information that has not been processed

Glossary

to represent/representation to describe in written or picture form

tabular like a table

Synonyms

affected .... influenced

The graph of results is accurate, clear, and directly relevant to the aim of the study.

Make sure that the graphs have a title, a legend (a key), and a clear label for each axis. They should be simple **representations** of the results (descriptive) not the raw data.

The graph should show whether the experiment's DV is **affected** by the change in the IV. This could be as simple as showing a bar chart representing the mean of IV1 and the mean of IV2.

It is often better to draw the graph by hand (with a pencil and ruler) and paste it into the report. You should not simply enter the data set into Excel and then print out the most interesting-looking graph. It would be better to use a scanner to convert a hand-drawn graph into an electronic version.

In order to make sure that the graph is clear:

- Make it large.
- Give it a title, and include (N = …) after the title to show how many participants.
- Give it a border.
- Label the axes (include units).
- Label the data either on the graph or with a key (legend).
- Show the measure of central tendency and the measure of dispersion, if possible.

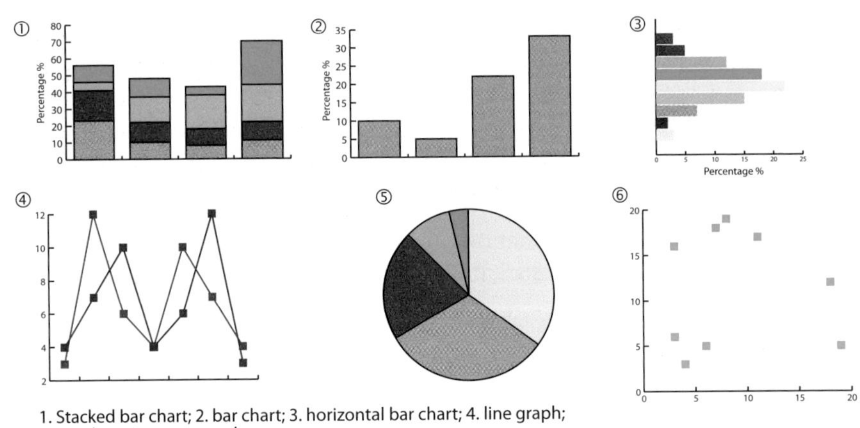

1. Stacked bar chart; 2. bar chart; 3. horizontal bar chart; 4. line graph; 5. pie chart; 6. scattergraph

---

Results are presented in both words and tabular form.

Example sentence:

Results

The median estimate of speed for the question using smashed was XX mph, while the median estimate of speed for the question using hit was XX mph. The standard deviation of the data set associated with 'smashed' was XX mph. The standard deviation of the data set associated with 'hit' was XX mph.

Results	IV1 (Smashed), mph	IV2 (Hit), mph
median		
standard deviation		

Discussion

Suggested word count: 600

Discussion of results is well developed and complete (for example, differences in the results of calculations of central tendency and/ or dispersion are explained).

Repeat the description of the descriptive results. Write the same sentence that you used below the graph. State how the results support or **refute** the aim of the study.

Example sentence:

The aim of the experiment was to measure the effect of leading verbs on speed perceptions of a car crash. The results demonstrate the extent to which changing the leading verb can influence the participants' estimates of speed. The average estimation of speed changed with the different verbs. The variance in speed estimates of 48.5 km/h between the verbs 'smashed' and 'hit' demonstrates a change in speed perception.

The findings of the student's experimental study are discussed with reference to relevant background studies and/or theories.

In the discussion section, you must refer to all of the studies you mentioned in the introduction. You should include a statement about whether the results from your experiment support or refute the studies.

Example sentence:

Loftus and Palmer (1974) aimed to investigate the effect of **leading questions** on the accuracy of speed estimated in, and perceived consequences of, a car crash. The results, which ranged in mean speed estimates on a range of 40.8 mph for smashed and 31.8 mph for hit, indicated that the speed estimates were indeed influenced by the wording used. Our study clearly supports Loftus and Palmer as a significant difference was found between the verbs smashed and hit (estimates for smashed being considerably higher). The results of both studies clearly question the extent to which perception is reliable.

Limitations of the design and procedure are highly relevant and have been rigorously analysed.

You must give at least three problems with the design and procedure and say why they occurred.

Example sentence:

The participants consisted of mostly 16-year-old students with limited experience of driving and so limited skill in estimating traffic speeds. This is suggested in the large range in speed estimates in the raw data.

The experiment lacks ecological validity. It was conducted in a classroom, and the car accident was watched in video format. A real-life traffic accident would have included more stimuli such as realistic sounds, realistic distances, etc. A real-life accident would have been witnessed after the participants had likely been outside and amongst the traffic for some time, whereas the video was shown in isolation.

The participants were aware that they were in an experiment being conducted for the researcher's IB Diploma and so demand characteristics may have **affected** the participants' responses.

Similarly, the researcher may have influenced the experiment with researcher biases such as unintentionally placing more stress on some words in the instructions, or body language when showing the videos.

Glossary

to refute to prove that a statement is incorrect

leading question a question that encourages the desired answer

rigorously carefully, thoroughly, and exactly

Subject vocabulary

ecological validity having realism and being able to generalize to real-life situations

demand characteristics participants form an interpretation of the experiment's purpose and then change their behaviour to fit that interpretation. It is why deception is sometimes necessary

researcher bias a behaviour or expectation on the part of the researcher that influences the experiment particularly the results and conclusions

Synonyms

affected .... influenced

Synonyms

modifications...... changes

recap.................. repeat

Glossary

varied including different types (of things or people)

eyewitness testimony a formal statement in which a person describes something they have seen

scenario situation

physical assault attacking someone, e.g. hitting or punching

Subject vocabulary

data sets groups of data (e.g. groups of themes generated from interview; responses to questions on specific topics)

Modifications are suggested and ideas for further research are mentioned.

You must include a solution for each of the problems mentioned above.

Example sentence:

If the study was to be conducted again, certain modifications could be made. The participants may be chosen from an older or more **varied** age group with driving experience. This would allow for participants to be more familiar with car speeds, and thus provide more accurate estimates and with possibly less variance within the **data sets**. Furthermore, the participant may be asked more questions in addition to the speed of the car, in order to reduce the focus on the speed estimate and perhaps reduce the likelihood of response bias. However, the use of the video allowed a standardized presentation of the data and so while it lacked ecological validity, it should remain as a basic procedural guideline for this experiment. In future, one of the participants can be selected to act as the presenter, to read instructions and so avoid any researcher influences.

Further research can be in the form of future research questions.

Example sentence:

This experiment concludes that **eyewitness testimony** can be affected by leading questions. More research is needed into whether certain verbs carry more influence than others. Other research could be carried out on whether verbs influence perception in other **scenarios** such as **physical assaults**.

If eyewitness testimony is affected by verbs, is it also affected by other variables such as the type of vehicle involved in the accident, such as delivery vans versus sports cars, motorcycles, taxis, school buses?

The conclusion is appropriate.

The conclusion can be very similar to the abstract. You should include a full **recap** of the aim, the relevant aspects of the procedure, and the main findings.

Appendices

The appendix (plural: appendices) contains relevant information that cannot fit into the other areas, for example, raw data; consent and debrief forms; calculations; examples of apparatus such as questionnaires. Appendices should be labelled appropriately and referenced in the body of the report. You should use Roman numerals (I, II, III, IV, etc.).

Example:

Appendix I: Raw Data

Referencing

A reference section is strongly recommended and not a bibliography. A reference section means you cite the author in the main body of your IA (usually the introduction) and then provide full details at the end of the work (with the details listed alphabetically) under a heading of 'References'. You have a choice of referencing styles. However, this book recommends the Harvard referencing system (or author-date system). The Harvard referencing system uses an author-date reference in the text, e.g. '(Smith, 2000)', being inserted after the cited idea within parentheses and the full reference to the source being listed at the end of the essay. If you quote directly (and this should happen rarely) then you need to include the surname, date, page number, e.g. '(Smith, 2000: 24)'.

- Only use page numbers when you quote directly.
- If you use this system then you do not need to have 'footnotes'.
- Do not include any other information in the author-date reference. For example, do not use initials (Smith, J.S., 2000); do not mention universities (Smith, University of Bath, 2000); do not mention qualifications (Smith, PhD, 2000).
- For SL students the reference section will usually only include the study being replicated. Make sure you find the original study and read it thoroughly and then reference fully in your reference section.
- You can use the author's surname in the text and then include the date in parentheses, e.g. 'Smith (2000) argued...'

Example:

Loftus, E.F., and Palmer, J.C. (1974) Reconstruction of automobile destruction: An example of the interaction between language and memory. *Journal of Verbal Learning and Verbal Behavior*, **13**, 585–589.

Referencing has exact rules about the information to be included, where to use a comma (,) and where to use a semi-colon (;), where the date goes and how the page numbers appear. Journal articles, books, and websites are all referenced differently. Please see the Extended Essay section for further details.

Introduction to the Internal Assessment (Higher Level)

The Internal Assessment (IA) should be a simple experiment. An experiment is a method where a variable (an independent variable - IV) is changed to measure the effect on another identified variable (the dependent variable - DV) while controlling for other variables. Therefore, an independent variable (IV) is the variable an experimenter *manipulates*. The dependent variable (DV) is the variable an experimenter *measures*. **Manipulate** *one* IV and measure its effect on *one* DV. Students should note: The IA is *not* an opportunity for you to show you can conduct independent research - you are being measured on your ability to follow clear guidelines about how to write up a simple experiment. A good experiment has a clear IV and a clear DV. Students are very strongly advised to conduct a very simple, safe experiment such as those found in the Psychology course guide or the following:

Examples of research include:

1. **Aim:** To measure the effect of leading verbs on speed **perception**.
   Source study/idea: Loftus and Palmer.
   IV: The **intensity** of a leading verb.
   DV: Speed perception as measured by **estimation** of speed.
   Design: Independent measures.
2. **Aim:** To measure the effect of **context** on **recall**.
   Source study/idea: Godden and Baddeley.
   IV: The context of recall.
   DV: Amount of recall.
   Design: Independent measures.
3. **Aim:** To measure the effect of interference on cognition.
   Source study/idea: The Stroop effect.
   IV: Word lists are congruent or incongruent.
   DV: Interference as measured by the time taken to complete the task.
   Design: Repeated measures.
4. **Aim:** To measure the effect of physiological **arousal** on perception of attractiveness.
   Source study/idea: Dutton and Aron.
   IV: Presence or absence of physiological arousal on perception of attractiveness.
   DV: Perception of attractiveness as measured by attractiveness **rating**.
   Design: Independent measures.

Abstract

Suggested word count: 200

The abstract is a clearly written summary of the experimental study, including the results.

State the relevant aspects of the procedure and the main findings.

What was the experiment's aim?

What was the experiment's **scope**; what did it do, and to whom?

What were the results?

What is the experiment's conclusion?

Subject vocabulary

to control for experimenters control variables and the experimental settings so they can be sure they are manipulating and measuring what they *assume* they are manipulating and measuring

to manipulate to change

independent measures different participants are used in the different conditions of the research process

interference disruption

cognition/cognitive related to mental processes (such as perception, memory, problem-solving)

congruent similar

incongruent dissimilar

repeated measures the same participants are used in every condition of the research process

physiological related to the body

Glossary

to manipulate/manipulation to control something or someone to your advantage

to perceive/perception to see or understand information

intensity how strongly you feel about something

context situation in which something happens

arousal bodily and psychological alertness

rating a measurement of how good or interesting something is

scope the extent/range that a subject deals with

Synonyms

estimate............. guess

recall .... remember

Introduction

Suggested word count: 600

The introduction should contain the academic background to the study. It should clearly show where the main ideas came from and how the aim and hypothesis are based on previous research.

Background theories and/or studies are adequately explained and highly relevant to the hypotheses.

Background theories and/or studies should be logical and focused around your central idea. You must explain them in-depth. A minimum of three studies should be examined. Explain the aims, methods, results, and conclusions. Aim can be defined as the overall research goal (usually the research question). It does not need to be copied from the original study; you can use your own words. Method can be defined as what happened in the study. Results can be defined as exactly what was found in terms of their data. Conclusions can be defined as the broader meaning that comes from the results.

Example paragraph:

Loftus and Palmer (1974) aimed to show that **eyewitnesses** do not accurately 'replay' what they saw. Instead they reconstruct events based on their schemas or simplified mental representations. Loftus and Palmer aimed to show that participants' perceptions of a car's speed could be manipulated by **leading questions**. An independent measures laboratory experiment was conducted, with 45 undergraduate students being presented with seven **film clips** of traffic accidents. The experiment's IV was a key verb that took five conditions in the question: 'About how fast were the cars going when they smashed into each other?' 'Smashed' was substituted with 'collided', 'bumped', 'contacted', and 'hit'. The mean speed associated with 'smashed' was 40.8 mph while the mean for 'hit' was 31.8 mph. Loftus and Palmer (1974) concluded that eyewitness **testimony** can be manipulated by using different words in a leading question.

The aim of the study is clearly stated.

The aims are statements of what the research tries to show. Do not use the word 'investigate' when stating the aim because the IA is an investigation. You should state the aim precisely, so use words such as measure, discover, explain, and evaluate. You can also use the aim of the IA in the title.

Example sentence:

Aim: To measure the effect of leading verbs (IV) on speed perceptions (DV).

Subject vocabulary

hypothesis the idea being tested by the study

schema a frame for understanding the world

participant someone who takes part in a research study

condition the experimental situation the experimenters have created to test something

mean a form of central tendency usually referred to as the 'average'

Glossary

(eye)witness a person who sees something, usually a crime

leading question a question that encourages the desired answer

film clip short extract from a movie

testimony a (formal) statement of what is true

Subject vocabulary

to operationalize *how* the IV is manipulated and *how* the DV is measured

significant difference a difference that has been identified by using mathematical tests and that can be considered large enough for social scientists to look for causes

Glossary

to predict/prediction to say what will happen in the future

outcome the result

to expose to see/to be shown

The experimental and null hypotheses are appropriately stated and operationalized. The prediction made in the experimental hypothesis is justified by the background studies and/or theories.

The hypothesis is a statement that predicts the experiment's **outcome**. An operationalized hypothesis clearly contains the IV and shows the effect on the DV. There should be two: an experimental hypothesis (H1) and a null hypothesis (H0). The null hypothesis predicts the independent variable will have no effect on the dependent variable. The experimental hypothesis predicts that there will be an effect. You should clearly state what this effect will be, and indicate how it will be observed. Based on the results of the experiment, one hypothesis will be rejected. The hypothesis should follow logically from previous research.

Example sentence:

H1: Participants **exposed** to the leading verb 'smash' when asked to estimate the speed of a car crash will have significantly higher speed estimations than participants who are exposed to the verb 'hit' when asked to estimate the speed of a car crash.

H0: Participants exposed to the leading verb 'smash' when asked to estimate the speed of a car crash will have no significant difference in their speed estimations than participants who are exposed to the verb 'hit' when asked to estimate the speed of a car crash.

Method

Suggested word count: 400

The Method section contains information on how and why the experiment was designed, how it was carried out, and who it was carried out with (the participants). The word 'method' should appear at the top of the new section in the middle of the page and then each sub-section should have clearly labelled sub-headings of *design*, *participants*, and *procedure*.

Design

The independent variable and dependent variable are accurately identified and operationalized.

State the IV and DV and then describe how they will be operationalized. Operationalizing an IV means showing how it will be manipulated. Operationalizing a DV means showing how it will be measured.

Example sentence:

The IV is leading verbs. It will be manipulated by changing the verb. Participants will be exposed to the verb 'smashed' or 'hit' in a question about a traffic accident. The DV is perception. It will be operationalized by asking participants to estimate a car's speed in miles per hour (mph).

You can use a table to make them clearer.

	IV	DV
Identified...	The IV is the verb in the question, i.e. ...	The DV is the car's estimated speed
Operationalized...	IV1 = hit IV2 = smashed	Measured in miles per hour (mph)

The experimental design is appropriate to the aim and its use is appropriately justified.

Experimental designs are usually either:

Repeated measures (the same participants experience the IV's two conditions) or

Independent measures (different participants experience the IV's two conditions)

'Justified' means to give reasons for using a particular design. Repeated measures are used because they require fewer participants, and variables such as participants' intelligence can be controlled in each condition. Independent measures avoid demand characteristics such as participants guessing what the experiment is trying to find out and then not responding naturally.

Example paragraph:

Independent measures were used to control for demand characteristics. Participants would probably guess the nature of the study if they were **exposed** to both verbs and so their responses would be unnatural.

There is clear indication and documentation of how ethical guidelines were followed.

The IBO publishes ethical guidelines. If your IA breaks these guidelines you could receive zero marks.

You must include clear evidence that your experiment is ethical.

In practice, the term ethical guidelines refers to how participants **consented** to be involved, whether the experiment was safe, whether the participants were **deceived**, and how participants were debriefed. Mild deception is often necessary but must be reasonable. A simple guide is to ask yourself how you would feel if you were the participant?

Example sentence:

Mild deception was necessary so the participants did not guess the nature of the experiment. The deception did not cause **discomfort** or **humiliation** and so was considered by the researcher and his supervisor to be reasonable, and was clearly addressed in the debriefing session.

You should put **blank** consent and debrief **forms** in the Appendix.

Example sentence:

Participants were asked to read and sign an **Informed** Consent form (Appendix I). Participants were debriefed after the experiment (Appendix II).

Synonyms

appropriate .... suitable

forms................. official documents

Subject vocabulary

participant someone who takes part in a research study

condition the experimental situation the experimenters have created to test something

demand characteristics participants form an interpretation of the experiment's purpose and then change their behaviour to fit that interpretation. It is why deception is sometimes necessary

to control (for) experimenters control variables and the experimental settings so they can be sure they are manipulating and measuring what they *assume* they are manipulating and measuring

ethical relating to the idea of right or wrong behaviour

to debrief to give out information after an event (e.g. experiment)

Glossary

to expose/exposure to see/ to be shown

to consent to agree to something

to deceive/deception to cause someone to believe something that is not true

discomfort a feeling of not being at ease

humiliation making a person feel stupid or ashamed

blank nothing written on it

informed having a lot of information about something

Sample informed consent form (to be included in the IA's Appendix)

To whom it may concern,

As part of my IB Diploma Psychology course I am **conducting** an experiment that investigates the cognitive process of **perception** and I would like to invite you to participate.

The experiment will involve you watching a brief video of a traffic accident. There are no disturbing images of injuries in the video.

You will then be asked to complete a brief questionnaire.

The experiment is being supervised by the school's Psychology teacher and he has approved the study as being safe for participants. No personal information will be kept.

If you agree to participate, please sign below.

____

Do not tell the participants what the experiment is about on the consent forms. Put a blank consent form in the Appendix.

Synonyms

conducting .... carrying out

estimate............. guess

concerns............ worries

Glossary

to perceive/perception to see or understand information

intensity how strongly you feel about something

to affect to influence

Example debrief form

Dear Participant,

Thank you for participating in the experiment. Its aim was to measure the effect of leading verbs on participants' perceptions of speed. As participants, you were asked to watch a traffic accident and then **estimate** a car's speed. I averaged these estimates to make a concluding statement about the effect of the leading verb on speed perception.

The experiment's conclusion is that the **intensity** of the verb used in the question (hit or smashed) **affects** participants' perception of the car's speed. In general, participants who were asked how fast the car was travelling before is smashed into the other car estimated a higher speed than those who were asked how fast the car was travelling before it hit the other car.

The experiment's results will only be used in my internal assessment. Participants were assigned a number and so cannot be identified in the report. No personal information was collected about participants.

If you have any questions or **concerns** about your involvement in the experiment, please contact me or my supervisor, in the school's Psychology Department.

Participants

Relevant characteristics of the participants are identified.

You must identify relevant characteristics to describe the group of participants who took part in the experiment. Relevant characteristics of participants in Loftus and Palmer (1974) include driving experience, exposure to **urban** traffic situations, experience with/in traffic accidents, exposure to speed-related interests such as go-kart racing, playing WRC on the PlayStation, studying Physics. Before including a characteristic, you should think about whether it is relevant.

It is important that you think about this assessment **criterion** before you set up your experiment. How will you collect this information about the participants?

Example sentence:

> Twenty participants were included in the experiment: 12 girls and eight boys, aged between 16 and 17, all students at the International School of [...]. The speed limit around the school is 40 mph and so all the participants are regularly exposed to traffic speeds in the range of the car shown in the experiment's video. Eleven of the participants were Hungarian, but nine were Chagos Islanders. There are no cars on the Chagos Islands and so these participants had very little exposure/experience of estimating speeds. Eight participants drive themselves to school and so they have a high level of experience of estimating traffic speed. Four have been involved in traffic accidents and seven more have witnessed traffic accidents recently. Twelve have been participants in other psychology experiments and six of the participants have studied psychology.

The sample is selected using an appropriate method and the use of this method is explained.

Sampling means choosing participants from the wider population and this section requires you to describe how and why you chose the participants.

Purposive sampling: Purposive sampling targets a particular group of people who would make good study participants because of their characteristics. 'Appropriate' characteristics would depend on the aim of the study.

Example sentence:

> We chose purposive sampling because the experiment required a good command of English. We deliberately approached good English speakers who we knew because having some participants with native English skills and others who have English as a second or third language would make the results less reliable.

Opportunity sampling: This is where members of a **target population** are asked to take part just because they are available. In this situation, you ask possible participants that you see in the corridor or in lessons. This is sometimes called convenience sampling.

Example sentence:

> We chose an opportunity sampling method because it is quick and convenient and because we needed the full agreement of a teacher in advance to use their classes for our experiment. We approached a supportive teacher and agreed in advance to use their lesson time for our experiment. We used 22 participants because this was the class size.

Synonyms

characteristics ..... traits/features

urban .... towns/cities

Glossary

criterion a standard by which you measure something

Subject vocabulary

target population the group a researcher is interested in and the group about which the researcher wishes to draw conclusions

Random sampling: Each member of a target population has the same chance of being sampled. In this situation, you write each name on a separate piece of paper and put them into a container and then pull out the required number of participants. Do not use the phrase 'random selection' as it is not a suitable way to describe this process.

Example sentence:

We chose a random sampling method to achieve an unbiased sample. We placed every name from our grade level onto a piece of paper and then put them in a hat and pulled out 20.

The target population has been identified and is appropriate.

The target population is the group who the results can be generalized to. It will usually be students from a particular grade level.

Example sentence:

The target population is all students from Grade 11 at the International School of [. . .].

Procedure

The procedural information is relevant and clearly described, so that the study is easily replicable.

You should include a step-by-step guide of how the experiment was conducted. Include details of when and where the experiment was carried out. Make sure that you only describe the experiment's procedure, not the whole IA.

Details of how the ethical guidelines were applied are included.

You should state when you handed out the informed consent forms. You should also explain how and when you debriefed your participants.

Example sentence:

Participants were given consent forms and then asked to read and sign them. These were then collected by the researchers and filed for later reference. After the experiment was over participants were each given a debriefing form and asked to read it. Consent and debriefing forms can be found in the appendices (I and II).

Necessary materials have been included and referenced in the appendices.

Necessary materials can be written as a list. After each one, add the appendix Roman numeral reference in brackets. Necessary materials include: questionnaires, consent and debrief forms, pens, scrap paper, recording equipment, video references, raw data forms (which can include print outs from websites and/or Excel worksheets).

Example sentence:

Example of questionnaire (Appendix IV)

Raw Data forms (Appendix V)

Subject vocabulary

unbiased free from personal influence or opinion

to generalize/generalization the extent to which we can apply results to other circumstances

procedural referring to the method used to carry out an experiment

raw data information that has not been processed

Synonyms

replicable .... repeatable

materials .... equipment

Results section

Suggested word count: 300

Results: Descriptive

Results are clearly stated and accurate and reflect the hypotheses of the research.

The results section must show whether the IV caused a change in the DV.

Appropriate descriptive statistics (one measure of central tendency and one measure of dispersion) are applied to the data and their use is explained.

A common mistake is to calculate more than one measure of central tendency (mean, median, mode) and one measure of dispersion averages (range, standard deviation, variance, inter-quartile range). Use one of each.

A measure of central tendency shows the most likely, the most probable, the typical piece, or the average piece of data. Choose from the mean, median, or mode.

Use the mean to describe the typical, most likely, piece of data. If there are extreme outliers (unusually high or low pieces of data), the mean will be distorted. As a result, it does not describe the typical data. If there are outliers, use the median.

If the data is not continuous, use the mode. If a group includes five girls and 15 boys, the most likely gender is male. It would not make sense to say that the typical gender is 0.75 male.

A measure of dispersion shows how **varied** the group of data is or how dispersed the data is from the normal or central data. The actual measure used depends on the data set you have collected.

Use the standard deviation if the data is continuous and the data set is normally distributed and use the inter-quartile range if the data is skewed.

Make sure that you include information on *what* the statistics are describing. For example, the mean speed is not 35.5, it is 35.5 miles per hour.

Example sentence (if the score is low):

> The low value indicates the data tends to be very close to the mean suggesting there is a great deal of similarity in the data set.

Example sentence (if the score is high):

> The high standard deviation indicates the data is spread out over a large range of values suggesting there is less similarity in the data set.

Subject vocabulary

results data that has been processed – for example, turned into a mean

hypothesis the idea being tested by the study

descriptive statistics statistics which summarize the data

dispersion measures how spread out a data set is

mean a form of central tendency usually referred to as the 'average'

median the middle value separating the higher half of a data set from the lower half

mode the value that appears most often in a data set

standard deviation shows how much variation, spread, or dispersion exists from the average or expected value

variance the average of the squared differences from the mean

inter-quartile range an accepted measure of dispersion

outliers results/responses that are very different form the other results/responses

distorted changed

continuous data data that can be measured on a scale and compared with other data

normal distribution refers to a type of data that is symmetrical around the mean

data sets groups of data (e.g. groups of themes generated from interview; responses to questions on specific topics)

skewed a lack of symmetry in the data set

Glossary

varied including different types (of things or people)

Subject vocabulary

axis the vertical and horizontal lines on a graph

raw data information that has not been processed

condition the experimental situation the experimenters have created to test something

Glossary

to represent/representation to describe in written or picture form

tabular like a table

Synonyms

affected .... influenced

manipulating ...... changing

The graph of results is accurate, clear, and directly relevant to the hypotheses of the study.

Make sure that the graphs have a title, a legend (a key), and a clear label for each axis. They should be simple **representations** of the results (descriptive) not the raw data.

The graph should show whether the experiment's DV is **affected** by the change in the IV. This could be as simple as showing a bar chart representing the mean of IV1 and the mean of IV2.

It is often better to draw the graph by hand (with a pencil and ruler) and paste it into the report. You should not simply enter the data set into Excel and then print out the most interesting-looking graph. It would be better to use a scanner to convert a hand-drawn graph into an electronic version.

In order to make sure that the graph is clear:

- Make it large.
- Give it a title, and include (N = ...) after the title to show how many participants.
- Give it a border.
- Label the axes (include units).
- Label the data either on the graph or with a key (legend).
- Show the measure of central tendency and the measure of dispersion, if possible.

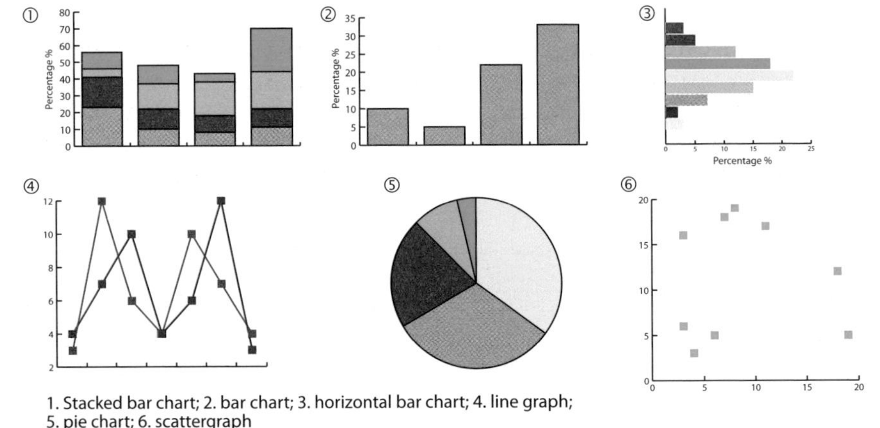

1. Stacked bar chart; 2. bar chart; 3. horizontal bar chart; 4. line graph; 5. pie chart; 6. scattergraph

Results are presented in both words and tabular form.

Example sentence:

Results

The median estimate of speed for the question using 'smashed' was XX mph, while the median estimate of speed for the question using 'hit' was XX mph. The standard deviation of the data set associated with 'smashed' was XX mph. The standard deviation of the data set associated with 'hit' was XX mph.

Results	IV1 (Smashed), mph	IV2 (Hit), mph
median		
standard deviation		

Results: Inferential

Social scientists need to know if the difference seen in the DV data sets is large enough to be the result of them **manipulating** the IV. If it is, they can be confident the manipulation of the IV caused the effect on the DV and their hypothesis has been supported. In statistical terms, they need to know if the difference between the two conditions is *significant* enough. Therefore a statistical test needs to be applied to the data.

An appropriate inferential statistical test has been chosen and explicitly justified.

There are two questions that need to be asked before a statistical test can be chosen:

1. Which design was used (repeated measures or independent measures)?
2. Is the data nominal, ordinal, or interval/ratio?

Nominal data

Nominal data is where the values/observations can be given a number. The numbers are simply labels. For example, in a data set, males could be coded as 0, females as 1. The marital status of an individual could be coded as Y if married, N if single. Where people are required to estimate speed of cars they could be asked: 'Are they going fast or slow?' Participants' responses could be coded 'f' for fast or 's' for slow.

Ordinal data

Ordinal data is where the values/observations can be put in order. For example, asking people to estimate the speed of cars on a scale of 1–10 (10 being the fastest). In this way, the data can be ranked (placed in order). In ordinal data, the order is important (e.g. large to small; slow to fast) but not the difference between the values because there is no standardized way of measuring the difference.

Interval data

Interval data is where the values/observations can be put in order and the difference (or interval) between the values is standardized and is the same. Miles per hour (mph) and temperature (Celsius) are examples of interval data. They are standardized measuring scales which are recognized throughout the world.

	CHOOSING A STATISTICAL TEST	
	INDEPENDENT MEASURES DESIGN	REPEATED MEASURES OR MATCHED PAIRS DESIGN
NOMINAL DATA	CHI SQUARED TEST	SIGN TEST
ORDINAL DATA	MANN WHITNEY U TEST	WILCOXON SIGNED RANKS TESTS
INTERVAL OR RATIO DATA	UNRELATED T-TEST	RELATED T-TEST

Subject vocabulary

inferential statistical test experimenters need to know if the difference seen in the DV is large enough to be the result of the manipulated IV. If it is, they can be confident the manipulation of the IV caused the effect on the DV and the hypothesis has been supported. This difference is known as a significant difference and is found by applying inferential statistical tests. The result allows them to make in-depth conclusions (or inferences) about the data

to code to label a theme or idea generated by research

to standardize to make the same from one condition to the next

Glossary

to justify to give an acceptable explanation

Results of the inferential statistical test are accurately stated.

Each statistical test produces different values. It is important that you include all of the values. For example, Wilcoxon Signed Ranks test produces an N value, a critical value, and an observed value.

Example sentence:

I used a repeated measures design and my data was at least ordinal status. Therefore, the appropriate statistical test to use was Wilcoxon Signed Ranks test. All calculations can be found in Appendix III.

The observed value (T) was calculated to be 0 because none of the paired scores had a negative value when the differences were subtracted.

The critical value was calculated to be 3 for a one-tailed hypothesis at the 0.005 level of significance when N = 10 (Wilcoxon and Wilcox, 1964). N is the number of paired scores used.

T must be equal or less than the critical value for the results to be considered significant. Therefore, my results can be considered to be highly significant.

The null hypothesis has been accepted or rejected appropriately according to the results of the statistical test. A statement of statistical significance is appropriate and clear.

You must include a sentence where you accept or reject the null hypothesis based on the results of the test.

Subject vocabulary

condition the experimental situation the experimenters have created to test something

Example sentence:

Statement of significance:

The difference between **condition** A and condition B is significant at the 0.05 level of significance when N = 10. I can reject my null hypothesis and accept my experimental hypothesis.

Discussion

Suggested word count: 700

Glossary

to refute to prove that a statement is incorrect

Discussion of results is well developed and complete (for example, descriptive and inferential statistics are discussed).

Repeat the description of the descriptive results. Write the same sentence that you used below the graph. State how the results support or **refute** the experimental hypothesis. Repeat your statement of significance.

Synonyms

affected .... influenced

Example sentence:

The aim of the experiment was to measure the effect of leading verbs on speed perceptions of a car crash. The results demonstrate the extent to which changing the leading verb can influence the participants' estimates of speed. The average estimation of speed changed with the different verbs. The variance in speed estimates of 48.5 kmph between the verbs 'smashed' and 'hit' demonstrates a change in speed perception. These results indicate that people may be significantly **affected** by the wording of a question; a change in the leading verb led to different speed estimates. The difference between condition A (smashed) and condition B (hit) is significant at the 0.05 level of significance when N = 10 for the Wilcoxon Signed Ranks test. I can reject my null hypothesis and accept my experimental hypothesis.

The findings of the student's experimental study are discussed with reference to relevant background studies and/or theories.

In the discussion section, you must refer to all of the studies you mentioned in the introduction. You should include a statement about whether the results from your experiment support or refute the studies.

Example sentence:

Loftus and Palmer (1974) aimed to investigate the effect of **leading questions** on the accuracy of speed estimated in, and perceived consequences of, a car crash. The results, which ranged in mean speed estimates on a range of 40.8 mph for 'smashed' and 31.8 mph for 'hit', indicated that the speed estimates were indeed influenced by the wording used. Our study clearly supports Loftus and Palmer as a significant difference was found between the verbs 'smashed' and 'hit' (estimates for 'smashed' being considerably higher). The results of both studies clearly question the extent to which perception is reliable.

Limitations of the design and procedure are highly relevant and have been rigorously analysed.

You must give at least three problems with the design and procedure and say why they occurred.

Example sentence:

The participants consisted of mostly 16-year-old students with limited experience of driving and so limited skill in estimating traffic speeds. This is suggested in the large range in speed estimates in the raw data.

The experiment lacks ecological validity. It was conducted in a classroom, and the car accident was watched in video format. A real-life traffic accident would have included more stimuli such as realistic sounds, realistic distances, etc. A real-life accident would have been witnessed after the participants had likely been outside and amongst the traffic for some time, whereas the video was shown in isolation.

The participants were aware that they were in an experiment being conducted for the researcher's IB Diploma and so demand characteristics may have affected the participants' responses.

Similarly, the researcher may have influenced the experiment with researcher biases such as unintentionally placing more stress on some words in the instructions, or body language when showing the videos.

Modifications are suggested and ideas for further research are mentioned.

You must include a solution for each of the problems mentioned above.

Example sentence:

If the study was to be conducted again, certain modifications could be made. The participants may be chosen from an older or more **varied** age group with

Glossary

leading question a question that encourages the desired answer

rigorously carefully, thoroughly, and exactly

varied including different types (of things or people)

Subject vocabulary

ecological validity having realism and being able to generalize to real-life situations

demand characteristics participants form an interpretation of the experiment's purpose and then change their behaviour to fit that interpretation. It is why deception is sometimes necessary

researcher bias a behaviour or expectation on the part of the researcher that influences the experiment particularly the results and conclusions

Synonyms

modifications...... changes

driving experience. This would allow for participants to be more familiar with car speeds, and thus provide more accurate estimates and with possibly less variance within the data sets. Furthermore, the participant may be asked more questions in addition to the speed of the car, in order to reduce the focus on the speed estimate and perhaps reduce the likelihood of response bias. However, the use of the video allowed a standardized presentation of the data and so while it lacked ecological validity, it should remain as a basic procedural guideline for this experiment. In future, one of the participants can be selected to act as the presenter, to read instructions and so avoid any researcher influences.

Further research can be in the form of future research questions.

Example sentence:

This experiment concludes that **eyewitness testimony** can be affected by leading questions. More research is needed into whether certain verbs carry more influence than others. Other research could be carried out on whether verbs influence perception in other **scenarios** such as **physical assaults**.

If eyewitness testimony is affected by verbs, is it also affected by other variables such as the type of vehicle involved in the accident, such as delivery vans versus sports cars, motorcycles, taxis, school buses?

The conclusion is appropriate.

The conclusion can be very similar to the abstract. You should include a full **recap** of the aim, the relevant aspects of the procedure, and the main findings.

Subject vocabulary

data sets groups of data (e.g. groups of themes generated from interview; responses to questions on specific topics)

Glossary

eyewitness testimony a formal statement in which a person describes something they have seen

scenario situation

physical assault attacking someone, e.g. hitting or punching

Synonyms

recap .... repeat

Appendices

The appendix (plural: appendices) contains relevant information that cannot fit into the other areas, for example, raw data; consent and debrief forms; calculations; examples of apparatus such as questionnaires. Appendices should be labelled appropriately and referenced in the body of the report. You should use Roman numerals (I, II, III, IV etc.) for this.

Example:

Appendix I: Raw Data

Referencing

A reference section is strongly recommended and not a bibliography. A reference section means you cite the author in the main body of your IA (usually the introduction) and then provide full details at the end of the work (with the details listed alphabetically) under a heading of 'References'. You have a choice of referencing styles. However, this book recommends the Harvard referencing system (or author-date system). The Harvard referencing system uses an author-date reference in the text, e.g. '(Smith, 2000)', being inserted after the cited idea within parentheses and the full reference to the source being listed at the end of the essay. If you quote directly (and this should happen rarely) then you need to include the surname, date, page number, e.g. '(Smith, 2000: 24)'.

- Only use page numbers when you quote directly.
- If you use this system then you do not need to have 'footnotes'.
- Do not include any other information in the author-date reference. For example, do not use initials (Smith, J.S., 2000); do not mention universities (Smith, University of Bath, 2000); do not mention qualifications (Smith, PhD, 2000).
- You can use the author's surname in the text and then include the date in parentheses, e.g. 'Smith (2000) argued. . .'

Example:

Loftus, E.F., and Palmer, J.C. (1974) Reconstruction of automobile destruction: An example of the interaction between language and memory. *Journal of Verbal Learning and Verbal Behavior*, **13**, 585-589.

Referencing has exact rules about the information to be included, where to use a comma (,) and where to use a semi-colon (;), where the date goes and how the page numbers appear. Journal articles, books, and websites are all referenced differently. Please see the Extended Essay section for further details.

Introduction to the Extended Essay

Synonyms

significantly .... greatly

The guidance and examples offered in the following pages are not complete. They are intended as an introduction to the Extended Essay and to give students ideas about possible direction and focus. They are designed to help students *begin* the researching and writing process. Students should **significantly** expand on the ideas presented. Essays that do not do this are unlikely to receive passing marks. Students can use the reference sections to develop their own research paths. They should not be used exclusively.

Dos: the following are suggestions for what you *should* be doing

- Do: Have a focused research question that will allow you to come to a conclusion in 4000 words.
- Do: Make sure you can find research from appropriate sources that will help you answer it *before* you decide on a question.
- Do: Avoid 'pop' psychology topics, questions, and resources. Pop psychology is published in 'self-help' books, magazines, and websites. Pop psychology resources cover many of the same topics as academic psychology but they do so with a mainstream audience in mind. Academic psychology is the product of clearly defined and accepted research methods. It is taught in universities and the work is published in academic journals.
- Do: See the Extended Essay as a series of small sections, each with their own focus and purpose. Each section will have different research attached to it.
- Do: Use sub-headings to demarcate your essays. The sub-headings should be small questions that can be addressed in about 600 words.
- Do: A lot of broad reading from a variety of sources.
- Do: Use a journal (digital or pen and paper) to keep track of your research.
- Do: Give yourself realistic personal deadlines and stick to them. 'This Saturday I will write one paragraph on emotion.'
- Do: Get a 'study-buddy' (peer reviewer). They should check for small errors and overall structure. They help you see things you missed like poor spellng.
- Do: Return the favour and be a study-buddy for someone else.
- Do: Have more ideas than you need. Read more authors than you need. Your problem should be trying to fit all of your ideas into your essay not trying to fill out the essay with very little research.
- Do: Use formal language. This is not a creative writing exercise, nor are you talking to your best friend. You are *not* trying to project your personality through your writing. You are presenting other people's ideas and research to make an argument. Use cold, dry, academic language. The ideas themselves are interesting, not your style of writing. Use the style you find in academic journals.

Subject vocabulary

mainstream audience non-experts who have not studied the topic or subject

academic journals academic magazines used by scholars/academics to introduce new research and then have it reviewed and criticized by others in their specific field

journal a diary that records what you did and when you did it together with new ideas and *thought-bursts*

deadline a date and time when work has to be finished by

Don'ts: the following are suggestions for what you should not be doing

- Do not: Try and change the world and invent new ideas. You are a Diploma psychology student who has been asked to write a 4000-word essay. This is all. Your job is to organize existing ideas into a logical whole with appropriate evaluation under a reasonable question. You won't find or invent anything that has not been found or invented before. Not yet.
- Do not: Use the same author more than three or four times to illustrate an idea. If you are doing this then you need to do more research.
- Do not: See the essay as a 4000-word assignment. Instead, see the essay as a series of 600- (× 5) word sections with a 500-word introduction and a 500-word conclusion. Each section should address a clear point.
- Do not: Ignore small mistakes. Small mistakes lose marks and detract from the overall judgement of the essay (e.g. poor referencing, lazy presentation, poor use of quotes to fill up space, sections that lack focus). Use your study-buddy to help you. You should always have another pair of eyes mark your work other than your teacher.
- Do not: Overuse quotes. Always ask yourself, *can I change this slightly and then reference it so I don't have to quote it?*
  - Bad: 'Do not: Overuse quotes. Always ask yourself, *can I change this slightly and then reference it so I don't have to quote it?*' (Bryan and Law, 2013: 233).
  - Good: Bryan and Law (2013) argue students should avoid quotes wherever possible. They encourage them to always ask, can I change this slightly and then reference it so I don't have to quote it?
- Do not: Write a big idea without a reference. For example, you can't have big ideas such as *memory* or *depression* and not define them. You are not expected to define them yourself. You are expected to find different definitions, reference them, and then choose one. If you don't reference them this is considered plagiarism.
- Do not: Write a sweeping statement or a generalization without a reference. For example, you can't write 'most people experience depression at some point in their lives...' without a reference and without a researched statistic.
- Do not: Start a sentence with 'most people...' or similar phrases. It is not considered academic.
- Do not: Use a source if you can't find the author's name. If you cannot find an author's name on a piece of work (usually a website) do not use it.
- Do not: Write author's initials, author's universities, author's qualifications (e.g. PhD) in your in-text referencing (see below). The surname and date is all that should be included. Keep your sentences and references simple and to the point.

Subject vocabulary

referencing the process where you acknowledge the authors that contributed to your work. It is to avoid being accused of plagiarism, to correctly label where you found your ideas, to allow the reader to determine whether the work supports your argument in the way you claim it does, and to help the reader decide how worthy your argument is by checking on the quality of the sources you have based it upon

plagiarism stealing other authors' ideas and/or words and claiming them as your own. You are automatically committing plagiarism if you don't reference correctly

sweeping statement generalization you may use in conversation but not in an academic essay

in-text sentences and paragraphs in the main body of your essay

Correct referencing

A reference section means you cite the author in the main body of your essay and then provide full details at the end of the essay (with the details listed alphabetically) under a heading of 'references'. You have a choice of referencing styles. However, this book recommends the Harvard referencing system (author-date system). The Harvard referencing system uses an author-date reference in the text e.g. '(Smith, 2000)', being written after the cited idea within parentheses and the full reference to the source being listed at the end of the essay. You can also write the author and date as part of a sentence if you wish. When there are more than three authors than use the first three names that appear on the original source and then use 'et al.' for the other names.

If you quote directly (and this should happen rarely) then you need to include the surname, date, page number, e.g. '(Smith, 2000: 24)'.

- Only use page numbers when you quote directly.
- If you use this system then you do not need to have 'footnotes'.
- Do not include any other information in the author-date reference. For example, do not use initials (Smith, J.S., 2000); do not mention universities (Smith, University of Bath, 2000); do not mention qualifications (Smith, PhD, 2000).
- You can use the author's surname in the text and then include the date in parentheses, e.g. 'Smith (2000) argued...'

The reference section comes at the end of the work and places the cited authors in alphabetical order. You must include important information such as author's surname and initials, date, full title of the piece being cited, and publishing information.

There are different rules of using work from journals, books, newspapers and websites.

Work from a journal: Cite the surname, initials, date, the title of the article, the volume number and pages.

Example:

Hochschild, A.R. (1979) Emotion work, feeling rules, and social structure. *American Journal of Sociology*, **85** (3), 551–575.

Work from a book: Cite the surname, initials, date, the title of the book, place and name of publishers.

Example:

Hochschild, A.R. (1983) *The Managed Heart: the commercialization of human feeling, 20th anniversary edition*, reprinted (2003). Berkeley, CA: University of California Press.

Work from a newspaper: Cite the author's name, publishing date, title of the article and name of the newspaper.

Example:

Gray, R. (4 May 2013) Magnetic pulses may help treat depression. *The Telegraph* (UK edition).

Work from a website: Cite the author and/or organization, the date the article was written, the title, the website address, the date you accessed it on.

Example:

BBC News (24 April 2013) Why do so many people want cosmetic procedures? <http://www.bbc.co.uk/news/health-22277890>. Accessed 7 May 2013.

Work from a secondary source. For example, you read about an interesting study in a book but you have not read the original study. Cite the book/journal you got it from in the usual book reference format and the use roman numerals and write the study you wish to reference and the page number.

Vaughan, G.M., and Hogg, M.A. (2008) Attraction and close relationships. *Introduction to Social Psychology*. Frenchs Forest, NSW: Pearson Education Australia, 487–525. Print.

i. de Munck (1996) page 517.

Or: Cite the original study which you will find in the reference section of the book/journal and then state 'cited in' and then reference the book/journal where you got it from.

Hawkins, B.S.R. (1990) The management of staff development in a contracting education service. Unpublished PhD thesis, Birmingham Polytechnic. **Cited in** Mercer, J. (2006) The challenges of insider research in educational institutions: wielding a double edged sword and resolving delicate dilemmas. *Oxford Review of Education*, **33** (1).

Extended Essay example 1

To what extent have Western ideas of 'slimness' affected women living in cultures-in-transition?

Introduction

An outline of why the topic is important could include why 'slimness' is considered important. Fouts and Burggraf (1999) found thin women to be linked with wealth, health, control, and beauty whereas being overweight was **correlated with** weakness, laziness, lack of control, and unhealthy lifestyles. Other studies have shown how reading fashion or fitness magazines, viewing television and music videos were connected to unhappiness towards one's body because of the constant **exposure** to the '**ideal stereotype**' of a slim male and female body (e.g. Cusumano and Thompson, 1997; Hatoum and Belle, 2004). Then, you would move onto the cultural part of the question. For example, Frith et al. (2006) argued 'ideal beauty' would vary depending on the culture in question, as different cultures establish different norms. Therefore a single **concept** of an 'ideal body' cannot be assumed to be universal. For example, Soh et al. (2006) found that traditional Asian, Arabic, and African cultures have the tendency to not require slimmer body styles as being an essential factor in terms of feminine beauty.

The essay would focus on how (and possibly *why*) traditional ideas in non-Western countries concerning the 'ideal body' have started to change. The why question could form the second half of an essay and would look at Western media influences. The inclusion of the 'why' question is a more **sophisticated** essay and it is not addressed below.

For example: Western media influences have begun to spread on a global scale, meaning that women in other cultures around the world are beginning to be exposed to the same pressures women in Western cultures experience. An example of this is research carried out by Becker (2004) in Fiji. The traditional and standard norm for women in Fiji is that they are large and **voluptuous** and it was believed that having a slim body was thought to be unhealthy. However, in 1995, television, broadcasting mostly Western programmes, was introduced into this culture. Consequently, after only 3 years, the people of Fiji report a significant increase in eating disorders and a common unhappiness with physical appearance.

Definitions

You would need to find clear definitions for *cultures, transition, slimness,* and what you mean by *Western cultures.*

Glossary

slimness being thin

transition changing from one process or situation to another

exposure have contact with/ experience of

stereotype a belief about what a particular person or group of people is like

voluptuous having large breasts and a curved body

Synonyms

correlated with ... linked to

ideal .... best/perfect

concept .... idea

sophisticated ..... complicated/ developed

Use of examples

You should centre your essay on clear examples.

Example 1: South Africa

South Africa has been exposed to very many Western influences, such as new role models, which have been suggested to be creating a new identity for black **adolescents** and forming a westernized approach to culture among the youth (Stevens and Lockhat, 1997). Allwood and Szabo (2006) investigated the eating attitudes in adolescent South African females and found Western influences imposed on the black females in a private school played a role in their body dissatisfaction and the risk of developing an eating disorder.

Example 2: Egypt

Ford, Dolan, and Evans (1990) showed that Egyptian women were beginning to find their ideal body shape to be a slimmer one, which is a more recent **phenomenon** because Egyptian society has never been one to place a great importance on slimness in the past. Nasser (1993) carried out a study with Egyptian schoolgirls in Cairo where he asked them to take the EAT-40 (Eating Attitudes Test 40; Garner et al., 1982)

From the 420 351 female students at the school in Cairo around 88 per cent completed the EAT-40 (Garner et al., 1982) self-report questionnaire and around 11.4 per cent of those students were found to have some sort of eating disorder or body image problem. Comparisons showed there were more EAT-40 (Garner et al., 1982) positive cases in the school in Cairo (11.4 per cent) than there were in the UK.

Conclusion

Summarize your findings. What do they show? ('The findings show Western ideas of slimness are spreading and this is leading to an increase in eating disorders in cultures-in-transition...') Show the important parts of the research ('This research is important because...' and 'I have given these important issues attention because...'). **Emphasize** future areas of research ('Future areas of research include the **mechanisms** which spread ideas about slimness, for example, print media, social media and TV...'). You can also list a series of future research questions that your essay has influenced.

Synonyms

adolescents......... teenagers/young people

phenomenon...... occurrence/trend

emphasize.......... stress/highlight

mechanisms........ ways/processes

References

Allwood, C.W., and Szabo, C.P. (2006) A cross-cultural study of eating attitudes in adolescent South African females. *World Psychiatry*, **3**(1), 41–44.

Becker, A.E. (2004) Television, disordered eating, and young women in Fiji: negotiating body image and identity during rapid social change. *Culture, Medicine and Psychiatry*, **28**, 533–559.

Cusumano, D.L., and Thompson, J.K. (1997) Body image and body shape ideals in magazines: exposure, awareness, and internalization. *Sex Roles*, **37**, 701–721.

Ford, K.A., Dolan, B.M., and Evans, C. (1990) Cultural factors in the eating disorders: a study of body shape preferences of Arab students. *Journal of Psychosomatic Research*, **34** (5), 501–507.

Fouts, G., and Burggraf, K. (1999) Television situation comedies: female body images and verbal reinforcements. *Sex Roles*, **40**, 473–481.

Frith, K., Shaw, P., and Cheng, H. (2006) The construction of beauty: a cross-cultural analysis of women's magazine advertising. *Journal of Communication*, **55**, 56–70.

Garner, D.M., Olmsted, M.P., Bohr, Y., and Garfinkel, P.E. (1982) The Eating Attitudes Test: psychometric features and clinical correlates. *Psychological Medicine*, **12**, 871–878.

Hatoum, I.J., and Belle, D. (2004) Mags and abs: media consumption and bodily concerns in men. *Sex Roles*, **51**, 397–407.

Nasser, M. (1993) Screening for abnormal eating attitudes in a population of Egyptian secondary school girls. Leicester: Department of Psychiatry, University of Leicester, Leicester Royal Infirmary, UK.

Soh, N.L., Touyz, S., and Surgenor, L. (2006) Eating and body image disturbances across cultures: a review. *European Eating Disorder Review*, **14**, 54–65.

Stevens, G., and Lockhat, R. (1997) 'Coca-Cola kids' – reflections on black adolescent identity development in post-apartheid South Africa. *South African Journal of Psychology*, **27**, 250–255.

Extended Essay example 2

What is the role of cultural factors in the formation of interpersonal relationships?

Introduction

An outline of why the topic is important could include a reference to an increasingly interconnected world where many different cultures are living in closer **proximity** to each other.

You may want to use the introduction to clearly define your terms. Cavazos (2010) defines interpersonal relationships as the **interaction** between individuals, such as friends, family, co-workers, and strangers, who fulfil each other's needs, both physical and emotional by interacting in different ways. Culture can be defined as *'attitudes, values, beliefs, and behaviours shared by a group of people, but different for each individual, communicated from one generation to the next'* (Matsumoto, 1997).

Suggestions for structure and/or focus

You can use a combination of the following suggestions or take one and expand it to form an entire essay.

Suggestion 1: Focus on Hofstede's scales

For example, the impact of **collectivism** versus **individualism**. Gupta and Singh (1982) compared **arranged marriages** and non-arranged marriages, finding that *love can be learnt if the couple feel that they need to make their relationship work.* De Munck (1996) found that Sri Lankan Muslims *preferred* arranged marriages and they were found to be very successful. Alternatively, individuals within individualistic cultures are more independent and can make greater choices regarding who they marry. From this, love is valued more in individualistic terms (Simmins, vom Kolke, and Shimizu, 1986).

Suggestion 2: Focus on one culture

For example, in Japan there are multiple terms to describe interpersonal human relationships: the feeling of connection, *fureai*; the feeling of familiarity, *shitashimi*; the feeling of respect, *sonkei* (Markus and Kitayama, 1991).

Suggestion 3: Focus on gender differences

Mead (1935) is used widely to illustrate the socially constructed nature of gender roles. She studied different tribes in New Guinea to illustrate how gender roles are specific to culture and place. Gender can be seen as a cultural **construction**, and this in turn will affect relationship formation. Tanner (2010) claims genders approach situations differently and therefore seek different qualities in a partner. For example, Buss (1989) studied 10000 participants from 37 cultures. He concluded that males generally preferred younger mates as they are more capable of reproducing. Females on the other hand generally preferred older mates as they are more protective and seen as a provider of resources. His large sample size and deliberate attempt to involve diverse cultures are methodological strengths of his work. Remember: Mead has serious **flaws** with her methods and she ignored gender **universals**. It is widely accepted that gender has a significant biological element.

Synonyms

proximity .... closeness/nearness

construction .... understanding/creation

flaws .... faults

Glossary

to interact/interaction to act in close relationship with

arranged marriages parents choosing a husband/wife for their children

universals general truths

Subject vocabulary

collectivism in collectivist cultures, the social is emphasized more than the personal, and self-expression is not encouraged

individualism the personal is emphasized more than the social, self-expression is encouraged and people are viewed as unique

Suggestion 4: Focus on the role of geographical proximity

Individuals are more likely to get to know someone if they have regular contact (Newcomb, 1961). For example, Festinger, Schachter, and Back (1950) found that individuals living on the same floor as one another would have a closer relationship than those that live on another floor or in a different building. Interestingly, the location of staircases within a building can affect the process of relationship formations. You would use this approach to talk about the relationship between culture and geographical proximity and how this is changing due to an interconnected world - people from different cultures are living closer to one another or where internet-based relationships are more common - and how this might impact on interpersonal relationships.

References

Cavazos, M. (2010) 'What is the meaning of interpersonal relationship?' LIVESTRONG.COM - *Health, Fitness, Lifestyle | LIVESTRONG.COM*. Ed. David Bill. 9 Feb. 2010. Accessed 25 Oct. 2010.

Matsumoto, D. (1997*) Culture and Modern Life*. Belmont, CA: Thomson Brooks/Cole Publishing Co.

Mead, M. (1935, 2002*) Sex and Temperament: In Three Primitive Societies*. UK: HarperCollins.

Tanner, M. (2010) 'Gender and grief - how men and women handle grief.' *Parenting - Natural Parenting*. <http://www.naturalparenting.com.au/flex/gender-and-grief-how-men-and-women-handle-grief/7818/1>. Accessed 2 Nov 2010.

Vaughan, G.M., and Hogg, M.A. (2008) Attraction and close relationships. *Introduction to Social Psychology*. Frenchs Forest, NSW: Pearson Education Australia, 487–525. Print.

i. de Munck (1996) page 517.
ii. Festinger, Schachter, and Back (1950) page 491.
iii. Gupta and Singh (1982) page 517.
iv. Newcomb (1961) page 495.

Worchel, S., Cooper, J., Goethals, G.R., and Olsen, J.M. (2000) Culture and behaviour. *Social Psychology*. Ed. M. Taflinger. Wadswork: Thomson Learning, 435–461. Print.

i. Buss (1989) page 453.
ii. Hofstede (1980) page 437–8.
iii. Markus and Kitayama (1991) page 452.
iv. Simmins, vom Kolke, and Shimizu (1986) page 453.

Extended Essay example 3

*To what extent can a **definitive** personality be identified for cult membership?*

Introduction

An outline of why the topic is important could include why cults make use of practices that are beyond the normal in **universal** religions. For example, the amount of psychological control believed to be damaging to the individual (Walsh and Bor, 1996). Alternatively, cults are also popular because they are often friendly and welcoming in a family-like environment, leaving some members with greater emotional well-being after joining (Aronoff, Lynn, and Malinoski, 2000).

Suggested sections

1. Definitions

Outline working definitions of cults and personality, and briefly discuss how you arrived at the choices you made.

For example:

Cults:

Cults can be defined as 'small religious groups lacking in organization and **emphasizing** the private nature of personal beliefs' (Campbell, 1998: 122–123). The definition does not however provide much structure of who is likely to be part of a cult. Another definition is a 'group that **deviates doctrinally** from a "parent" or "host" religion; that is, cults grow out of and deviate from a previously established religion' (Gomes, 1995: 7). A further definition suggests cults have to: Be led by a **self-proclaimed** leader who claims to be led by a higher power; accept the leader's right to establish rules and lead; members must **pledge** and maintain complete **allegiance** to the leader (Singer, 1978, in Robinson and Bradley, 1998).

Personality:

Feist and Feist (2002) define personality as a pattern of characteristics that are relatively permanent and contribute with some **consistency** to an individual's behaviour. They also suggest the consistency of each individual's behaviour varies with various situations. The general concept of personality suggests that people can be categorized into different 'types' of individuals and these types are consistent across time and space.

2. Personality traits and cult membership

Discuss the different personality traits and characteristics found in individuals and members involved in cults, and conclude how individual traits affect cult membership. You may wish to choose two or three and discuss them in-depth.

For example:

You may wish to link certain personality traits with cult membership.

For example:

Neuroticism - defined as a tendency to experience negative emotional states (Walsh and Bor, 1996); sociotrophy - defined as a personality trait associated with high levels of dependence and a need to please others.

Spero (1982), when investigating the joining of cults, found that current cult members treated at a clinic with **psychodynamic therapy** showed signs of unhappiness, depression, and **anxiety** before joining their therapy groups. Gard

Glossary

definitive something that doesn't change/is fixed

universal the same everywhere

to deviate from to move away from

doctrinally the rules of the religion

pledge a serious promise

to be consistent/consistency to remain or always behave in the same way

Synonyms

emphasizing .... stressing/highlighting

self-proclaimed... self-chosen/selected

allegiance .... loyalty/commitment

anxiety .... nervousness/fear

Subject vocabulary

psychodynamic therapy therapy based on Freud's teachings. There is a focus on childhood experiences and unconscious drives

(1997) supports this claim by pointing out that young people especially who are going through uncertainty in their lives (such as doubts about their future) are therefore more likely to be attracted by a strong leader or group membership.

Wever-Rabehl (2006) argues from an evolutionary view that our ancestors tended to seek membership in small groups which would protect from weather and **predators** and increase their chances of success and survival.

Robinson and Bradley (1998) argue that the need for *acceptance* and *avoiding rejection* are the reasons for many of our decisions.

Subject vocabulary

evolutionary relating to the theory of evolution where traits have developed because they help survival

Glossary

predator an animal that eats or kills other animals

3. Ways of measuring personality

You may wish to discuss ways of measuring personality such as the Eysenck Personality Questionnaire and the Sociotrophy-Autonomy Scale (Beck, 1983, in Walsh and Bor, 1996).

You also may wish to discuss a problem with cult personality research: research takes place during people's cult membership or after people have left groups. There is a lack of research into how personality affects people's judgement *before* they join a cult.

4. Conclusion

Conclude the findings.

References

Aronoff, J., Lynn, S.J., and Malinoski, P. (2000) Are cultic environments psychologically harmful? *Clinical Psychology Review*, **20** (1), 91–111.

Campbell, C. (1998) Cult. In W.H. Swatos Jr. (Ed.). *Encyclopedia of Religion and Society*. Walnut Creek, CA: AltaMira, pp. 122–123.

Eysenck, H.J. (1998) *Dimensions of Personality*. New Brunswick, NJ: Transaction Publishers.

Feist, J., and Feist, G. (2002) *Theories of Personality* (5th ed.). New York, NY: The McGraw-Hill Companies, Inc.

Gard, C. (1997) The power and peril of cults. *Current Health*, **2** (23, 9), 18–21.

Gomes, A.W. (1995) *Unmasking the Cults*. Grand Rapids, MI: Zondervan Publishing House.

Robinson, M.D. (2010) Personality as performance. *Current Directions in Psychological Science*. <http://cdp.sagepub.com/content/13/3/127>. Accessed 30 Oct. 2010.

Robinson, B., and Bradley, L. (1998) Adaption to transition: Implications for working with cult members. *Journal of Humanistic Education and Development*, **36** (4), 212–222.

Spero, M.H. (1982) Psychotherapeutic procedures with religious cult devotees. *Journal of Nervous and Mental Disease*, **170**, 332–344.

Walsh, Y., and Bor, R. (1996) Psychological consequences of involvement in a new religious movement or cult. *Counseling Psychology Quarterly*, **9** (1), 47–51.

Wever-Rabehl, G. (2006) The anthropology of belonging. <http://suitelol.com/article/the-anthropology-of-belonging-a3931>. Accessed 25 Oct. 2010.

Potential extended essay questions

To what extent does media influence the perception of body image?

An investigation into cultural differences in the context of academic success.

To what extent does culture influence academic success in China and how can this be compared with an American approach?

To what extent do cultural norms influence the perception of beauty in contemporary France?

To what extent do Western cultural norms influence 'big is beautiful' concepts in traditional cultures?

To what extent is physical 'beauty' a universal concept?

To what extent can criminal behaviour be linked to biological/sociocultural/cognitive (choose one and use the others to evaluate) factors?

To what extent can case studies of patients with brain damage provide insight into memory processes?

Why is there a difference between people's beliefs about happiness and what psychological research shows?

To what extent can prejudice be linked to biological/sociocultural/cognitive (choose one and use the others to evaluate) factors?

To what extent can academic psychology contribute to the reduction of violence?

Why are there gender differences in depression?

Is it possible to effectively treat PTSD in war veterans with a virtual reality approach?

To what extent can attraction be explained by biological/sociocultural/cognitive (choose one) factors alone?

Why are some relationships less stable than others?

To what extent do men and women have different expectations in relationships and what are the ramifications for relationship stability?

To what extent does culture affect relationship formation?

To what extent does maternal deprivation explain development of anti-social behaviour?

To what extent can domestic help foster secure emotional attachment in their charges?

To what extent do physiological factors determine pathological behaviour?

To what extent does visualization affect sports performance?

To what extent does permissive parenting affect academic performance?

To what extent does measured intelligence change over time?

To what extent can dietary changes effectively tackle ADHD?

To what extent does physiology influence male aggression?

To what extent is Stockholm syndrome a valid psychological construct?

To what extent does learning a musical instrument impact academic performance?

To what extent can falling in love be seen as an OCD?

To what extent can battered person syndrome be compared with Stockholm syndrome?

To what extent does battered person syndrome have more constructive validity than Stockholm syndrome?

Assessment Objectives and Command Terms

Having followed the Psychology course at Standard Level (SL) or Higher Level (HL), students will be expected to demonstrate the following.

Knowledge and comprehension of:

1. **Specified content**

- Demonstrate knowledge and comprehension of key terms and concepts in psychology.
- Demonstrate knowledge and comprehension of psychological research methods.
- Demonstrate knowledge and comprehension of a range of appropriately identified psychological theories and research studies.
- Demonstrate knowledge and comprehension of the biological, cognitive, and sociocultural levels of analysis.
- Demonstrate knowledge and comprehension of one option at SL or two options at HL.

Command Terms associated with *knowledge and comprehension* are:

Define Give the precise meaning of a word, phrase, concept, or physical quantity.

Describe Give a detailed account.

Outline Give a brief account or summary.

State Give a specific name, value, or other brief answer without explanation or calculation.

2. **Application and analysis**

- Demonstrate an ability to use examples of psychological research and psychological concepts to formulate an argument in response to a specific question.
- At HL only, analyse qualitative psychological research in terms of methodological, reflexive and ethical issues involved in research.

Command Terms associated with *application and analysis* are:

Analyse Break down in order to bring out the essential elements or structure.

Apply Use an idea, equation, principle, theory, or law in relation to a given problem or issue.

Distinguish Make clear the differences between two or more concepts or items.

Explain Give a detailed account including reasons or causes.

3. **Synthesis and evaluation**

- Evaluate psychological theories and empirical studies.
- Discuss how biological, cognitive and sociocultural levels of analysis can be used to explain behaviour.
- Evaluate research methods used to investigate behaviour.

Command Terms associated with *synthesis and evaluation* are:

Compare Give an account of the similarities between two (or more) items or situations, referring to both (all) of them throughout.

Compare and contrast Give an account of similarities and differences between two (or more) items or situations, referring to both (all) of them throughout.

Contrast Give an account of the differences between two (or more) items or situations, referring to both (all) of them throughout.

Discuss Offer a considered and balanced review that includes a range of arguments, factors or hypotheses. Opinions or conclusions should be presented clearly and supported by appropriate evidence.

Evaluate Make an appraisal by weighing up the strengths and limitations.

Examine Consider an argument or concept in a way that uncovers the assumptions and interrelationships of the issue.

To what extent Consider the merits or otherwise of an argument or concept. Opinions and conclusions should be presented clearly and supported with appropriate evidence and sound argument.

4. **Selection and use of skills appropriate to psychology**

- Demonstrate the acquisition of knowledge and skills required for experimental design, data collection and presentation, data analysis and interpretation.
- At HL only, analyse data using an appropriate inferential statistical test.
- Write an organized response.

Learning Objective 4 is fulfilled with the Internal Assessment component of the course.

Authors' note:

The book has been written with the Learning Outcomes and Command Terms addressed as they appear in the IB Diploma Psychology guide. Students and teachers should always consider how Command Terms can change. In the Learning Outcomes the Command Terms are associated with Assessment Objectives 1, 2 or 3, and indicate the depth of understanding required of students.

A Command Term used in an examination question will be:

- the same as that specified in the related Learning Outcome, ***or***
- another Command Term associated with the same Assessment Objective, ***or***
- a Command Term of less cognitive demand.

For example, if a Learning Outcome begins with the Command Term 'explain', an examination question based on this Learning Outcome could contain the Command Term 'explain', another Command Term associated with assessment objective 2 (such as 'analyse'), or a Command Term associated with assessment objective 1.

It is particularly important to note a Command Term of 'compare' could become 'compare and contrast' or 'contrast', which changes the meaning of the Learning Outcome considerably and will acquire additional learning of new content to address the Learning Outcome sufficiently.

Index

D

E

F

T

V

W

Y

Z